RIDLEY SCOTT

RIDLEY SCOTT
A BIOGRAPHY

Vincent LoBrutto

UNIVERSITY PRESS OF KENTUCKY

Editorial and Sales Offices: The University Press of Kentucky
663 South Limestone Street, Lexington, Kentucky 40508-4008
www.kentuckypress.com

All photos courtesy Photofest.

Cataloging-in-Publication data available from the Library of Congress

ISBN 978-0-8131-7708-3 (hardcover : alk. paper)
ISBN 978-0-8131-7710-6 (pdf)
ISBN 978-0-8131-7711-3 (epub)

This book is printed on acid-free paper meeting
the requirements of the American National Standard
for Permanence in Paper for Printed Library Materials.

Manufactured in the United States of America.

  Member of the Association
of University Presses

To Tony Scott (1944–2012)

People say I pay too much attention to the look of a movie but for God's sake I'm not producing a Radio 4 play for today, I'm making a movie that people are going to look at.

Ridley Scott

The word "religion" is only a label. What lies behind that, the most important thing of all, is the word "faith." You either have faith, or you don't have faith, or you have degrees of faith—and if you have degrees of faith, then you become agnostic. You're kind of in-between, or you're on the fence.

Ridley Scott

I've gradually realized that what I do best is universes. And I shouldn't be afraid of that.

Ridley Scott

CONTENTS

Contents

PROLOGUE

March 25, 2001: Oscar night in Hollywood. *Gladiator* had twelve nominations. Ridley Scott walked from his limo to the red carpet and then to his seat in Los Angeles's Shrine Auditorium. Scott had never won the Oscar for Best Director—would this be his night?

Ridley Scott has been nominated for the Academy Award for Best Director three times. First, in 1992, he was chosen for *Thelma & Louise*. Scott's third nomination was in 2002 for *Black Hawk Down*, but it was Scott's second nomination, for *Gladiator* in 2001, that seemed destined to bring home the coveted gold-plated statue. His competition that night was Ang Lee for *Crouching Tiger, Hidden Dragon*, Steven Soderbergh, double-nominated for *Traffic* and *Erin Brockovich*, and Lasse Hallström for *Chocolat*.

As Scott waited during the lengthy and often tedious internationally broadcast ceremony, he watched as *Gladiator*, a film about warriors, a theme he would revisit many times, lauded critically and at the box office, won Oscars for Costume Design, Visual Effects, Sound, Best Actor in a leading role, and finally Hollywood's Holy Grail—Best Picture, but when the name was called for Best Director, it was Steven Soderbergh for *Traffic*—not Ridley Scott. Ridley Scott must have been incensed that night. Much later, in 2014, he told the *San Francisco Chronicle*, "I remember one year when *E.T.* got best film and Steven Spielberg didn't get best director. I said, 'What? Where did they think he was?' . . . You can't separate best film from best director, that's crazy."

Ridley Scott seems headed for one of three Oscar destinies. First, the Scorsese syndrome, in which a passed-over director finally wins a Best Director Oscar for a film that may not be as good as those overlooked in the past. Second, he could be a member of the Alfred Hitchcock group and never win the competitive Best Director award. Finally, he could receive a special Oscar for Lifetime Achievement, as was the Academy's acknowledgment to directors Orson Welles, Sidney Lumet, and Robert Altman.

Prologue

Oscars are symbolically important in the motion picture industry; they also can be a source of pride, accomplishment, and recognition for the recipients. It can be assumed that Scott would appreciate such recognition, but regardless of Ridley Scott's Oscar destiny, the director's body of work will continue to speak for itself.

INTRODUCTION

In film, it's very important to not allow yourself to get sentimental,
which, being British, I try to avoid. People sometimes regard
sentimentality as emotion. It is not. Sentimentality is unearned emotion.

Ridley Scott

I don't ever blink. Honestly.

Ridley Scott

The problem about making movies is, when you go away, your life stands
still.

Ridley Scott

All film directors have a bit of the businessperson in them—after all, it is
called the film business—but Ridley Scott truly is a businessman as well as a
filmmaker. At 6:00 each morning he is on the phone to one or more of his
offices: London, New York, Los Angeles, or Hong Kong. He talks for one to
two hours. He makes the calls from a chauffeur-driven car designed to replicate an executive suite with all the accoutrements. If he is shooting a film, he
puts pencil to paper wherever he is—at home, in the car, on the set—and
when he wraps for the night, Ridley Scott is back in the car on the phone,
often in conversation with his Los Angeles company. When he arrives home
he eats dinner, watches a film other than one of his, sketches out plans for the
days to come on the work in progress, and retires by 10:00, so he can be up
the next day at 5:30 a.m. to start all over again.

Ridley Scott lords over Ridley Scott Associates (RSA), which creates
countless commercials, music videos, TV series, and movies and employs as
many as sixty directors at any one time. He also rules over Scott Free, a production company reserved for his personal feature film directing projects.
Scott is a top shareholder in a consortium that owns Pinewood and Shepperton Studios and The Mill. He has had success in television as an executive
producer of numerous shows, including the long-running hit legal drama

series *The Good Wife*. "I'm a dyed-in-the-wool businessman," he told Tim Walker.[1] He claims that if he were not a filmmaker, he would be Lord Alan Sugar, the billionaire British magnate, media and political adviser, and host of the BBC's *The Apprentice*.

Scott has directed both large and small movies. His choice of project varies, as does his method of choosing; sometimes he receives an offer to direct a film, other times he adapts a book or an original script, sometimes he looks for a particular subject or genre. He has been a director-for-hire, but rarely, if ever, does he make a selection solely based on market demands. Given his track record, body of work, and the enormous amounts of money his films have yielded to a wide range of backers and distributors in the studio system, he seldom struggles to get a film made or to attract investors. There are not many British or American film directors at eighty-one years old who are still steadily plying their trade. Scott's power as a filmmaker lies in his incredible stamina, his ability to make one film after another while overseeing his business ventures and developing series and special projects for television. He makes the movies he wants and has myriad projects ahead of him and in development ready to convert into the next Ridley Scott project. This assures him that he will always have the next venture on tap—no unimportant feat in itself.

Ridley Scott is both an auteur and a visualist. Andrew Sarris, a key American advocate of the auteur theory, states that a film director is the author of a film through the force of a consistent creative vision. Critics rarely attempt to evaluate Ridley Scott as an auteur because they can't seem to hunt down recurring themes or a consistent style in his films. This book will identify and explore these themes and analyze the style of Ridley Scott's movies. Scott has rightly been labeled a visualist, and some critics infer a negative connotation to the work of directors identified as such. But Ridley's work as a visualist is not necessarily accomplished at the price of content, story, and character development. Critics claim he is not an actor's director; nevertheless, in his work with major stars, character actors, and masses of extras, he is regularly praised by performers who believe he trusts their talent and contribution.

British film critic John Grierson summed up the industry's attitude toward visualists in 1932 when he wrote, "When a director dies, he becomes a photographer." The criticism suggests that if a director pays extreme attention to the camera and lighting, he or she is akin to a photographer, not a moviemaker. Nevertheless, Ridley Scott is in good company with renowned visualists Josef von Sternberg (the classic director of *The Scarlet Empress*

[1934] and *The Shanghai Gesture* [1941] known for his elaborate lighting and camerawork), Stanley Kubrick, and Andrei Tarkovsky. In fact, the components embraced by the visualist are there for all film directors, but it is the emphasis on pure visual storytelling, and the artistry and intensity with which this is applied, that separates the visualist from those practicing a generalized cinematic storytelling model.

By observation and his own acknowledgment, Scott is a film director obsessed with light. It is light that illuminates both the screen and the story being told. Combined with location and production design, light creates the mood and atmosphere in which Scott's film narratives live and breathe. The quality of light in a film is often taken for granted, but there is no seeing without light. The visualist paints with light while others present a wash with an occasional dramatic shading. Ridley Scott has talked about being a student of light, a study he conducts endlessly whether making a movie, walking outside, or simply sitting in a room in his home.

Still photography came before cinematography. Light striking a plate, film, or digital component produces an image. Of the many arts within this magic box are two critical aspects: angle and size are essential aspects of composition. Where a figure, object, or land or water mass is placed is the art of composition. The visualist painstakingly composes shot after shot complementing and contrasting them to visually tell a specific story. The angle is the way the subject is approached. Whether it be from the right or left, side view, or other, the angle sends a dramatic message of how the shot should be read—for power or weakness, distinction, or for another way of seeing what has been shown. Movies are about time and space—how long a shot is held and the varying of size work with the story to visually comment on the narrative and the people in the narrative.

And before still photography, of course, there was art. The first painters to work in a square or rectangular format, regardless of the length and width, were leading the way for filmmakers. Early in his career Ridley Scott worked as a production designer and expanded his visualist skills which, because he was a student of art, included painting. A visualist must select the palette of the film, the colors and shades of colors that will have an emotional and psychological impact on the audience. Ridley Scott's continual practice of painting sharpens his eye for "painting" each shot with the proper hue and tone.

In her book *If It's Purple, Someone's Gonna Die: The Power of Color in Visual Storytelling,* Patti Bellantoni shares her deep understanding of the narrative and emotional meaning put forth by color in a motion picture. Red can

3

be powerful, lusty, and defiant. Yellow can be obsessive, daring, and exuberant. Blue can be cerebral and powerless, and purple could be mystical, ominous, and ethereal. As examples she cites *Blade Runner* and its use of blood-red and orange to depict the polluted air to demonstrate the degradation of the environment of Los Angeles. In *Gladiator* purple is used to convey an ominous sense, a growing threat from a corrupt and evil leader.

Ridley Scott is a workaholic who rarely socializes. Writer Lynn Barber of the *Guardian* suggested to the director that perhaps he has not won an Oscar for Best Director because he's admired but not liked in Hollywood, to which he replied, "Possibly, but that puts me on the cutting edge, which is useful!"[2]

Ridley Scott is a man whose life is dominated by the creation of moving images in long and short form. *Ridley Scott: A Biography* investigates the man and his films, revealing the intersection of his personal life and his tenacious work ethic, with the intention of balancing the criticisms of his work with his decades of success. Recognizing that Scott's oeuvre is not without failures, this biography's objective is to celebrate the overarching career of one of cinema's shining talents.

In this book I will crosscut between the biographical facts of Ridley Scott's life and times and his work life as a director and producer of short films; television commercials; TV series, movies, and miniseries; and feature film motion pictures. I will also explore Ridley Scott as media businessman, son, brother, husband, father, painter, production designer, drawer of Ridleygrams, and total filmmaker. My goal is to establish a connection between the aesthetics, intellect, and emotions that drive Ridley Scott's film obsession and make them work.

As of 2018, Scott has directed twenty-five films covering many genres: historical/period, film noir, science fiction, horror, dramedy, comedy, and religious epics. In his feature film work Ridley Scott continually returns to war as his content. *The Duellists, Black Hawk Down, Kingdom of Heaven, G.I. Jane, Gladiator, Robin Hood,* and *Body of Lies* are all about some aspect of the military and war. As a boy in England, Scott witnessed the terror of World War II as he experienced the Blitz. The darkness produced by war can be found not only in the films mentioned above but in the dark countenance of nonwar Ridley Scott films such as *Alien, Hannibal,* and *Black Rain.*

Ridley Scott is both a cinematic storyteller and a visualist. All film directors tell stories visually in the motion picture medium, but some put greater emphasis on the script and performers, while others are more likely to use elements of the film crafts including cinematography, production design, sound, costumes, editing, and music. *Ridley Scott: A Biography* will identify and trace those elements that form each Scott film and examine the personal characteristics of the man who made them.

A critical biography of a filmmaker follows the artist's life and the art he or she practices. It is my hope that by the end of this journey, the reader will understand the yin and yang of the exceptional entirety of Ridley Scott as man and as director, including his misunderstood and underappreciated motion pictures, and will value the depth of Ridley Scott's accomplishments.

1

MOTHER'S MILK
The Early Life of Ridley Scott

A work of art is the result of a unique temperament.

Oscar Wilde

Ridley Scott was born on November 30, 1937, in South Shields in Northumberland, northeast England, to Elizabeth and Francis Percy Scott. His mother was born in 1906, an under-five-foot dynamo and a miner's daughter. She had an iron will and a love for the cinema that she shared with her son. During the 1930s Ridley's father, known in the family as Frank, was a partner in a successful commercial shipping business based in Newcastle. The onset of World War II and the threat of a German U-boat presence put a halt to the company. Frank Scott entered the military, where he was one of those responsible for the Mulberry Harbour operation—part of the intricate planning of the Normandy invasions. Because of his knowledge of shipping and transportation, Frank rose to the rank of brigadier general. He was a member of the Royal Engineers, a corps of the British Army tracing back to the time of William the Conqueror that provided military engineering and other technical support to the British armed forces.

Ridley Scott believes he was influenced by his father's nature. He told Steve Szkotak of the Associated Press, "His whole mindset on simplicity and order and reliability, I guess set into me. It's part of my upbringing, part of my schooling."[1]

In postwar defeated Germany, Colonel Scott was part of the Allied Control Council; therefore Ridley spent his early school years in Germany. After experiencing years of food rationing during the war, with no access to produce and other foods, the young Ridley found the US supermarket on the military base a special place. "I fuckin' loved that place: polished apples, gleaming fruit, bananas. We hadn't seen that in England for years," Scott told John Patterson of the *Guardian*. "Three smells always remind me of America:

Juicy Fruit gum, Coca-Cola and raspberry milkshakes. They defined that time. And then it was back to Stockton-on-Tees for the next 13 years."[2]

While in Germany, Ridley Scott avoided taking the eleven-plus exam required in England to determine the secondary school he'd attend. A mediocre student, Scott thought he would not have passed. His father's status allowed the family to bypass many of the class strictures that could have constrained his future plans.

As Ridley Scott told Paul M. Sammon, author of the indispensable *Ridley Scott, Close Up*, "So Dad got a job in the Army and became a commissioned officer . . . during the last two years of World War II he was attached to the War Office, and associated with Churchill."[3]

Because of his father's assignments, Ridley attended ten schools before he was ready for college. He was enrolled in a school for expatriate children nestled in a former U-boat barrack. "I walked to school past 100 U-boats every morning," Scott explained to John Patterson. "They were still cocooned in plastic because they didn't know what to do with them."[4]

Like many an English schoolboy, Ridley played conkers, a game in which a hole is drilled into a large horse chestnut then threaded with a large piece of string knotted at one or both ends to secure the conker. It is a two-person game. Each player takes turns hitting the other's conker. One player lets the conker hang from the full length of string while the opponent swings at it, taking turns until one breaks the other's conker to score a point. Ridley Scott's competitive spirit began early, as he explained to the *Guardian* in 2005. "I'm afraid I was quite competitive and used to cheat by baking my chestnut in the oven until it was very hard, then polishing it with bootblack so it looked shiny and new. Then I'd have this lethal missile like granite on a string."[5]

Ridley's older brother, Frank Scott, born in 1934, became a shipping captain. Frank was in the merchant navy from a young age, and he and Ridley didn't see each other much while Ridley was growing up.

Scott was just a tyke during the horrendous Nazi bombing blitz. "We were living in Ealing and they were bombing the streets," Scott told the *Hollywood Reporter*'s Stephen Galloway. "I was 2, 2½, 3 and we hid behind the stairs. I remember I had a little lamp, and we'd sing songs while we heard the bombs."[6]

Studies point to the monumental effects the war had on children, although the complete emotional impact and aftereffects can't be quantified. Statistics from 1940–1941 reveal that during the Blitz approximately one in ten children were killed by deadly air attacks. The lives of those who survived were drastically changed. Birthday and Christmas presents were sparse. Food was rationed. Recreational trips were limited. The warning sirens were loud and blaring. The threat from the skies made going to bed especially frightening. The overall stress lasted for years and took a toll on everyone, but most especially on the little ones.

Anthony David Scott, Ridley's younger brother, was born on June 21, 1944, in Stockton-on-Tees, England. For the majority of his life he was known as Tony. In the same *Hollywood Reporter* article by Stephen Galloway, Tony Scott recalled, "We had a brilliant upbringing and we never wanted for anything. Dad was a gentle sweet man. Mum was the matriarch and the patriarch of the family. She ran the roost with a steel fist, but at the same time there was respect and love for her. The driving force Ridley and I have comes from Mum, but they were chalk and cheese. There was a real big, sweet heart to her and at the same time a determination and toughness . . . like Ridley. We were a very, very tight family."

In an interview with Kenneth Turan in 2010, Ridley Scott confessed to secret thoughts about being a film director as a boy watching films in the local cinema. He kept his dreams quiet, however, "because in the North of England, the part of the woods where I came from, that would be unthinkable. The film industry and all that stuff was the other side of the moon." He also thought about acting but reflected, "That was too silly for words, I wouldn't dare. But at school, even like 7 or 8 years old, if there was some kind of play, like a nativity play, I'd always get involved. And though I totally enjoyed it, I never really thought there was any road ahead."[7]

Scott explained to Kenneth Turan his belief that his ability to handle high levels of stress came from his mother, describing her as "the master stresser." As to his own reputation as "master and commander," as Turan describes him, this can also be traced to his mother. Producer Brian Grazer, with whom Scott has worked twice, says definitively, "Nothing stops him, nothing." Paradoxically, Ridley Scott has been described as reflective and low-key in conversation, but on the set and whenever he is working he has a strong, relentless leadership presence.

Ridley Scott and his family spoke in the "Geordie" accent characteristic of people from the larger Tyneside region of northeast England. Geordie speech evolved from the Old English spoken by the Anglo-Saxon settlers of the region, together with Scottish and Irish influences. (Musicians Sting and Mark Knopfler are also Geordies.) At this point, with so much exposure to American accents, Scott's speech has been described as a blend of Geordie and the sound of the West Coast; the *Telegraph's* Mark Monahan noted, "His Geordie accent remains, beneath a drizzle of California." During the making of *Exodus: Gods and Kings,* actor Joel Edgerton observed that Ridley Scott's heritage helped shape his demeanor: "He's a Geordie, so he's not a big man for compliments—very dry."

The origin of Ridley Scott's surname is likely traceable to the Boernician clans of the Scottish-English border region. The Boernicians were one of the ancient tribes from which many Scottish names are derived. The first family of Scotts on record was found in Brabourne during the fourteenth century. The name means "painted warrior" in Celtic.

At the turn of the twentieth century, Ridley's great-uncle Dixon Scott started building a cinema theater empire. Dixon Scott strove to educate his audiences by presenting local stories and newsreels from global sources. His immediate family worked with him to bring moving pictures to Newcastle and the surrounding areas. Dixon Scott believed he had created a business that represented the lower classes rather than the wealthy and snobbish. Dixon Scott died in 1939 when Ridley Scott was only two years old, and Tony Scott was not yet born. It's uncertain what precisely the boys knew firsthand about their late great-uncle and his empire, but it is perhaps more than a coincidence that both Ridley and Tony became moviemakers who created films for the masses. It was in movie theaters that Ridley Scott learned about the cinemas of America and Europe, and they fueled his passion to make films of his own.

South Shields is a cold and harsh place where the people are tough, industrious, and taciturn. It is a coastal area where the river Tyne meets the North Sea. The children of South Shields, like Ridley Scott, learn to be sturdy and self-reliant.

During the Victorian era, there was a coal-mining boom in South Shields. The population grew from twelve thousand in 1801 to seventy-five thousand in the 1860s. In the 1850s shipbuilding was a leading industry. During World War II repeated Nazi air raids caused destruction and loss of life in the area.

Ridley Scott inherited a quality bred in most British men of his era: the well-known "stiff upper lip," referring to an individual who displays strength and fortitude in adversity. Brits with this trait are considered unemotional. As Scott matured he developed a reserve often associated with this British characteristic. He was frequently perceived as taciturn, cool in nature, and even enigmatic. Actors and crews accustomed to working for outgoing, loquacious, and personable directors found Scott a bit mysterious—a man who kept his state of mind hidden. He could talk, discuss, and interact with others; still, the overall impression was that his thoughts and sentiments were tightly held. In discussion with Lynn Barber for the *Guardian* he said, "As an Englishman, I'm aghast at emotional intensity."[8]

Ridley Scott's passion for art and drawing came early. At age six he was drawing ships and horses. At nineteen, however, he wanted to follow his father's track and join the military. Frank persuaded his son to go to art school instead. Frank himself was a talented artist in pen and ink. Scott believes his father may have influenced his own deep love of drawing and painting. Ridley had a particular interest in comic strips. He studied the compositions in the panels and how the characters were placed and related to their environment. His favorites were those that dealt with the dark side of life, like *Little Orphan Annie,* a perspective he would explore in many of his films. "My safety valve was art," Ridley Scott told the *Hollywood Reporter.* "My parents thought I was a bit strange because when someone else would have gone dancing, I was always painting. . . . I never thought about the future at all."[9]

At this time Ridley Scott was very shy and had no involvement with girls. Tony Scott reflects on his brother's early drive and talent in the BBC documentary about Ridley Scott, *Eye of the Storm*: "He was the older brother; I always looked up to my older brother. He was tough; he always seemed to have a fire, a focus on where he wanted his life to go at a very early age. I didn't. I was always sort of scrambling a little bit. Rid was constantly drawing and when everyone else was watching television, he sat off in the other room doing beautiful little drawings; he had as a child a photographic memory which he could transfer down to his fingers and did these great very real reproductions of life. At his age it was amazing that he had that skill."[10]

"My one real talent from a very early age was that I was able to draw pretty well, that was a constant," Ridley Scott explained to Kenneth Turan. "I was doing oils by the time I was like 8 or 9. I was one of those kids who tended to stay in on Saturday nights. My mother used to come and say, 'Why don't you go to the dance with the boys?' And I'm going, 'no, I'm perfectly happy.' I think my parents thought I was definitely weird."

Scott's early school career was not successful; he did poorly in most classes due to lack of interest. One teacher, Mr. Cleeland, told the boy that he should go to art school—that was what Ridley did best. "That was the best advice I ever got in my life, as soon as I entered art school, it was like the sun rose," Scott told Turan.

Elizabeth and Francis Scott were loving parents who wholeheartedly accepted Ridley's desire to go to art school and supported the decision completely. They knew they had a talented, artistic boy and they wanted him to develop those interests and abilities.

The very first film Ridley Scott remembers seeing was the pirate movie *The Black Swan* starring Tyrone Power and Maureen O'Hara, directed by Henry King and written by Ben Hecht. It was released in 1942 when Scott was five years old. The film was in Technicolor, and the bright, heavily saturated colors caught Ridley's nascent artist's eye. Scott talks about being "gonged" by Rita Hayworth in *Gilda* (1946). Although as an adult he knew he'd been too young to see this sophisticated and very sexy film, his reaction seemed to lie between a cinematic one and that of a very young male. "When she sang, 'Put the Blame on Mame,' something funny happened to me. I think I was about 7, but I definitely got the urge. I realized there was something special about Rita," he told Kenneth Turan.

Scott has strong memories of his mother taking him to see the Orson Welles masterpiece *Citizen Kane*. As a boy he didn't totally comprehend the plot, but he perceived there was a conscious artistic mind behind the film. He told Lynn Barber for the *Guardian*, "Everything in the screen from left to right, and right to left was considered."

Later he would go to the cinema every week—alone, because he didn't want any distractions. He stayed to watch the A and B pictures over and over, starting at 2:00 in the afternoon. He'd finally leave for home at 10:00 at night. He always read the credits carefully, noting that the job of art director might be something he could do.

Ridley Scott studied graphic design and painting at the West Hartlepool College of Art at West Hartlepool in Stockton-on-Tees, Teesside, from 1954 to 1958. He received a BA diploma in design. Stephen Crowther, a teacher at the West Hartlepool College, thought Ridley Scott was talented, deeming his work comparable to the best American illustrators. Some on the school's staff thought his work was slick and not really appropriate for painting.

After graduation, Scott decided to enter national service as a marine for two years. He was at a crossroads in his life. Art was in his blood, but so was the military, which had been a tremendous influence in his life through his father's service and his brother Frank's career in the merchant navy. Below the surface young Ridley Scott was attracted to self-discipline and organization. The inner workings of war fascinated and obsessed him and would surface in two major ways during his career. In terms of content, he would make at least seven films and produce other projects that were solely or partly about war. His directing style, while not militaristic in the fullest sense, is based on high organization, orderly planning, and disciplined execution.

His father talked him out of joining the marines, convincing him instead to continue to study art. There were no film schools in England at the time. The Royal College of Art (RCA) in London accepted him in 1958, offering him a liberal scholarship. The Royal College of Art was a public research university that specialized in art and design. The college's objective was to advance learning, knowledge, and professionalism in art and design and to create a standard compatible with the industry while promoting social awareness.

Of the college Scott declared to Kenneth Turan, "It is without any question the best art school in England, if not the world." In the three years he spent there, Scott explored arts other than drawing. He investigated photography, sculpture, and industrial design. At the RCA Ridley Scott took a step toward moviemaking by studying set design for television. His professor was George Haslam, a theater and television designer who taught him the fundamentals and the important skill of how to read a play.

Scott received his MA in graphic design from the Royal College of Art after attending from autumn 1958 until 1961. He adored art school. He would say that he'd go five days a week—then five nights a week—all in the same five days. While studying, Ridley Scott began to understand how the arts were interrelated. He became aware of music and writing and many other disciplines.

Scott had originally wanted to be a painter, but when teachers argued that his aptitude for illustration showed more promise, he believed he would never fully succeed as a painter. The argument lies in the work's commercialism, the expressive detail and content. *Slick* was a word often used to describe Scott's talent. Of course, this is a subjective engagement with the nature of what art is. With fine training, Ridley Scott created art as he saw it and developed his own vision.

Graphic design attracted him in part because the RCA had a strong department in that area. Scott thought it provided "a more specific target and a broader canvas," as he said in an interview for rca.ac.uk. He recalled,

> I was struck by the professionalism and the highly competitive nature of graphic design. . . . All the students were of a very high standard. Putting us all together was the beginning of my being

aware of the competitive nature of my chosen profession. I realized from very early on that I would have to fight hard and do very well if I was going to make it. . . . The mood of the college at the time was rebellious and politicized [as well as] studious and introverted. It could be very competitive with not much being given away and everything kept close to your chest. You observed all the time, watched what everyone else did and tried to do better and be the most original. . . . A lot of the staff had been war artists so for Bob Gill [advertising executive and graphic designer] to come in with button-down shirts, black suits and talking in a sharp Madison Avenue way was incredibly attractive. U.S. advertising was way out, and I realized very early the need to learn fast and absorb all that I could and then make my own decisions. I had strong views even then and could sort the wheat from the chaff, and that's still important today in everything I do.[11]

2

BROTHER AND BROTHER
Boy and Bicycle

Your battles inspired me—not the obvious material battles but those that
were fought and won behind your forehead.

James Joyce

When Ridley Scott was in London at the RCA, he became what he calls a serious, hardcore movie buff. Every weekend Scott would go to the National Film
Theatre, a leading repertory house, or the Academy Cinema, a prestigious, if
weather-beaten, art house cinema located on Oxford Street, where he was
exposed to a wide range of moviemaking including Japanese, French, Indian,
and Hollywood cinema. Scott was so enamored with Hollywood that while
he was at school he wanted most to direct a western, a dream he still has. He
was an ardent admirer of Ingmar Bergman films and especially liked *Summer
with Monika* (1953), which concerns teenagers who fall in love and go off to
an isolated island.

There was no formal film department at the Royal College of Art. Scott
was in the television department. George Haslam, head of the television
design area, was a talented designer and tutor, adviser, and supporter of his
students' dreams. However, it was not in his skill set to analyze or break films
down. He would provide the students with scripts, and they came back with
a set design and models.

One day, while rummaging around the design department, Ridley found
in a steel cabinet an old spring-loaded sixteen-millimeter camera and light
meter with an instructional manual. Realizing he had the opportunity to
make a movie, Scott set off to write a screenplay about a boy who skips school
on his sixteenth birthday, gets on his bike, and explores a seaside town. He
presented the script for the proposed short film and was given a cash budget
approved by Haslam and the go-ahead to direct his first film.

The script was written in stream-of-consciousness, which Scott intended
to record as voice-over. Scott was an avid admirer of the literature of James

Joyce and Henry Miller. He was especially taken with Joyce's masterwork *Ulysses*. The project, *Boy and Bicycle,* starred Ridley's younger brother Tony and cost about $100 to make.

Ridley Scott began his film directing career as an auteur—he wrote, directed, and produced *Boy and Bicycle,* which he also storyboarded in its entirety and photographed as well. The storyboard process was natural for Scott, who was adept with a pencil; he was aware that he needed to understand his film on a shot-by-shot basis. He could use the storyboard during production, which would tell him where to put the camera and how to frame the shot. Throughout his career Ridley Scott would utilize this storyboard process during preproduction and into production to communicate with his production designer and director of photography.

It was a bold choice to voice the film in stream-of-consciousness style, which was considered rather experimental and not the kind of conventional narrative usually chosen for a student short at that time. Scott was looking to penetrate the thoughts and feelings of an unnamed young boy. It also gave Scott a rare opportunity to probe his own deep and unconscious feelings about boyhood freedom and the environment in which he lived. This technique as used in the film is an inner monologue. Scott's study of Joyce, in particular, taught him that thoughts could, at times, be disjointed, poetic, and irrational.

The film is lean and concise: a journey, a boy's adventure. It has a clean commercial look, and the story is told in a superb way. Visually *Boy and Bicycle* is stark, but it includes lyrical images akin to the 1960 British New Wave film *Saturday Night and Sunday Morning,* photographed by master cinematographer Freddie Francis in the north of England. The film was enormously popular with Ridley Scott's generation.

Boy and Bicycle is a freedom ride away from the constraints of family, religion, and society—a brief excursion in a young man's life. It took the boy in the film a day out of his routine to realize that he was outside his own idea of the law—that he was suddenly isolated. While riding his bicycle, the boy hears students sing the familiar hymn "All Things Bright and Beautiful." The voice-over is filled with immediate responses, childhood memories, and imaginative speculation. These are comingled with nursery rhymes and favorite books of Ridley's, such as *Little Women* by Louisa May Alcott. One can fathom a connection between *Ulysses* and *Boy and Bicycle.* Like Joyce's protagonist in *Ulysses,* the boy perceives the external world through the physical environment while he hears disconnected, internalized voices.

Scott was aware that even a short film would take a lot of organization. He decided it made the most sense to shoot close to home. The school gave Ridley the camera for six weeks during the 1961 summer holiday. *Boy and Bicycle* was shot on location within two miles of the art college. As the star of the film, Tony had his summer constantly interrupted by his older brother waking him up every day at five or six in the morning so they could start shooting. "We'd drive up to Hartlepool with the gear that I'd manage to rent at 12 pounds a week. Arriflex legs, no-battery stuff because it was all like winding a clock. The whole film cost 60 quid," Scott told Kenneth Turan.[1] In adulthood and as a film director in his own right, Tony was proud to have been in his brother's first film. Ridley's father drove the camera car while Scott filmed his brother's bicycle journey. The film was shot on locations nearby on the streets of Billingham in the northeast of England. The bicycle trip's final scenes take place on the coast. The elder Scotts each had a role in the film. Ridley's father played a tramp and his mum played the boy's mother.

On "set" the brothers smoked Woodbines, strong English cigarettes that were popular during World War I and World War II. Ridley's directorial method with actors was nascent and untrained. He told Kenneth Turan he dictated, "Right, Tony shut up complaining, ready, ready, action! Next time go stand back over there. Shut up. Okay. By the way go and get lunch while I think about what I'm going to do. So I'd give him money to go and get sandwiches."

Scott was inspired by the high contrast black-and-white look of the films of Akira Kurosawa. He was especially taken with the Japanese master's *Throne of Blood* (1957). Scott observed that Kurosawa would let the sky go black in some of his black-and-white films. Research determined that this striking effect was achieved by the use of filters—in this case a red filter. Scott picked up a red filter and used it while shooting the film. Scott hand-held the camera, in part to follow the movement of the bike, and in part because he was limited in his choice of equipment. A camera technique employed in *Boy and Bicycle* that Ridley Scott later utilized in most of his feature films is shooting into a light source—most often the sun—so the lens elements show and dazzle the eye. This technique was considered a mistake during Hollywood's golden era and any such footage would be discarded. But in the late 1960s it became an artistic tool in such movies as *Butch Cassidy and the Sundance Kid* (1969), shot by Conrad Hall, and *Easy Rider* (1969), photographed by László Kovács. It is a sign of Scott's cinematic intelligence that he attempted such a technique in his first film.

Almost twenty-seven minutes, *Boy and Bicycle* was screened for teachers and classmates at RCA. After Ridley Scott graduated, he had the film warehoused. He then received a traveling scholarship to the United States, where he stayed for nearly two and a half years. While he was away his professor George Haslam retired and was replaced by Peter Newington. In 1964 Newington found the print of *Boy and Bicycle.* The soundtrack was raw and lacking in subtlety. Scott was offered a grant of £250 from the British Film Institute (BFI) in order to smooth out the editing and the mix. Scott took the opportunity to sweeten the track by adding sound effects of seagulls, tide, and street noises. Thus, although the film was made in 1961, the copyright for *Boy and Bicycle* is 1965.

The soundtrack had a composition by John Barry of James Bond fame—"Onward Christian Spacemen," recorded in 1963. Scott couldn't afford the rights. After Scott begged and cajoled the composer for seven months, Barry finally called the young man down to a recording session during which he recorded a new version of the piece for Scott to use in his film.

Boy and Bicycle begins with the camera circling the boy's bedroom, immediately establishing Scott's free use of the camera. The boy passes merry-go-round animals, birds, a beach, Stonehenge shapes, and reflections in water—then circle ripples that relate visually to the circular wheel of his bike. Also in the opening are the off-screen voices of Ridley's parents calling the boy to come to breakfast.

Boy and Bicycle creates a social picture of northeast England in the early 1960s when industry still flourished in the region. The images of an industrial landscape would be explored again by Scott in *Blade Runner* and *Black Rain.*

During his odyssey, the boy feels as if he is the only boy in the world, lending a sense of freedom combined with feelings of isolation. We learn about the boy's emotional life and his fight with isolation as he moves beyond his home to explore new landscapes, alternately beautiful and scary, and as he communes with nature.

Scott's short student film can be classified in several genres. It is a semi-autobiographical film because it is likely about the emotional life of Ridley Scott. It also is a road movie since much of its screen time involves the bike trip. *Boy and Bicycle* is a coming-of-age movie; we learn of the boy's growth and ideas concerning the world around him through his thoughts. It is an experimental film, although there is a framework of a story; the cinematic method is also nonnarrative, using images to create a mood and structure.

Boy and Bicycle does not contain any obvious DNA that can be traced to the feature films Ridley Scott would make in the manner that a short like Martin Scorsese's *The Big Shave* is directly reflected in that filmmaker's later work. What it does reveal is the technical artistry of Ridley Scott as a visualist.

Although Scott lists many films as having an influence on him, including *Saturday Night and Sunday Morning, The Seven Samurai, Citizen Kane,* and *The Third Man,* he told rca.uk, "There aren't too many visual metaphors or devices I employ cinematically that I can trace back to my student days. You try not to repeat yourself. Or I try not to. Perhaps curiosity and determination are the key factors I needed then, and need now, on every film I develop and make."[2]

Boy and Bicycle became a lost film for many years until the British Academy of Film and Television Arts (BAFTA) discovered it. When Scott screened it, he was pleased that it stood up well. *Boy and Bicycle* is available as an extra on *The Duellists* DVD, a British Institute Experimental Film Fund presentation.

During the period in which the short was made, Tony, an avid mountain climber, persuaded his older brother to join him for a trek in the nearby Cleveland Hills. The conditions that day were foggy. Tony easily climbed the two-hundred-foot face of the cliff and then disappeared into the fog. "Then a rope came down, and I could hear his voice saying, 'Tie it 'round, up you come,'" Scott told Scott Foundas of *Variety.* Ridley started to climb, but almost immediately his arms became numb. "I said, 'I think I'm going to peel off.'" Ridley fell as far as a hundred feet, his body flipping backward and the rope entangling him. "I could hear Tony at the top saying, 'I think I've got you.' He lowered me to the ground, and he had burn marks on his hands."[3] Ridley Scott never climbed a mountain again, but Tony Scott kept up the dangerous and invigorating sport, climbing El Capitan peak in Yosemite National Park three times.

3

THE PROFESSIONAL
From the BBC to Television Commercials

My idea of professionalism is probably a lot of people's idea of obsessive.

David Fincher

Ridley Scott graduated from London's Royal College of Art with first-class honors. His years at the RCA coincided with a tumultuous time of social upheaval in London, and there was a divide among the students. The counterculture movement began in England in 1958 with a march on February 17 for the Campaign for Nuclear Disarmament. Younger people began to challenge the established social and political norms. Scott, with his north-of-England roots, remained traditional, dressing in a conservative tweed jacket and sensible shoes, while many of the other students grew their hair long and affected a rebellious look.

After graduation in 1961, Scott was awarded a year-long traveling scholarship to America from Schweppes, the beverage company. Scott traveled eleven thousand miles throughout many states on a Greyhound bus. The scholarship to the US helped him land a position at the Drew Associates advertising agency in the US, where he had the opportunity to work with legendary documentary filmmakers Richard Leacock (*Primary*, 1960, and *Chiefs*, 1968) and D. A. Pennebaker (*Don't Look Back*, 1967, *Maidstone*, 1970, and *Jimi Plays Monterey*, 1986).

Later Scott was a trainee set designer for the BBC (British Broadcasting Company) assigned to design the second *Dr. Who* serial, *The Daleks*. Ironically, the assignment would have involved creating alien creatures, which would later come to have an association with Scott as a feature film director, but just before the start date a schedule conflict blocked him from getting the job.

"Ridley started in the design department at the BBC," recalls former BBC designer Geoffrey Kirkland in *Eye of the Storm*. "We were sentenced to six months of the *Tonight* programme and we all liked those sentences when we were that young. But like all designers in a big monolith, he wasn't satisfied. We weren't getting the best programs."[1] The *Tonight* program was a current events show, which offered limited creativity for a young set designer.

Scott was moonlighting during this period, designing sets for commercials until six in the morning, and then arriving at the BBC for seven. Fearing burnout, he decided to choose between the two, opting for commercials because the money was better and they presented greater artistic challenges.

Felicity Heywood, Ridley Scott's first wife, was born in London to an Austrian mother who was a nurse and a British father who was a bartender. During World War II Felicity was evacuated to Wales; this turned out to be a happy time in her childhood. Ultimately the family was reunited and moved to Montreal, Canada, where her father worked at Ruby Foo's, a Chinese nightclub. Four years later the family moved back to the UK, where Felicity attended a strict convent school. After graduation, she made a swift turn toward the flower-power, hippie freedom of the swinging '60s in London and enrolled as a painting student at the Royal College of Art. Her father burst with rage at the news. He wanted his daughter to work in a factory or office. Felicity, a strong-minded young woman, stood her ground. She recalls being the only girl admitted to the prestigious art college that year. After the repression of convent school, she found it liberating to ride the train every day to London. She enjoyed this life of freedom, sipping coffee with fellow student David Hockney, and working with him in a bar. Heywood describes Hockney, who became a noted painter, draughtsman, printmaker, stage designer, and photographer, as a very clever, somewhat awkward, bumbling gentleman. (Scott also painted while he was the RCA but had difficulty facing a blank canvas every day and rarely felt satisfied with his results. Today he regards Hockney as one of the era's most important painters.)

Heywood was an aficionado of the revolution in fashion. She borrowed clothes from RCA textile design students Ossie Clark and Zandra Rhodes (now Dame), who became two swinging '60s vogue giants. Once she spent most of her money allotted for the year on a pair of slacks at the renowned Harrods.

Heywood became Ridley Scott's first serious girlfriend. The couple was part of a circle of friends that included designers and artists on the rise. As art students, however, the couple had little money. She and Ridley lived in a modest flat in Barnes. Felicity worked as a waitress in Kensington High Street in the evenings. Nonetheless, the couple threw large parties—always inviting all the neighbors so there would be no one left to complain.

Felicity Heywood and Ridley Scott married in 1964. The next year Felicity gave birth to their first child, a boy they named Jake. Three years later, in 1968, a second son, Luke, was born. The two were married for eleven years but eventually the marriage unraveled, and they divorced in 1975.

Heywood's second marriage was to film director Bosie Vine-Miller. She herself has become an artist of some note. Her work has been widely recognized and exhibited. She recognizes the influence of Scott's work and world on their sons and is proud of Jake's and Luke's achievements, referring to the two as "very nice, gentle blokes."

Both boys followed their dad into the family business. Jake has made a name for himself directing commercials, notably some well-recognized Super Bowl spots. He also has directed many high-profile music videos for artists such as No Doubt, Radiohead, REM, George Michael, U2, Lily Allen, Massive Attack, and the Strokes. Luke is an integral part of Black Dog Films, part of Ridley Scott Associates (RSA), which produces music videos. He has worked with Beyoncé, Jamie Scott, and Imogen Heap.

Tony Scott also followed in his brother's footsteps, attending the same schools as Ridley. When Tony enrolled at London's Royal College of Art, his older brother urged him to make a film for the British Film Institute. "Ridley gave me an Ambrose Bierce short story and said, 'If you are interested in doing a film you can beg, borrow or steal a Bolex camera,'" Tony told Chris Lee of the *Daily Beast*.[2] The twenty-six-minute short, entitled *One of the Missing*, was released in the UK in January 1969. Ridley may have suggested this particular story because it was in a genre in which Ridley would later excel—war, in this case the American Civil War. The story concerns a Southern soldier who, sent on a reconnaissance mission to discover the enemy's position, is trapped in the rubble caused by Northern cannon fire. As it happens, his own gun is pointed at his forehead: at any time it might go off and annihilate him.

Ridley Scott maintained a frenetic pace during these developmental years. In 1963 Scott shot commercials at night and during the day was educated by the BBC in directing. He shot a short test version of Stanley Kubrick's 1957 World War I film *Paths of Glory*. Like Kubrick, Scott was fascinated by war—later reflected in *G.I. Jane* (1997), *Gladiator* (2000), *Black Hawk Down* (2001), *Kingdom of Heaven* (2005), and *Body of Lies* (2008). "I remember I did a potted version of *Paths of Glory*," Scott relates in *Eye of the Storm*. "I managed to get the fundamentals of the story of the Kubrick film down to battle, outrage, and trial and execution. And I managed to get that into a half an hour."

Scott was the production designer, wrote an adapted and compressed screenplay, and found all the correct props for the World War I period. He designed every shot. A thirty-five-millimeter motion picture camera was borrowed to shoot the film. When the film was screened for students and instructors in the BBC's director's program, they were duly impressed and full of praise for Scott's accomplishment.

Geoffrey Kirkland recalls this production in *Eye of the Storm*. "It was a lot of smoke—a half a dozen extras. . . . I was forced to be one, and we could have done with at least another twenty or thirty. Six of us had to be running around and back to camera again to have charged over the wire. He always wanted to direct, there was no question about that."

During his early years at the BBC, Scott constantly sought to direct and convinced the station to allow him to take a director's course. He pressed the management to give him a promotion. "I was such a bloody nuisance for three years as a designer, always complaining, that the BBC finally gave me a director's course and out of that got me a programme," Scott told Lynn Barber of the *Guardian*.[3] Scott's inaugural television program was *Softly, Softly* (1963), a spin-off of the then-popular crime series *Z Cars* (1962–1978). In 1965 Ridley Scott was given the chance to direct television episodes, including some for *Z Cars* about the work of mobile uniformed police in the fictional town of Newtown (based on Kirby) on the outskirts of Liverpool. Scott also directed episodes of the television series *The Informer* from 1966 to 1967 and a few episodes of *Adam Adamant* during the same period.

Scott had no experience directing actors and at the beginning found the process difficult. "I learnt to talk to actors simply by being handed two books, which were *Spotlight*—Male and Female, which were fundamental casting directories. I was given an office at the BBC with an experienced PA and told to get on with it because my show would be up in three weeks. And so I would sit in my room flicking through pages and saying, 'What do you think of him?' and then I'd meet them and somehow learned the process of putting a cast together. Of course, I had no idea where they were coming from," Scott told Barber.

At first Scott found himself on set primarily talking about the visual aspects of a project. His first attempts at directing actors were more as a traffic cop telling them where they should move. When challenged by an actor as to the nature of the character or how that character was feeling, he was at a bit of a loss and would say something generic like "You're sad." When asked why, he had no real answer other than "Because." Things changed when he directed actor Ian Hendry in *The Informer*. The renowned actor, who had worked extensively in BBC television, watched Ridley on set. He knew he wasn't a trained director so he took the care to take him aside and talk to him. Scott reported Hendry's advice to Kenneth Turan: "Your voice is too quiet. You are too apologetic. Take no prisoners. Apologize for nothing. And be assertive. Above all things, any decision is better than no decision." Scott concluded, "And from that moment on, I just changed gear."[4] He thought back to the way he had directed Tony in *Boy and Bicycle*, and although his methods then were far from totally effective for a now professional director, he remembered telling his actor-brother some specific commands about the state of the character. "So I learned engagement with an actor, where you assume partnership. It's not Svengali, it's partnership. The best results are with partnership. If the actor says, 'But . . .' you learn to listen. See? It's a good idea. Then they love the fact you accept them," Scott told Turan. One of Scott's issues at this early point in his career was that he felt he didn't speak the same language as actors. He was never an actor, nor had he studied acting. His world was filled with light, cinematography, and design. He was concerned with character and story, but he perceived acting as a job like any other in the filmmaking process. He would always hire the best actors he could find, but in the earlier days of his career he expected them to just do the job and act. His lessons from Ian Hendry were critical; ultimately experience would support Scott's path to a way to properly deal with actors.

Scott worked on the science fiction series *Out of the Unknown*, an anthology drama with adaptations from major genre writers such as Isaac Asimov, Ray Bradbury, and Kate Wilhelm. Scott designed the episode "Some Lapse in Time" that ran in the series' first year in 1965. Ridley Scott was less successful at BBC2, known for more "highbrow" programming; during a job interview he revealed he knew nothing about Shakespeare. Dissatisfied with his small salary of £75 a week, he left the BBC and transitioned into advertising, where he would shine, directing thousands of commercials and honing his craft as a future motion picture director.

"The BBC didn't pay very well in the 1960s," Scott told John Patterson of the *Guardian*. "You could look at your pay stubs and know exactly where you were going to be 40 years hence. So I did a commercial and it paid me so much I thought, 'I'm going to do this for a living.' I had my own company by the time I was 27 or 28—Ridley Scott Associates."[5]

After eight years of art school, Tony Scott at first wanted to make documentaries. His elder brother told him, "Don't go to the BBC, come to me first." Ridley provided the younger Scott an incentive. Tony was very much in debt. Ridley knew Tony liked fast cars. "Come work with me and within a year you'll have a Ferrari. And he did."[6]

Television commercial spots, whether sixty seconds or thirty, are sources of sizable income for advertising agencies, the directors, the product company, and the television networks that run them. Over the decades supporters of spot commercials and those in the field have classified commercials as mini-movies. Ridley Scott approaches the commercial as an art that uses cinematic storytelling to show the client's wares. Frequently viewers find commercials an intrusion, but occasionally one comes along that entertains or moves them. Film industry professionals questioned whether directors of television commercials had the chops to direct a feature film.

In the early years of American cinema, there was no training ground for directors. Directors came from various occupations and diverse backgrounds; when they were hired they learned on the job, and those who adapted rose in the profession. Even the moguls who ran the studios were originally business-men transplanted from other industries. Later, directors came from the theater and literature. In the 1950s live television, then in its golden age, became a vital training ground, producing esteemed film directors such as Sidney Lumet and John Frankenheimer. Later, film schools institutionalized the profession. Baby-boomer directors such as Francis Ford Coppola, Martin Scorsese, and Brian DePalma were among the early crop of film school graduates.

The hit movie *Flashdance* (1983) brought tremendous attention to British director Adrian Lyne, who had started his career directing commercials in England. Directors of commercials began directing music videos. These directors established another category that made its mark in feature film-making. Directors who made this transition include Wes Anderson, Sofia Coppola, Darren Aronofsky, David Fincher, Michel Gondry, Spike Jonze, Alan Parker, and Howard Zieff.

In general, the features crafted by directors of commercials emphasized rapid imagery and scenes that could be, like commercials, read quickly by the audience. Old school film purists complained, but there was a steady pipeline of such directors and many were successful at the box office.

Ridley Scott became a director of commercials because he could make a living and because he truly loved the form. He thought he could contribute something to it. He described the state of the commercials industry in the 1960s:

I was making commercials in New York in 1965 when they brought us in to get what was called the "English light," but when I was starting off with the BBC, I couldn't ever get the bloody sets lit properly. I used to be very critical. I thought commercials looked awful. The interiors were always lighter than the exteriors. It looked completely ridiculous. When I was getting into commercials, some of the people I encountered did not take them seriously. They were taken as a drudge. And the difference was that I took commercials very seriously. I loved every moment of the 20 years I was passionately engaged in television commercials. Derek Van Lint [director of photography] who did my second film *Alien* must have done at least 100 commercials with me. Frank Tidy [director of photography] did *The Duellists* and probably 150 commercials with me. I think I can safely say that what we did [in commercials] has changed the way feature films look today. That includes lighting, as well as editing. Do I need to see the hand go on the door handle, the feet going up the stairs? No. Communication in television is a story in 30 seconds. That's why it's harder frequently for a feature film director to move back and try to do television commercials. It's hard to grasp that language. For a television commercial director to suddenly be given two hours to tell and pace a story—that can be difficult as well.[7]

Directing and cinematography are inexorably linked in the creation of a motion picture, yet there are few directors in the history of cinema deeply involved in shot-by-shot photography or in the operation of the camera. Notable exceptions are Josef von Sternberg, Stanley Kubrick, Peter Hyams, Steven Soderbergh, Nicolas Roeg, and Robert Rodriguez. In commercials the hybrid director/cinematographer is quite common. This gives one person the creative control, guaranteeing the director will get the exact shots he or she wants in terms of lighting, composition, framing, lens choice, and use of filters or tools to move the camera. It made sense to Ridley Scott when he transitioned from commercials to feature films that he would choose his director of photography wisely, at times someone he had worked with on many commercials, and, as the director, he could also be the camera operator, or one of them. Scott brought speed to making movies; his extensive experience crafting commercials accelerated what can often be a tedious process, moving it along at a brisker pace. He was already an experienced production designer and, although there are vast differences between storytelling in a commercial and in a full-length feature film, he was keenly aware of how one image after another tells a motion picture story.

Years after leaving the BBC, Scott worked as an independent in television production. In late 1967, he created Ridley Scott Associates, a film and television commercials production company in London. Its goal was for Scott and other filmmakers to make state-of-the art commercials. Eventually he brought his brother Tony into the company as co-owner. During this period Ridley Scott directed, often produced, and often even shot hundreds of television commercials.

The first four weeks of RSA were touch and go, and the possibility of closing the shop hung over Ridley Scott because no money was coming in. He hadn't negotiated a bank loan and didn't have any investors. RSA was bought and paid for from the savings Scott gathered from his previous work in commercials. Fortunately, a big agency contacted Scott and asked if he could design a commercial. The business started to grow. It was at RSA that Ridley Scott learned the producing skills that would carry him throughout his career. RSA built a cadre of talented filmmakers; Scott would produce a commercial that another director helmed. He also continued to direct commercials at a furious pace. "It was almost like being in sport. I thought, 'How many tournaments can I play?'" Scott told Scott Foundas of *Variety*.[8]

In *Omni's Screen Flights/Screen Fantasies: The Future According to Science Fiction*, edited by Danny Peary, Ridley Scott talked about the importance of directing commercials in his career. "If you're a filmmaker and you're not filmmaking, that's a fallow period. It's like being an athlete. If you're not running around the track, you're losing your edge. It is like doing a pocket version of a feature film. The advantage with advertising is you don't have to live with something for months on end. . . . My training in commercials was really my film school." Scott went on, "It helped build my awareness of how to present suspense and—'manipulate' is a bad word—fascinate the audience and hold it in a kind of dramatic suspension. I learned how to communicate immediately, to use every conceivable visual and aural device to work on the senses and grab the viewer's attention for a particular time-span."[9]

Before Ridley Scott became the owner of an agency, he was on the other end. "I was the guy who carried out the agency's wishes," he told Sean Woods of *Rolling Stone.* "It was very, very competitive, because it's all about cost against creativity against 'what are you going to deliver?' The hot agencies would go after these so-called hot directors, and I was one of them for 20 years."[10] In 1999 filmmaker Richard Natale spent time at RSA. He found the culture there very warm for developing filmmakers and a dedication to the art of the commercial. "RSA has been a prime contributor to our visual vocabulary. RSA's commercials (and even its music videos for the likes of Madonna, REM, Janet Jackson, Mariah Carey and Sean "Puffy" Combs) are easy to spot: high gloss, stunning cinematography and conspicuously fast-paced editing. There have been hundreds of variations on two basic approaches: a barrage of highly-charged, sophisticated images creating a contemporary visual tone poem (any Nike commercial), or a series of sensuous dissolves, exotic, dreamlike and provocative (Calvin Klein's Obsession ads)."[11]

Barry Day, an associate of Ridley Scott's, observes in *Eye of the Storm,* "His commercials are an evocation . . . of a time people his age and mine didn't live through, but maybe that was the way it was. He was giving us that feeling, taking life, idealizing it, soft-focusing it, but this is the way you want it to be. Advertising has to do with hope and promise and happy endings and he was giving it to us in a very, very beautiful way you'd never quite seen before."

"I first worked with Ridley in the late 1960s," remembers Barry Day, director of international advertising and development, in *Eye of the Storm*:

> We were making a film for ice cream in glorious black-and-white
> and there was this young director who was managing to make it
> look like it was real ice cream. He was getting movement and
> appetite appeal for something that most people just shot, and he
> said "Let's just make it and get on with the next thing." He obviously
> cared. The first time I was aware of someone who brought the love
> of film and a sense of composition and framing and detail to it and
> it got to the point quite soon where people were looking at a reel
> and somebody said, "Who did that?" "Oh, it's bloody Ridley again!"

Money came into the company from ads directed by Ridley Scott and from directors Alan Parker and Hugh Hudson. It was a great time for British advertising, with Tony Scott, Alan Parker, Adrian Lyne, and Hugh Hudson all working at the same time. Scott says he got the itch to direct feature films when he saw fellow commercial directors Alan Parker and Adrian Lyne get film projects before him. "When someone told me Alan was doing *Bugsy Malone*, I couldn't sleep for weeks," Scott told Tim Walker. "Then Adrian started doing *Foxes* and I couldn't sleep for weeks again. I thought, 'I'm thirty-nine and I'm never going to get to direct a film.' So I stopped making commercials completely for almost a year and a half to get *The Duellists* going. It cost me a fortune."[12]

4

FENCERS

The Duellists

I see beauty in everything.

Ridley Scott

The creation of Ridley Scott's first feature film, *The Duellists,* began when after fifteen years of directing television commercials, Scott decided to move into the world of feature-length motion pictures. *The Duellists* was not the director's first attempt. Scott had planned a project based on the 1605 Gunpowder Plot—a failed plan to assassinate King James I, a Protestant, and blow up the Houses of Parliament. A screenplay was written—a collaboration between Scott and Gerald Vaughan-Hughes (*Sebastian,* 1968), but Scott could not obtain funding.

Another Scott-Vaughan-Hughes collaboration was based on the true story of an American nineteenth-century paleontologist, "Indian" Capwell. Considered too intellectual for Hollywood, it was rejected. Scott wrote two scripts: *Castle Accident,* for the Bee Gees, cowritten with John Edwards, and a heist genre picture, *Ronnie and Leo* (aka *Running in Place*), which he wrote solo in 1972. *Castle Accident* was a romp set in medieval times, an era to which Scott was drawn. Robert Stigwood, the Bee Gees' manager, thought a movie could pull his then fractured group together and do for them what *A Hard Day's Night* did for the Beatles. Stigwood bought the script but eventually pulled out. No funding was found for either project, but Scott got close on *Ronnie and Leo,* which got as far as preproduction with commitments from Michael York and Ernest Borgnine. Scott described the project to Trevor Hogg as "a very black, very violent comedy heist film somewhat influenced by Nicholas Roeg's *Performance,*" a film Scott greatly admired.[1] *Ronnie and Leo* almost came to fruition but ran into financing problems. The powers-that-be in British movie studios viewed Scott as too inexperienced to direct a theatrical feature. Scott believed he was ready but decided to play their game and first direct some filmed television.

Ridley and his brother Tony began to develop ideas for television series. They negotiated with a French television company, Technicinol, to produce a one-hour version of a Henry James story, "The Author of Beltraffio," a macabre narrative of a desperate family fighting among themselves with a tragic conclusion, as an episode in a six-part series of literary classics. Tony and Ridley flipped for the director slot, and Tony won the coin toss. The proposed project was received with such enthusiasm that the French offered a second program for Ridley Scott to direct. Scott decided he would turn this second project into his first feature. He began hunting through literary sources to find nineteenth-century writers with good stories. These properties were in the public domain, so there were no fees to pay.

Scott revisited the work of Henry James and delved into Jack London, a writer he greatly appreciated, known for his tales of adventure. Ultimately, although Ridley Scott had little taste for Joseph Conrad, he responded to a 1908 short story, "The Duel," in which two men duel periodically for twenty years. The themes of "The Duel" would allow Scott to pursue the ideas of obsession and the art of dueling and to closely examine two men under intense pressure.

Scott and Vaughan-Hughes began writing a sixty-minute teleplay, now titled *The Duellists*. Technicinol offered a budget of £150,000. However, as the script grew in scale, the company was not able to stay committed to Scott's project. Out of his own pocket, Scott paid Vaughan-Hughes to write the script for *The Duellists*, relying on his ideas to improve the script, develop the characters, and set the tone of the piece as well as to expand it to feature film length.

Conrad's short story "The Duel," aka "The Point of Honor: A Military Tale," was perfect for Scott. It had two main characters and plenty of action. As it was a period piece, Scott could apply his exquisite sense of imagery. The story was long for a short story form, more like novella, which was easier to adapt without leaving much out. Conrad had based "The Duel" on the actual duels of two French Hussar officers who battled during the Napoleonic era: Dupont and Fournier-Sarlovèze. Conrad fictionalized them as D'Hubert and Féraud.

Joseph Conrad (1857–1924) was born Józef Teodor Konrad Korzeniowski in Poland and was the machismo man's man. Conrad probed the thoughts and actions of the male psyche in a myriad of difficult circumstances. Conrad's literary work centers on man's frequent malevolence and individual battles with good and evil.

There are many Conrad screen adaptations, most famously Francis Ford Coppola's *Apocalypse Now* (1979), based on the writer's masterwork *Heart of Darkness*. Others include *An Outcast of the Islands* (1951), directed by Carol Reed, and *Lord Jim*, which has been filmed twice, in 1925 by Victor Fleming and in 1965 by Richard Brooks.

"To be truthful I am not an admirer of Conrad," Scott explained to Trevor Hogg. "I find him heavy going, because I think that generally he has a low level of humor." Actually, close examination of *The Duellists* and many of Scott's "manly man" films, such as *1492: Conquest of Paradise, White Squall, Gladiator, Black Hawk Down, Kingdom of Heaven,* and *Body of Lies,* reveal an affinity for the dark heart and examination of the complex male as seen in Conrad's writings.

In *The Duellists* D'Hubert, played by Keith Carradine, seems obliged to follow the fashion and rules of his position, but the Féraud character, played by Harvey Keitel, is driven by deep-seated anger and misguided machismo that results in the incessant confrontations between the two men. D'Hubert is motivated by honor, while Féraud is addicted to danger, violence, envy, and malevolence.

Financing and producing a first feature film is a tremendous undertaking. Scott sought financing in the United States, but, encountering difficulties, he eventually approached David Puttnam at his British company Enigma. The National Film Finance Corporation (NFFC) was involved in the financing. An agreement to produce *The Duellists* was reached.

David Puttnam produced low-budget films such as *That'll Be the Day* (1973), *Stardust* (1974), and the controversial *Bugsy Malone* (1976), a mob musical featuring child actors. Puttnam had been in advertising, so he was aware of Ridley Scott's talents and accomplishments; this softened the risk factor of backing a first-time feature director.

While at the Cannes Film Festival with *Bugsy Malone,* Paramount Pictures executive David Picker asked Puttnam if he knew any bankable directors. Puttnam contacted Scott, who immediately hopped on a plane to France to meet Picker. Producer Puttnam and director Scott offered Picker *The Gunpowder Plot* at a budget of $2 million and *The Duellists* for a reported $900,000 to $1.2 million, a low-ball figure for a studio film. Scott's biggest selling point was his reel featuring ten years of quality commercials he directed and mostly photographed. Although Paramount didn't perceive *The Duellists* as a prestige project, the studio thought the script sophisticated and Scott's reel sufficiently impressive to green-light the project. In keeping with the Hollywood philosophy of buying cheap and reaping high, David Picker inaugurated Ridley Scott's feature career by selecting the lesser budgeted project.

Scott advised Paramount that preproduction would start immediately. He was concerned that if they waited until spring to shoot, the picture would not get made, so he insisted on commencing shooting in the fall. The studio brass was shocked and told Scott a location film like *The Duellists* couldn't be shot in the winter. Scott was adamant and replied, "We do it now, or we don't do it," as he recalled to Paul Sammon in *Ridley Scott, Close Up*.[2] Although it was a risk to make his first feature at this time, he played hardball, which worked in getting the film made, but because of Scott's demand, the studio used its leverage to force Scott to pay for the completion bond, a critical production requirement most often picked up by the corporate backers. Ridley Scott looks back on his ultimatum as reckless. He didn't fully understand the financial consequences or the hazards and had no idea what it would be like to shoot a complex period movie in winter. But he knew the studio wanted the project and wanted him, so at that moment he dared to make an ultimatum. There was a lot at stake, but in the end the stress and anguish made *The Duellists* a better picture.

Principal photography on *The Duellists* began in late September 1976. Through hard work the company was able to wrap production on Christmas Eve 1976. Mounting the production took six weeks. The film was shot under a tight three-week schedule. Although Scott did some preplanning about the shooting, he proceeded one day at a time. He thought any other approach would have overwhelmed the small production unit. Although Paramount was financing *The Duellists*, while in production Scott felt the studio soon forgot it was being made, which worked in his favor; a studio can negatively interfere in a picture that is tightly under its radar.

A debut directorial film is more typically a young person's game. Orson Welles was twenty-six when he directed *Citizen Kane*, Martin Scorsese a year older when he directed *Who's That Knocking at My Door* (1969/1970), and Steven Spielberg was at the quarter-century mark when he directed *Duel* (1971). Ridley Scott turned forty while directing *The Duellists*, thus embarking on his feature film career in midlife. Although less typical, there was precedent— Michelangelo Antonioni started his career in features at forty-one, Jim Sheridan at forty, Clint Eastwood at forty-one, and Robert Bresson at forty-two.

Ridley Scott was in awe of Stanley Kubrick's *Barry Lyndon* (1975), released two years before *The Duellists*. *Barry Lyndon* is considered one of the most accurate, believable, and handsome period films ever made. Ridley Scott states it is one of the most beautiful films he's ever seen. Like many admirers of *Barry Lyndon,* Scott believes the film takes the viewer back in time. *Barry Lyndon* is acclaimed for its production design and photography—its use of color, lighting, and composition. Scott had photography in common with Kubrick. Both men were skilled with the still camera and had great abilities in composing a frame, capturing light and chiaroscuro, the art of light and dark. Both men also deftly handled the motion picture camera. Scott was ready to bring his sense of beauty to the feature film. Ridley Scott has stated he was attempting to emulate the style of *Barry Lyndon,* which created imagery that recalled naturalistic paintings of the era. Both Kubrick and Scott had the ability to reinvigorate literary works and bring screenplays to life in a manner that heightened their original qualities, creating cinema that is both highly visual and rich in content.

For Ridley Scott light is all important in creating images. Wherever he may be, Scott is acutely aware of the qualities of natural light, how it shifts and the atmospheric effect it has on his surroundings. On location or in a studio or on a practical interior location, Scott's eyes see the quality and effect of light and how it impacts psychologically and dramatically on a scene. One of the reasons Scott spends so much times either lighting a set or waiting to control natural light is that it is so complex and so vital in its support of characters and the story.

Scott had lived in a seventeenth-century stone house and observed how light functions when refracted on limestone. Scott moved around the house and its grounds at different times of the day, following full sunlight or the sun shrouded by clouds, to observe and document in his mind's eye how the house and its parts absorbed and refracted natural light.

Period films have always been a particular challenge for filmmakers. Scott's confidence was fortified by the many period commercials he had directed. The most renowned is the 1973 twenty-nine-second spot for Hovis bread, "Bike Round," shot on location on Gold Hill in Shaftsbury, Dorset. It is set in the late 1920s/early 1930s. A boy on a bicycle (as in Scott's first short *Boy and Bicycle*) travels on cobblestones to a bread shop. Laurence Raw, in his indispensable *The Ridley Scott Encyclopedia,* astutely suggests, "The use of lighting to create dramatic effect suggests similar techniques in *The Duellists,* especially the use of light and shade in the baker's shop, which recalls the third duel scene in Scott's film."[3] The spot is scored to Dvořák's *New World Symphony,* which heightens the nostalgic feeling about a product that was first developed in 1886. In 2014, the bread manufacturer's 120th anniversary, the commercial was aired on British television for ten days. In a poll, Scott's Hovis commercial was voted as an all-time favorite.

The boy was played by Carl Barlow, who forty years after appearing in the ad discussed the working method of Ridley Scott with Sara C. Nelson for the *Huffington Post United Kingdom*: "I remember he was very particular about everything with real attention to detail—even a door knob half way down the hill had to be perfect."[4]

Scott was also interested in the work of David Lean. "My model is David Lean whose characters never got lost in the proscenium," he told Michael Sragow.[5] Many fine directors admired David Lean, especially for the scope of his films and the control he exercised over the artistic content of his work. Ridley Scott was also a great admirer of Akira Kurosawa and Ingmar Bergman.

Balancing the large canvas between the environment and the people in the narrative would be a challenge well met in *The Duellists*. In revisiting the film in 2012, Sragrow said, "*The Duellists* is one of the most impressive directorial debuts in British movie history. It's as if having a central, magnetizing idea liberated Scott's imagination. In *The Duellists,* he works originally, on inspiration, as if he doesn't owe anything to anybody. He really seems scot-free." Scott is one of those rare film artists who doesn't let his inspirations show outwardly, but they are there for the astute critic and scholar to see.

For *The Duellists* Scott selected paintings that documented the period and place. From his extensive arts training Scott knew painters. His principal artistic inspirations were Napoleonic painters Carle Vernet and January Suchodolski as well as Georges de La Tour and classical still-life paintings. De La Tour was an eighteenth-century painter noted for making his subjects look as if they were illuminated by candlelight. Scott strove to get a candle-light effect in many of the interiors of his film, and period candles were used to illuminate those scenes.

Carle Vernet was a French painter who frequently painted hunting scenes, races, and landscapes. He was also known for his meticulous renderings of Napoleonic battle scenes. January Suchodolski was a Polish painter also renowned for his paintings of Napoleonic battles. Other painterly influences on *The Duellists* were Vermeer, a master of light; Willem Kalf, who captured still lifes with brilliant chiaroscuro; Franz Hals, also Dutch and known for his portraits rendered in loose brush strokes; and Jan Steen, again Dutch, known for his masses of color and humorous and psychological insights.

Another influence was Théodore Gericault, a French painter and pioneer of the Romantic movement.

Even though *The Duellists* was shot day by day within its tight schedule, eventually the entire movie, shot for shot, was storyboarded in Ridleygrams distributed to the key crew members, especially in the camera and design departments. Ridleygrams, often sketched quickly by Ridley Scott, capture the essence of a particular shot. He came up with the name to personalize the storyboard process and express the speed of this visual communication process.

Stacy Keach (*Fat City*, 1972) narrates *The Duellists*, basically speaking from Conrad's original text. In the opening a card reading "Strasbourg 1800" appears. There is a picturesque, painterly image of a young girl dressed in a skirt and floppy hat leading a flock of ducks through a path in the countryside. The image is reminiscent of a Dutch, French, or English painting. The director and the director of photography Frank Tidy shot with an Arriflex camera. Hollywood was using the American Panavision camera, which was sturdy, accurate, and came with a full complement of lenses. The Arriflex is a German-made motion picture camera that, although it had been used in Hollywood films over the years, was then most associated with independent films, documentaries, and shorts. The film was shot on the new Eastman color II 5247 stock to make the best out of the overcast conditions on location.

Scott's director of photography, Frank Tidy, making his feature film debut, had photographed 150 to 200 commercials with Ridley Scott as director. He was nominated for BSC (British Society of Cinematographers) and BAFTA film awards for his work on *The Duellists*. The production had only three trucks to haul around the equipment, as opposed to as many as fifty on an A-list production. Within these limitations, Scott managed to execute a plethora of camera techniques. He employed Tiffen low-contrast filters to add mood and coldness. "Graders" were used, which darkened and gave a tint to the upper region of the film frame while the lower section remained normally visualized. This dramatic technique is very painterly when used properly. Control over compositions is critical with use of graders.

When the commitment to make *The Duellists* at Paramount was sealed, David Picker initiated discussions with Ridley Scott and David Puttnam concerning casting. They were pleased when the executive put forth the names Harvey Keitel and Keith Carradine for the lead roles. Twenty-eight-year-old Keith Carradine was the first choice for the handsome and likeable

Lieutenant D' Hubert, and thirty-eight-year-old Keitel was the prime candidate for the malevolent Lieutenant Féraud.

At that time both actors were up-and-comers. Keitel had made a name for himself through an intense relationship with Martin Scorsese, who gave him the lead role in his first feature, *Who's That Knocking at My Door.* Keith Carradine was a member of the Carradine acting clan, which included his father, John, and brothers David and Robert. Keith was also associated with Robert Altman's repertory company, appearing in *McCabe & Mrs. Miller* (1971), *Thieves Like Us* (1974), and the seminal *Nashville* (1976). At the time Carradine was approached for *The Duellists,* his song "I'm Easy," written for *Nashville* and winner of the Golden Globe and Academy Award for Best Song in a Motion Picture, was number one on the charts. He was about to go on the road to promote it, but ultimately was persuaded to sign onto the film.

Both Keitel and Carradine had the same New York agent— Harry Ufland. Ufland had been sent the script by *The Duellists'* production company. Both actors very much liked the script. Nonetheless, it took Scott two and a half months to persuade Carradine and Keitel to accept the roles. During his stay in Los Angeles, Ridley Scott met with them many times, plying them with enticements, including the French food that would be a perk of the job. Keith Carradine was the easier sell. Although Keitel was happy with the script and liked Ridley Scott, he told the director he was wrong for the part. Keitel saw himself as a contemporary New York type and thought he would not fit in a European eighteenth-century environment. He was a stickler about playing a Frenchman with the correct accent; Keitel thought his inability to do so was a deal breaker. Scott went into full-throttle mode to convince Keitel he was the man for the role. Scott told Keitel the cast would be eclectic; he planned to cast Brits to play Frenchmen, so the audience wouldn't take a New Yorker to task. Scott was able to convince the mercurial actor that if the story played well on-screen, the audience would enter the world of the film and become involved with the characters—they wouldn't even notice the accents. Keitel bought this logic and signed on. At first uncomfortable in the skin of Féraud, he eventually settled in, applying Method acting techniques. Scott proved at the outset of his film directing career that he would persist no matter how long it took to get what he needed for the film, pursuing the actors he wanted without panicking or giving up and moving on to others that might have been second rate.

At the Virginia Film Festival as seen on YouTube, Keith Carradine recalls this early acting experience and reflects on Ridley Scott as a director.

I was struggling. I didn't always feel I was giving him what he needed. I think there were a few occasions where I felt this way—a kind of reaching for something. He was having trouble making me understand . . . and I was having trouble satisfying whatever it was he was after. Maybe it was because he couldn't articulate it properly or something. But on the whole to criticize Ridley as being a strictly visual filmmaker misses a very important point, which is the nature of cinema is visual—that's what it is about. It's interesting how people will try to minimize his importance as a filmmaker and you look out there and you will see many, many filmmakers who are imitating what he's done over the last twenty years.[6]

With his leads in place, Ridley Scott found the rest of the casting process simpler. His strategy was to engage stockpiled talent by sending out the word to actors he had met or worked with in commercials at Ridley Scott Associates or during his time at the BBC. Diana Quick, who was offered the role of Laura, D'Hubert's mistress, had worked with the Royal Shakespeare Company. Scott introduced this love interest to counter the morose quality of the endless conflicts between D'Hubert and Féraud and injected other female roles to stimulate audience interest. The female characters suggest Scott's understanding of strong women—a theme that would appear in subsequent Ridley Scott films inspired by his mother and other women in his life. As Scott told Marlow Stern of the *Daily Beast,*

I'm used to very strong women because my mother was particularly strong, and my father was away all the time. My mother was a big part of bringing up three boys, so I was fully versed in the strength of a powerful woman, and accepted that as the status quo. I think there are a lot of men who feel they're being emasculated by having the woman be in charge; I've never had that problem. All the relationships in my life have been with strong women, from childhood. The relationship I've had in my life for the past 30 years is with a very strong Costa Rican woman [longtime partner Giannina Facio—the couple married in June 2015]. . . . Oddly enough, I find it quite engaging to be working with a female when I'm directing. It's kind of interesting.[7]

Diana Quick was friendly with the legendary Albert Finney and convinced him to play a cameo involving one day's work as Joseph Fouché, a key member of Napoleon's empire. There are conflicting stories as to what Finney was paid for his appearance. Either he was given a framed check for £25 bearing the inscription, "Break glass in case of dire need" or, as Ridley Scott remembers the payment, he was given a case of champagne.

Tom Conti (*Merry Christmas Mr. Lawrence*, 1983, *Ruben, Ruben,* 1983, *Beyond Therapy,* 1987) made his feature film debut as Dr. Jacquin, a confidant of D'Hubert. Gay Hamilton, who featured in *Barry Lyndon* as Barry's flirty older cousin, plays Féraud's feisty maid and mistress in *The Duellists.*

A large number of extras was needed for a film requiring many soldiers and figures on the streets as well as interiors. The budget was so tight Scott used crew members as extras. For the scene of a cavalry charge Scott put producer David Puttnam and other crew members to work as soldiers. The costume and wardrobe departments were forced to wrap the men in hotel blankets because production couldn't afford uniforms.

For production and postproduction units Scott continued to dip into the talent well at Ridley Scott Associates. RSA personnel on *The Duellists* included dubbing editor Terry Rawlings, focus puller Adrian Biddle, and associate producer Ivor Powell (nephew of British film critic Dilys Powell). These valuable production members continued to work with Scott on future films.

For the cinematography on *The Duellists,* there was a bone of contention between David Puttnam and Ridley Scott when Puttnam discovered Scott intended to personally operate the camera, as he almost always did when he directed a commercial; it was not an uncommon practice in that field and a way of getting exact control over the image. Puttnam believed this was impossible on a feature film where the director needed to be involved with oversight and not focus on the shooting.

For Ridley Scott a camera was like an artist's pencil. The production started with a camera operator who quickly resigned, telling Puttnam and Scott the project was no fun when the director was so concerned with every aspect of the camerawork. To resolve the issue Scott and Puttnam struck a deal. Scott would operate the camera for five days as a test; if the results were unsatisfactory or they were behind schedule, they would hire an operator. After the trial period the photography was scrutinized, and Puttnam was convinced.

While he was shooting, Scott talked to the actors from behind the camera. He brought much élan to the photography, especially his skill for making the screen look full. Frank Tidy was in charge of the lighting. With justification, Ridley Scott is listed as a camera operator on *The Duellists'* end credits. "You're painting when you're operating. The proscenium, which is the viewfinder, is where the bells go off. If you are the actor, I'm actually engaging with you, I'm looking right inside you, and I'm seeing every goddamn blink. They like that. It's a bit like being a good still photographer. And they blossom, they blossom," Scott told Kenneth Turan.[8]

Scott would go on to operate the camera on *Alien* and *Legend*. Eventually Scott stopped the practice because he began shooting with as many as eleven cameras at once on a scene and found it was more effective to sit in the tented area with the monitors displaying the images captured by each camera. This gave Scott the ability to talk to the camera operators after a take and have them adjust a composition or change a lens.

Scott called himself a smoke demon because of all the smoke he used for many scenes. For Scott smoke was a natural diffuser of light and added atmosphere. A reputation for using smoke followed Scott from film to film. He would put almost anything in the air—smoke, dirt, or snow—to get the look he wanted. Smoke is a marvelous and atmospheric texture on film, but it could be hard on the crew and cause many health hazards, especially affecting the lungs, particularly when used in interior scenes. This extensive use of smoke for visual purposes was strictly an artistic tool for Scott, who may have ignored the comfort of others; certainly on *Blade Runner* this would become a problem and an issue for an already irate crew.

Scott's directorial behavior on the set emerged early. *Millimeter* magazine's Donald Chase said of Ridley Scott, "The man is part risk-taking dreamer and part pragmatist-pusher."[9] As for his temperament, Ridley Scott is now known for his appreciation of actors and his technical crew. The mature Ridley Scott does not raise his voice, yell at an actor or crew member, curse, badger, or in any way harass his team. In the early days it was different. Scott was known to be short-tempered, demanding, and especially hard on actors. Although he always achieved the results he wanted, lacking patience, experience, and trust, the young Ridley Scott exhausted himself and his company. Perfectionism came at a price.

For the first duel Carradine and Keitel were given car aerials to use for swords. They had to put a cap on the tips to avoid injuries. When real blades are used, the protective cap can't be left on because it will be seen by the audience and spoil the illusion. The swords were attached to batteries so as to produce sparks. On several occasions, an actor fell to the ground due to the shock produced by the electricity.

The story of *The Duellists* concerns two of Napoleon's army officers. A nasty feud is created when the mayor's nephew is nearly killed in a sword duel by the obsessed Lieutenant Gabriel Féraud. Lieutenant Armand D'Hubert is dispatched to put the maniacal Féraud under house arrest.

D'Hubert and Féraud do not meet again for six months, this time in Augsburg in 1801. Féraud wastes no time challenging D'Hubert to a duel and seriously wounds him. In their next duel, they fight to a standstill. Then D'Hubert is promoted to captain, and since the military does not allow officers of different ranks to fight one another, no duels occur.

In 1806 D'Hubert learns that Féraud is now a captain and in the same city. D'Hubert, learning he will soon be promoted to major, attempts in vain to avoid Féraud. The resulting duel, which D'Hubert wins, is fought on horseback.

Later D'Hubert, who has risen to the rank of brigadier general, marries and retires from military service, although he has been offered command of a brigade by Napoleon. After Napoleon is defeated at Waterloo, Féraud is arrested and is to be executed for his role in the Hundred Days' War, but, incongruously and unbeknownst to Féraud, D'Hubert intervenes on his behalf.

Ever in pursuit, Féraud challenges D'Hubert to a duel with pistols. Each duelist has two bullets. D'Hubert corners Féraud and is in a position to shoot him. Instead D'Hubert releases him and pronounces an end to their dueling bond. Féraud is a psychologically defeated man, and D'Hubert is free to live his life with his loving family. The duels at last are ended. In the BBC documentary on Ridley Scott, *Eye of the Storm,* Scott observes, "The irony at the end of it all is that they can't remember what the initial argument was about and I found that was a very intense take on the idea of obsession and mindless violence. . . . Obsession—it's really about obsession, not so much revenge."[10]

Although there were some sets that were dressed and art-directed by production designer Peter Hampton, outdoor locations were chosen and utilized by Scott based on convenience. On several occasions the crew dressed Scott's hotel room and shot a scene there. Economy was all. The budget couldn't sustain many sets. Scott used ingenuity to keep the shoot going.

The able fight director William Hobbs was recommended for the exhaustive task of choreographing the duels. Hobbs had a distinguished career in fight coordination. His credits included *Macbeth* (Roman Polanski, 1971) and *The Three Musketeers: The Queen's Diamonds* (1973). Scott and Hobbs felt strongly that each duel had to display its own dynamic and they collaborated intensely to achieve verisimilitude. They dueled on the ground with rapiers and flintlocks—at times on horseback. Both principal actors received training in the art of the duel. Keitel, with no experience in the sport, learned to fight as obsessively as his character required.

Unless there was a major critical reason to pause in the shooting, Scott and his team never stopped. The director kept a brisk pace. Speed was essential. Scott couldn't afford to let too much time pass as he had a deadline and he personally would pay for any overages. One of the duels was shot in only forty-five minutes. Scott photographed it wrapped in a hotel blanket because he kept getting whacked by Carradine and Keitel as they dueled with their swords. Scott and Tidy photographed everything on *The Duellists* with one camera.

The sky was almost always overcast. On rare occasions when the sun came out, Scott yelled for the crew to assemble so they could shoot in sunlight. One of those times was for the next to last shot. The framing was wide and high, looking down on the landscape. Keitel is in the shot and took Ridley's direction when he asked the actor to turn so he could be photographed in profile. He wears a Napoleonic hat and appears to be a defeated Napoleon looking off and contemplating his future. The image of Napoleon being very short projected over the centuries is not quite true. He was five foot seven inches. Harvey Keitel comes close to that height at five foot eight. Standing on the precipice was difficult for Harvey Keitel, who suffered from vertigo. The sun came out frame-right and kept moving for some time. This expansive shot has great beauty. It was captured in one take. Scott got the idea from an image he'd seen in a black-and-white picture of Napoleon on the top of a rise, looking off across hills, valleys, and fields. He felt it was appropriate for Keitel's character. The very last shot in the film is a tight close-up of Keitel looking into the distance contemplating his fate.

As Christmas was approaching Ridley Scott and company shot a horseback duel. It was cut to the quick in order to speed up production. If he didn't finish in time to release the cast and crew for the holidays, he would have to pay £100,000. Luckily he was successful.

For a snow scene Scott borrowed a shot from a toothpaste commercial he directed. It was perfect for the situation. Scott quickly learned that when you are not being paid much you become inventive.

The original musical score composed by Howard Blake (*The Riddle of the Sands*, 1979, *Flash Gordon*, 1980, *A Midsummer's Night Dream*, 1996) features a relentless, haunting theme filled with melancholy and deep sadness. The theme builds in intensity through repetition. Ridley Scott was more than pleased with the score, which gave the film such mood and atmosphere.

The music editor Terry Rawlings taught Scott much about what can be done with music. Scott was so impressed with Rawlings he promoted him to film editor. Rawlings cut Ridley Scott's next three films, *Alien, Blade Runner,* and *Legend.*

Postproduction on *The Duellists* began after the production wrap on Christmas Eve and concluded in mid-1977. The film was released late that year. One of the most audacious moments of editing comes in the horseback duel. Real time is intercut with Carradine's character flashing back to his past. This rapid editing at first seems out of place, but the viewer begins to realize the film is getting inside of D'Hubert's mind. This intricate intercutting took place in the editing room, where the idea was born. It is the only really fast cutting in *The Duellists,* which overall has an even and dedicated pace.

Scott has stated that nothing during the shooting was hard—it was fun. What was difficult was getting the film to a desired running time of one hundred minutes. The initial first cut came in long because Ridley Scott and editor Pamela Power put in every scene that was shot and then pruned down the cut until they reached the requisite time. There was a second editor on the picture, Michael Bradsell (*The Devils,* 1971, *Savage Messiah,* 1972), who was supervising editor. *The Duellists* was basically split in half, allowing Ridley Scott to go back and forth working with the two editors. *The Duellists* was Power's first editorial outing and her debut as a feature film editor. She would go on to cut *Legend* and *G.I. Jane* as an additional editor. She also worked for Tony Scott, editing his first feature, *The Hunger* (1983).

Discussing the editorial contribution, Scott observed to Trevor Hogg of the Flickeringmyth website, "The editors gave me a perspective on pace and kept me from falling into a standard commercial director's trap, that is, from feeling that you have to have a payoff every thirty or sixty seconds."

In terms of pace *The Duellists,* unlike other first films directed by television commercial directors, doesn't feel like a long commercial. It is paced like a feature film, with each scene finding its own rhythm based on content and action. This is quite an accomplishment and one of the reasons *The Duellists* is such a standout as a first film. Ridley Scott was able immediately to direct in the correct structure. As more directors of commercials directed feature-length films, critics began to type them as filmmakers who couldn't break out of their earlier methodology. There is some truth to this but not concerning Ridley Scott. His vast knowledge of the history of world cinema was a film school for him in understanding the long form of movies.

Three mega movie executives were at Paramount when *The Duellists* was completed: David Picker, Michael Eisner, president and CEO, and Barry Diller, chairman—they all adored the film.

The Duellists is a fine film, handsome and visually striking. As the first motion picture of a newly minted director it is breathtaking and astonishing. On his first film, Ridley Scott cemented his reputation as a visualist. Discerning film critic Pauline Kael would later call him a "visual hypnotist."

A lifelong theme of Ridley Scott films is the investigation of the world of men. They are the duelists during the Napoleonic Wars, the cops of *Black Rain*, the fighters and royalty in *Gladiator*, the soldiers of *Black Hawk Down*, the warriors of *Kingdom of Heaven*, the law and the lawless in *American Gangster*, and the doomed men of *The Counselor*. Like Conrad (whom the director continues to say he doesn't care for much), Scott is fascinated and perhaps obsessed with how men think and act. Through motion pictures he examines their strengths as well as their weaknesses.

Reviewers expressed various criticisms. Tom Milne in the *Monthly Film Bulletin* found the film an exciting adventure story but contended that *The Duellists* "clearly betrays the dampening influence of television" because it relies on close-ups and uses short static scenes. Moreover, he felt it confirmed once again "that Conrad at his best does not translate to the cinema too easily."[11] Dave Kehr of the *Chicago Reader* noted, "The pleasures are mainly pictorial: damp green landscapes and heavy gray skies."[12] In the *Los Angeles Times* Mark Chalon Smith offered a mixed critique, labeling the film ambitious but flawed. He praised the duels and noted that the cinematography, "with its gun-gray skyscapes and fire-lit interiors . . . evoke[s] something of Conrad's tortured realism."[13] Vincent Canby of the *New York Times* praised the film, stating that it "uses beauty much in the same way that other movies use soundtrack music, to set mood, to complement scenes and even to contradict them." Canby went on to extol the script: "it is precise, intelligent, civilized, and . . . it never for a moment mistakes its narrative purpose."[14]

"I think Ridley began by being more of a stylist," Barry Day explained in *Eye of the Storm*. "You've seen *The Duellists*—every frame was beautifully lit, beautifully arranged as it would have been in a commercial, but, for many of us, the development of the characters and the narrative flow was a little stilted. He's overcome that and happily ever since then. I think the criticism people have had with commercial directors making features is that they are lovingly caring for each frame, but do not really feel too much where these frames lead to and what happens to the motivation within it."

The notion of Scott overwhelming the story and characters with striking visuals would follow him throughout his long career. Day seems to believe he overcame this imbalance, but in the main critics especially let the director know he's more a visual than a narrative storyteller.

Close analysis of *The Duellists*, however, reveals a studied balance between the numerous sword fights, action scenes directly tied to the overall story, and the inner makeup of the two polar-opposite main characters. Each battle is like a separate short film. The weapons are different, the locations change, and most important, the intensity of the men and their state of mind progresses over a very long period of time.

Unfortunately, *The Duellists* was poorly distributed. Initially only seven prints were struck for the US opening. To Ridley Scott's dismay, the film was booked across the country on the art house circuit. Nevertheless, the film was distinguished by winning a special award for Best First Film at the 1977 Cannes Film Festival, and in 1978 the David di Donatello Award for Best Director—Foreign Film from the Academy of Italian Cinema.

It is unfortunate that *The Duellists* was not widely seen in its initial release. But many viewers and cineastes who did see it took note of the director's name. Ridley Scott had made a film that over the decades has gotten more attention and praise and easily sits among those considered the best first films of a director who went on to a substantive career. In a film that is more about a man's obsession to maintain honor at all costs, *The Duellists* features dueling sequences that rank among the best: *The Adventures of Robin Hood* (1938), *Scaramouche* (1952), and *The Three Musketeers* (1973). It functions as an action movie filled with inventive swordsmanship and gunplay yet at the same time is a deep psychological drama.

Ridley Scott told John Patterson of the *Guardian,* "I remember finishing *The Duellists* and thinking, 'That was easy.' Then I got to Cannes and thought, 'Oh, we're the English entry,' and then, 'Oh, we're gonna win!' Then the critiques came in, 'Too pretty, too arty, too gauzy.' I took it to heart because I'd always done that in commercials. Later, I realized I was just very lucky to have a good eye."[15]

Few who saw the first theatrical run of *The Duellists* had any idea that the Ridley Scott credited as director would go on to achieve a stellar career that endures, shines, and frequently overwhelms—and occasionally underwhelms. Decidedly, over multiple decades Ridley Scott has been recognized as a stylish and powerful maker of motion pictures.

5

ALIENATION

Alien

In space no one can hear you scream.

Tagline for original Alien *poster*

During the production of *The Duellists,* Ridley Scott began to consider his next feature project. He was in the Dordogne region in France admiring all the beauty when it dawned on him that this romantic setting would be perfect for the ancient tale of Tristan and Isolde. He approached David Puttnam about it for his second feature. They agreed and Gerald Vaughan-Hughes wrote a screenplay.

Dordogne is a beautiful and peaceful area known for its lush landscape and quiet, desirable qualities for filming a movie. More than one hundred movies have been shot in the Dordogne region.

Tristan and Isolde is a medieval romantic adventure poem based on an ancient Celtic fable. In the tale, the young hero Tristan travels to Ireland as a messenger to request the hand of Princess Isolde in the name of his uncle, King Mark of Cornwall. Tristan succeeds in his efforts, but on the journey home with Isolde the two accidentally drink a love potion meant for the princess and the king. The two become bonded by a deep love. When the king learns of this, he separates the lovers, who face tragic deaths. There are many variations on the story, but its essence is a tale of star-crossed lovers.

The screenplay was submitted to Paramount, and in spring 1977 *Tristan and Isolde* was placed in development. Scott began traveling back and forth between Ridley Scott Associates in London and Los Angeles, where David Puttnam assembled a production office. In England, producer Ivor Powell coordinated the developing project.

Powell, a science fiction buff, was instrumental in introducing Ridley Scott to a magazine that would impact the look of the director's next three films. Powell was an avid reader of *Heavy Metal.* The publication sported an

Ridley Scott and Sigourney Weaver on the set of *Alien*.

impressive roster of cutting-edge artists, most notably the French cartoonist Moebius, whose real name was Jean Henri Gaston Giraud: a man with the talent to design wardrobe, buildings, weapons, transportation systems—everything. He drew and painted images of the future, and his artistic signature was distinctive, often very detailed and architectural. Scott was so enamored with the *Heavy Metal* visual world that he even considered applying it to a period film like *Tristan and Isolde*. Scott combed the back issues of *Heavy Metal* with pencil in hand, trying to transplant the *Heavy Metal* aesthetic to the production design being developed for *Tristan and Isolde*.

In the middle of 1977, the storyboards and Gerald Vaughan-Hughes's revised screenplay were complete. *Star Wars* had just been released and was creating a huge buzz; David Puttnam suggested to Scott they go see this new film that was all the rage. Scott watched George Lucas's space epic unspool at the legendary Mann's Chinese Theater in Hollywood. He was devastated because Lucas's epic applied many of the design concepts Scott envisioned for *Tristan and Isolde*. Ridley Scott concluded that a medieval romance didn't have an audience in this new market. Lucas (along with Spielberg's *Close*

Encounters of the Third Kind) had opened the door wide to a new generation of science fiction film. The original plan for *Tristan and Isolde* was to place it in France, but after *Star Wars,* Scott sat down for weeks developing plans to set it in a futuristic environment.

Sandy Lieberson, then the London head of 20th Century Fox, had been at the screening of *The Duellists* at Cannes and was favorably impressed. He combed through Fox studio materials in development in hopes of finding a project he could offer to the promising new director. He had a list of directorial candidates for *Alien.* Even Robert Altman, an unlikely choice, was on the list.

Scott explained to Paul M. Sammon his decision to direct *Alien*:

I was intrigued by Lieberson's willingness to invite me to the
Hollywood dance. . . . I was somewhat baffled, because my
knowledge of science fiction at that point was barely minimal. I'd
only seen a handful of them—*The Day the Earth Stood Still, 2001,
Star Wars.* . . . As a rule, other than the ones I just mentioned, I didn't
really like science fiction pictures. . . . Lieberson thought I might be
able to bring something different to a sci-fi. . . . Once I started
reading *Alien,* I was immediately hooked. . . . I was impressed with
the script's vividness, the way things kept leaping off the page into
my mind's eye. I also responded to a subplot concerning the owners
of the human spacecraft, which was this sinister, Big Brother type of
corporation, and I was quite taken with the then somewhat novel
concept of the hero being a woman. [But] the thing that really
appealed to me most about *Alien* was its characters. . . . Everything
you needed to know about these people was beautifully set up within
the context of the story . . . [which] included an interesting social
subtext emphasizing the class differences between the command
officers and the guys sweating it out on the engineering decks.[1]

The decision to move into the science fiction genre by directing *Alien* was a career changer. Although Scott would make many different styles of films, he would become associated with science fiction and keep returning to it. Character and the interrelationships in a movie narrative were important to him. *Alien* was also significant for its female lead and the strength of that character, elements that marked several films he would make after *Alien.* He believed a strong female lead would appeal to audiences who were used to seeing submissive female characters and yearned for something different.

Lieberson believed the dark story would interest Ridley Scott. His invitation meant that Scott was now poised to become a Hollywood filmmaker. Ultimately, *Alien*'s brooding science fiction story was perfect for Scott. The script was cowritten by Walter Hill, a screenwriter of growing reputation (*The Getaway*, 1972, directed by Sam Peckinpah, and *The Mackintosh Man*, 1973, directed by John Huston). The story of *Alien* concerns a commercial spacecraft carrying a crew peopled by Captain Dallas (Tom Skerritt), Ripley (Sigourney Weaver), Lambert (Veronica Cartwright), Brett (Harry Dean Stanton), Kane (played by John Hurt, who replaced Jon Finch when the latter became ill), Ash, a robot (Ian Holm), and Parker (Yaphet Kotto). During their voyage Kane is infected by an alien creature that literally bursts through his stomach and kills him in the picture's most memorable and visually shocking sequence. The creature grows into a slimy giant who systematically kills every crew member, from an upper-deck elite officer to a grunge worker in the bowels of the ship. Only Ripley survives and fatally conquers the creature. The script was unusual; it was tight, gripping, and tense with stark horror. The vivid material stimulated Ridley Scott's acute visual sense.

Tristan and Isolde was losing momentum, so Scott appealed to Paramount to release him. *Tristan* and *Isolde* was eventually made in 2006 with Ridley and Tony Scott as executive producers. Director Kevin Reynolds mounted a handsome production, but the film failed at the box office.

From a production design standpoint, Scott knew he could apply the *Heavy Metal* magazine sensibility and graphic novel concepts in which he was immersed to the *Alien* project. Fueled by the design possibilities and well-drawn characters, Scott told Lieberson he was ready to direct *Alien* for 20th Century Fox. Lieberson contacted Alan Ladd Jr., Fox's LA-based production chief, and informed him of Scott's commitment. Ladd, known as Laddie, had already green-lighted the project on Halloween 1977 with Walter Hill as the potential director, but Hill had moved on to other projects and Scott was signed in February 1978.

When Scott accepted the director position, he was at the studio within thirty-two hours. Scott believed the script was perfect and that the film could be made right away. However, he was meticulous in casting the picture, a process that took a long time. "I didn't cast Sigourney Weaver until almost two weeks before principal photography. Laddie who is normally a paragon and absolute representation of calm and cool, lost his cool and said, 'Where the fuck is the leading lady?' I was ten days off. I tested her in the sets I was building for *Alien,* that's how close I was, and it worked out," Scott told Chris Hewitt of *Empire* magazine.

David Giler, Walter Hill, and Gordon Carroll were contracted as producers, but only Carroll and Ivor Powell would actually produce *Alien.* David Giler and Walter Hill were signed as producers because of their initial involvement with the project.

The original *Alien* screenplay had been entitled *Star Beast.* It was written by Ronald Shusett and Dan O'Bannon, whose first original screenplay, *Dark Star,* was directed by John Carpenter in his long-form debut in 1974. Giler and Hill rewrote O'Bannon's work, leaving the story outline and sequence of events but radically altering the dialogue. No small issue was their decision to change Ripley from a man to a woman. It was this screenplay that eventually reached Ridley Scott's hands. Brandywine, the production company, also made the critical decision to change the name of the script from *Star Beast* to *Alien.*

For the part of Ripley, Scott chose Sigourney Weaver, a New York stage actress with scant film credits. He saw strength and intelligence in the twenty-eight-year-old Weaver and trusted his judgment. The choice would pay off grandly. Weaver went on to star in a series of sequels that became a franchise.

Scott wanted to create a good environment for the cast on set. He believed that a well-designed set like the spaceship in *Alien* allowed the actors to inhabit their characters and drew out their best performances. Nevertheless, the atmosphere during shooting was tense and uncomfortable. Reportedly, Sigourney Weaver felt isolated and found Scott remote. For Weaver working on *Alien* was a trying experience: "I can't remember a happy moment, really," she commented in *Eye of the Storm.*[2]

Scott admits he generated an uncomfortable energy that had an impact on the cast and crew. As he explained to Paul M. Sammon, "I was twitching like crazy frankly because I was nervous. This was my first Hollywood picture. I was also frustrated because for the first time in my professional career there were hands other than my own on the film."

Tom Skerritt seemed to take everything in stride. In his assessment of Ridley Scott he told John Monaghan of the *Detroit Free Press*: "Ridley is an artist. . . . There is also poetry in his work, the way he works with images. 'It's all about the texture,' he would say."[3]

Scott's relationship with Brandywine/Fox was strained. Scott was constantly asked to justify his decision making, which caused him to want to just "get on with it," triggering a lot of collateral tension. Scott observed in hindsight that he was unable to ask for the trust of the cast and crew, and thus

Alien's results came at a price. Brandywine and 20th Century Fox maintained total control over the budget, quashing Scott's desire to go further in executing his directorial vision.

Alien was originally given a budget of $4.2 million. Scott knew this wasn't enough for his extensive visual plans, so he storyboarded the entire film himself with Ridleygrams to prove that the budget had to be increased; ultimately, the original figure was doubled to $8.5 million. In today's dollars, the budget is estimated at around $11 million.

Prior to shooting *Alien*, Scott listened to Dan O'Bannon's counsel on several matters. O'Bannon had preplanned and researched many of the elements of the story. He envisioned the screenplay as both science fiction and horror and suggested Scott screen the scandalous horror film *The Texas Chainsaw Massacre* (1974). Scott also watched the classic *The Exorcist* (1973) over and over for its portrayal of pure evil in an elegant setting. Influences from both these classics of the horror genre were absorbed into *Alien*.

The unadulterated bloody violence in *The Texas Chainsaw Massacre* being inflicted on victims from heartless and thoughtless creatures would give Scott the incentive to stage the Alien's merciless attacks on the crew members one by one. *The Exorcist* was a lesson in slowly and methodically building tension in a horror film as the young girl is transformed into a devilish beast.

The shooting schedule was set to begin on July 3, 1978, and conclude on October 21. Seventeen days were allowed for shooting inserts and pickups, planned for November and December. Scott was committed to detailing worlds on the screen that serve the characters and story and ultimately satisfy the audience. Especially on *Alien* Ridley Scott's training as a production designer would give him further collaborative options. He would exercise his design powers on *Blade Runner* and on other films to come, but here they would serve him in working with a talented team to fashion a beast with many moving parts and the ability to frighten audiences out of their wits.

To create an inimitable and visually enthralling atmosphere dominated by a unique creature, Scott required an exceptional crew of special visual effects artists and designers. Scott conceived *Alien* after his immersion in *Heavy Metal* magazine and graphic novels. Before Scott was on board, screenwriter O'Bannon had employed Ron Cobb, a well-known political cartoonist who was building a career as a film designer. On Cobb's résumé were several of the bizarre creatures in the memorable *Star Wars* cantina sequence. Scott was thrilled to have Cobb on his design team and gave him several assignments—the spaceship that carried the human crew, its mechanisms, and just about anything concerning earth culture. To design the human spacesuits and the crews' wardrobe Scott wanted Moebius. Scott also hired Michael Seymour, an RSA graduate, for the art department. The British Seymour had worked with Scott on countless commercials. As production designer he would meld the work of Scott, Cobb, and Moebius. This team and their assignments still left a design element behind—the Alien and its step-by-step transformation into an adult. The larger adult Alien kills its human victims by erotically thrusting a phallic tongue into their brain pads—death by penetration.

Scott began calling *Alien* a beast movie, and he strained his creative brain trying to imagine what the Alien would look like. The current standards for movie beasts were pretty bad, in Scott's estimation. They were often outsized and didn't scale in the environment (as in *Godzilla*), were shapeless (*The Blob*), wrapped in ancient bandages (*The Mummy*), oversized with a fashioned large head (*Frankenstein*), or appeared like an all-hair human (*The Wolfman*). Scott was looking for something high tech and with the ability to morph into different deadly shapes.

Dan O'Bannon had showed Scott a book by H. R. Giger, and enthusiastically Ridley Scott brought him on board. H. R. Giger was a Swiss surrealist painter, sculptor, and set designer influenced by Salvador Dalí and Ernst Fuchs. *Alien* was becoming a science fiction/drama/horror/beast movie. "I knew I was in dangerous waters regarding *Alien's* creature from the start, because almost all of the 'monsters' I'd seen in other films were pretty tatty," Scott told Sammon. "Therefore, I had to find someone capable of taking our own beast up to the next level. . . . Giger is a . . . surrealist, really, who's very technically accomplished but also drawn to grotesque imagery. Giger invented a remarkable style he called 'biomechanics' which combined organic life with machinery. . . . I started flipping through it and nearly fell off of my desk, because I'd lit upon a particular painting [Giger's *Necronomicon*] with this frightening, truly unique creature in it. This is our beast! . . . I'd never been so sure of anything in my life."

Necronom IV is half human, half reptile with a long skull. Giger often featured sexual images in his work, so here the cranium looks like a long gray penis. Later the creature would be fashioned with a pair of outsized lungs shaped like testicles. Horror and fantasy writer and filmmaker Clive Barker observes, "Giger seems to be painting aliens but the closer you look, the more you realize he's painting twisted versions of himself." Giger confirmed this to the *Guardian*, talking about the creation of the Chestburster: "It was Francis Bacon's work that gave me the inspiration. [It] would come tearing out of the man's flesh with its gaping mouth, grasping and with an explosion of teeth . . . it's pure Bacon."[4]

Director of photography Derek Van Lint was an RSA associate. His stylish and dynamic work on *Alien* would be his only credit as a director of photography on a feature film. Scott continued to operate the camera as he had in countless commercials and on his first feature *The Duellists*. Scott estimated that he shot about 80 percent of *Alien* himself. By operating the camera, Scott got close to his cast and the set design, always ready to make changes or give feedback because of his immediacy behind and in front of the video monitors.

There had been many suggestions for the name of the spaceship. Scott harkened back to Joseph Conrad's work and settled on *Nostromo*. He referenced Conrad again by calling the shuttlecraft *Narcissus* after Conrad's *Nigger of the Narcissus,* which concerns a boat crew infected with a deadly disease analogous to the Alien. The company that owns the *Nostromo* and cares little for its crew is called Wegla-Yutami after the riverboat company owners in *Heart of Darkness.* The fact that he adopted these Conrad monikers makes his negative comments about Conrad a bit perplexing.

The exterior of the derelict ship was built and photographed at Bray Studios, where model and miniature work was done. The portals of the derelict spaceship look like vaginas. The imagery of both insects and sexual organs can be seen on the sets throughout *Alien,* and egg shapes, skeletons, and skeletal structures permeate *Alien's* visual style.

Responding to what they believe is a distress call, the crew of the *Nostromo* lands on what is known as Moon LV-426. There the crew members find a giant Space Jockey, an alien who was the pilot of a space craft, with its chest hollowed out by what they believe to be a xenomorph. The creature was given the nickname "Space Jockey" during production by Giger. For the Space Jockey, H. R. Giger and Peter Voysey constructed a 1:24 scale prototype. The full-scale set was twenty-six feet high. Giger continued to detail the set up until filming.

The egg chamber was a matte painting by Ray Caple (*Superman*) based on H. R. Giger's design. Ridley Scott thought that thin membranes would signal the eggs out of which alien creatures would emerge. This was achieved with smoke and a pulsating scanner laser that the *Alien* production borrowed from the legendary British rock band the Who. One hundred and thirty eggs were constructed. Each had a vaginal opening. Nick Allder designed one of the eggs to open by way of a hydraulic mechanism he installed.

Chestburster departed from H. R. Giger's original design. Roger Dicken altered it to make an infant version of the Alien. On the day of the shoot the cast was not allowed on set until John Hurt was rigged with a false torso. The only information the rest of the cast had was what the script indicated.

Facehugger was designed by Roger Dicken, Ron Cobb, H. R. Giger, and Ridley Scott. A metal skeleton was created, and molded latex was applied. It was filled with acidic blood—a corrosive cocktail of chloroform, acetone, cyclohexylamine, and acetic acid that when dripped onto the Styrofoam floor ate right through it. Facehugger is the second stage in the Alien's life cycle. It has eight long tentacle-like fingers that allow it to move at a very rapid pace. Its only purpose is to make contact with a host's mouth for an implantation process. It wraps its tail around the subject's neck and cannot be removed until it completes its mission of planting an embryo; then it detaches and dies.

Jake Scott recalled in *Eye of the Storm* going to the studio on the day of the infamous Chestburster scene.

John Hurt is lying on the kitchen table and the Chestburster bursts through his rib cage. A hole had been cut into the table and John Hurt was slung into the hole. There was a fake chest piece and myriad blood lines, blood canisters covered in plastic sheeting. The actors hadn't been told specifically about the amount of blood and guts that would appear when the Chestburster broke through John Hurt's chest. Action is called and at the precise moment Ridley Scott shouts out, "Now!" Everyone reacted as the entire set was splattered with pieces and chunks of flesh, internal organs, blood and bodily fluids. It was disgusting, shocking and revolting.

Sigourney Weaver remembers that day well, recalling in *Eye of the Storm*, "I walked in and the two writers were off giggling—very excited like it was Christmas, which was a little weird. Then all the technicians including Ridley had on floor-length raincoats. We had no rehearsal . . . all of us . . . this thing jumps out of John Hurt's chest . . . and there it goes—it happened so fast we were all so astonished. . . . Ridley understands that you can manufacture that kind of surprise for yourself as an actor, but it's much better if someone can just sort of help you get there."

Ridley Scott told Sean Woods of *Rolling Stone* about the impact that scene had on an audience: "It was a birth. I walked the circuit of the theater when I was previewing *Alien,* and I knew I had the tiger by the bollocks. I'll never forget in St. Louis there was a group of couples that were literally entwined around each other in abject terror, and I knew I had done my job."

Jake Scott brings insight to his father's inner workings in *Eye of the Storm.* "I think my dad is interested in the darker side of life, darker people, darker characters and . . . the more morbid aspects of life. I don't want to make him sound like a weekend grave digger, but he certainly looks into the ground rather than up to the sky. I think he would choose William Blake over Constable. . . . He's just intrigued by a certain light and his light happens to be fiery dark and slightly foreboding." Jake Scott elaborates. "Black Dog is a term my father uses to describe darkness. It's a symbol for inactivity and depression and, 'my god, I've got to get on with something, I've got to get on with something.' He actually describes it as something that looms over his shoulder in the corner of his eye. This black dog drives him forward, so the faster he runs the harder it is for the black dog to keep up with him." "Black Dog" in British folklore is a kind of hellhound, a ghostly apparition associated with the devil and death.

Scott attributes his dark worldview in film to his early environment. "I was born in drizzling rain in the northeast of England. The northerners are the Celts, and they are all nuts. It's a Celtic thing, you know you tend to be a bit 'the glass is half-empty' rather than 'the glass is half-full.' That said, if you're going to make the big films, you've got to be a fuckin' born optimist," he remarked to Sean Woods.

Understanding the Black Dog concept is key to insights about how Ridley Scott's career would develop over the years. His work output is rare in a director of any era. The drive to create would push him to make one feature film after another, produce films by others, run RSA, and direct and oversee commercials, music videos, short films, and television movies and series. As Scott grows older this pace accelerates and his momentum continues to propel him. The influence of this drive showed up early on with bouts of temper and impatience, but eventually settled down into a steady work pattern that would earn him a reputation among his peers and audiences as a film director with a remarkable productivity. What might have been debilitating and unworkable for some became an unceasing creative streak for Ridley Scott.

The Alien was played by the six foot seven Nigerian graphic artist Bolaji Badejo, cast because he was so tall and slender. He was twenty-six at the time.

In an interview first published in *Cinefantastique* in autumn 1979, Badejo explained how the monster moved and functioned:

> It was all manual, remote-controlled. There's still a space in it for my head. I had it on just to make sure nothing goes wrong with the posture of the head or how tall it is in comparison to the other sequences. They must have had about 2000 tubes of K-Y jelly, just to get the effect of that slime coming out of his mouth. A lot of it was spread around the face. I could barely see what was going on around me, except when I was in a stationary position while they were filming. Then there were a few holes I could look through.[5]

Giger sculpted the alien outfit on stage B at Shepperton Studios. Carlo Rambaldi, who conceived the King Kong creature for the 1976 remake of *King Kong,* created the mechanics that brought the head to life. The suit was made of latex and cost in excess of $250,000. It consisted of ten to fifteen separate pieces worn over a one-piece bodysuit.

To enhance the quality of the miniature special effects photography, Scott made the decision to scrap all of the unit's footage and directed all the shooting of models during postproduction, pushing the crew to endure eighteen-hour days six to seven days a week.

When the first cut was put together by Terry Rawlings with Scott's input, the film was long. During the creation of the director's cut, when the editor and director work to get the released version, up to fourteen scenes or parts of scenes were deleted to make *Alien* better, tighter, and more articulate as a very scary science fiction horror film.

For the musical score Ridley Scott first considered New Age master Tomita's recording of Holst's *The Planets,* but he eventually decided on legendary Hollywood composer Jerry Goldsmith (*The Planet of the Apes,* 1968, *Patton,* 1970, *Star Trek: The Motion Picture,* 1979). Scott utilizes Howard Hanson's *Symphony No. 2 Romantic.* Others have pointed out that cues were swapped out from Goldsmith's 1961 *Freud* score.

Tension increased when just as *Alien* was to be released, Dan O'Bannon entered into a fierce Writers Guild arbitration with David Giler and Walter Hill over final screenplay credit. O'Bannon won, but many connected to the production believed that Giler and Hill made enormous contributions to the screenplay.

Alien premiered in the United States on Friday, May 25, 1979, at the Egyptian Theatre with mock-ups of the egg chamber, "The Mother" set, and a three-fourths scale model of the Space Jockey on display outside. It was given a huge advertising and merchandising budget. Worldwide the film grossed $183 million. At Oscar time it was nominated for the innovative production design and won the statuette for Best Visual Effects.

Reviews, however, were mainly negative. Vincent Canby of the *New York Times* praised the cast and design but also called *Alien* "an extremely small, rather decent movie of a modest kind, set inside a large, extremely fancy physical production." He wrote it off as an "old fashioned scare movie."[6] Jack Kroll of *Newsweek* likened Sigourney Weaver's Ripley to an old-time damsel in distress like Fay Wray in the original *King Kong* (1933).

Roger Ebert describes the motor behind the film:

> *Alien* uses a tricky device to keep the alien fresh throughout the movie: It evolves the nature and appearance of the creature, so we never know quite what it looks like or what it can do. We assume at first the eggs will produce a humanoid, because that's the form of the petrified pilot on the long-lost alien ship. But of course we don't even know if the pilot is of the same race as his cargo of leathery eggs. Maybe he also considers them as a weapon. The first time we get a good look at the Alien, as it bursts from the chest of poor Kane (John Hurt) [*sic*]. It is unmistakably phallic in shape, and the critic Tim Dirks mentions its "open, dripping vaginal mouth." Yes, but later, as we glimpse it during a series of attacks, it no longer assumes this shape at all, but looks octopod, reptilian or arachnoid. And then it uncorks another secret; the fluid dripping from its body is a "universal solvent," and there is a sequence both frightening and delightful as it eats its way through one deck of the ship after another.

The violence in *Alien,* notably the legendary Chestburster sequence in which the Alien breaks through Kane's chest, was considered controversial, as was the scene in which Ash has his head knocked off, revealing he's a robot.

To those critics and audience members who accused the film of wallowing in blood and guts, Scott argued that *Alien* is, with the exception of the Chestburster sequence, devoid of blood and guts and immersed in the design of the spacecraft and every other location. Ridley Scott has explained that *Alien* was a C movie done in an A way. Scott took a good script with good characters and elevated the production with eye-popping and scary special effects and a high level of craft in all aspects of the production.

Because of his work on *Alien* Scott nearly directed one of science fiction's most celebrated novels—*Dune,* written by Frank Herbert. This epic story takes place more than twenty-one thousand years in the future on the planet Arrakis, which has a desert environment hostile to human life. The intricate plot involves an emperor, duke, and baron in a complex struggle for political and social power.

After a mega-successful publication, Herbert found that film producers were hesitant to approach the material. In 1972 Arthur P. Jacobs, producer of the highly successful *Planet of the Apes* series, was the first to make an offer—a nine-year option on the book. He approached David Lean and Robert Bolt to write and direct *Dune.* Bolt dropped out, and Rospo Pallenberg, long associated with director John Boorman, replaced him. The start date was planned for sometime in 1974. Sadly, Jacobs died in 1973. For a period, the project was tied up with his estate. Then a French consortium bought the rights.

In 1975 *Dune* seemed like it had a green light. Surprisingly, the director was to be Alejandro Jodorowsky, the Chilean/French cinema madman/magician who surprised and offended audiences with *El Topo* (1970) and *The Holy Mountain* (1973). Jodorowsky did not read *Dune* but nevertheless pushed ahead gathering his crew. Salvador Dalí was offered a role, and Orson Welles, Mick Jagger, and even the band Pink Floyd were persuaded to join the production. For the look of the film Jodorowsky brought on cutting-edge artists H. R. Giger and Moebius. The script could have made an eleven- or twelve-hour movie, and it was vehemently anti-Catholic. Millions of dollars were needed for what has been called Jodorowsky's "trippy" take on Herbert's *Dune.* With insufficient funds and what was considered an unworkable script, Alejandro Jodorowsky was no longer the director of *Dune.*

In 1976, Dino De Laurentiis bought the rights to *Dune.* Years were spent developing the complex project. Raffaella De Laurentiis and her legendary father were solid fans of the book but realized making it into a movie was a risk. Raffaella De Laurentiis became the producer. In 1979 the De Laurentiis empire contacted Ridley Scott and asked him to come on board as director. He was intrigued by the endless design possibilities the material offered. Scott hired Rudy Wurlitzer (*Two-Lane Blacktop,* 1971, and *Pat Garrett and Billy the Kid,* 1973) to contribute to a screenplay adaptation for *Dune,* but Frank Herbert didn't approve it. H. R. Giger was tapped as production designer. Preproduction began. At that time there was no shootable script.

Then suddenly in 1980 Ridley's older brother Frank died of skin cancer—he was forty-five years old. It was an emotional time. Ridley Scott fell into a deep depression over the passing of his brother—because of his extreme grief he couldn't see staying on *Dune* for the long stretch it required, so he bowed out of the production. He had worked on *Dune* for around seven months. Scott turned his attention to RSA while coping with his brother's tragic early death, but eventually yearned to get back to features. He became attracted to material that pursued the deep emotions he was keeping inside. "I liked the idea of exploring pain," he told Lynn Barber of the *Guardian*.[7] He was experiencing a profound sense of loss and frustration. Frank left home at age sixteen and became a midshipman, later living in Singapore for fourteen years. Ridley was just getting to know his older brother when Frank was diagnosed with skin cancer. "When he was ill, I used to go and visit him in London, and that was really traumatic for me. But I still didn't discuss it with anyone. I'm of that generation that was brought up, you know, look after yourself, pull yourself together." The experience had a profound and overwhelming effect on Ridley Scott both physically and psychologically. Mentally he suffered paranoia and became very phobic. He couldn't sleep for almost two years. He resisted medical help. "I always believed in self-fixing. I was brought up stiff upper lip by Ma—very tough, my Ma," he told Lynn Barber.

Dune was eventually written and directed by David Lynch and released in 1984. It lost money at the box office and did poorly with the critics and audiences, but over time it became a cult favorite.

In 1979 Ridley Scott married his second wife, Sandy Watson, with whom he already had a daughter, Jordan. Watson began her career as a television producer at PKL, then worked on big-budget productions for the advertising agency Foote Cone & Belding alongside Alan Parker, Adrian Lyne, Ridley Scott, and other notable directors. Later, she had a short run with Collett Dickenson Pearce and KMP before forming her own production company in 1985, Lewin and Watson, with director Nick Lewin.

Like Scott, Watson developed a deep love of films as a child when she made weekly trips to the cinema. Her first career dream was to be an usherette, followed by film editor, then producer, then the head of a TV production company, and finally the owner of her own establishment. She eventually achieved all those goals (except usherette). She left school at the tender age of sixteen and worked in media, starting at the bottom as a runner at a production company where she caught the eye of her superiors by arriving at work every day decked out in a Givenchy suit, sunglasses, and high heels. She spent her days making sandwiches and trudging through Soho. Eventually she moved into the editing department, then was asked to go on shoots and became a production assistant, although she couldn't type. The next stop was at the PKL agency, where she landed a job as producer. She was offered more money at Foote Cone & Belding, with the opportunity to work on big-budget productions. She found this opportunity challenging and exciting but said working with Ridley was hard because their relationship was under scrutiny.

The couple divorced in 1989. Jordan was raised in London and first came to Los Angeles at fourteen. Sandy Watson was not particularly drawn to Los Angeles, and Jordan was not exposed to Hollywood parties or anything "decadent," as Jordan describes it. Due to his rigorous schedule Scott was not home as often as he wished. Jordan recalls, "I was aware of his absences, but since that was the way it always was, I never felt I was losing out, especially since I had more of his attention when he was home." Jordan, who is also a film director and photographer at RSA, was introduced to the business when her father was directing *Legend*. He told his daughter, "We'll let you be a fairy." Actually, when she got on set, she was put on a wire and performed as a stunt double. She was even paid £50. Although many children are adversely affected by the divorce of their parents, Jordan Scott says she wasn't. "I'm probably the only person on the planet whose parents' divorce didn't really have any lasting effect. I think they handled it perfectly, because it didn't seem to impact on my life at all." Although her older brothers Jake and Luke are technically Jordan's half brothers, the only girl in the family bristles at the term:

I get incredibly upset when people refer to them as my half-brothers because they've always been brothers to me. My mum helped raise them from a very early age, before she had me, and when I came along, because they were that much older, there was no jealousy. I was a novelty, this weird little specimen to show to their friends. It's always been a group effort and we've always lived about two minutes apart from each other in Hampstead. Our mums have always got on and it's an interesting set-up, but one that always seemed to work. Or maybe it's open-mindedness and everyone's inner hippie dying to come out. Whatever it is, we're lucky to have pretty groovy parents.

At eighteen Jordan left school and studied fine arts in California, but dropped out when she realized she wanted to work in film production. She worked for a music video producer, had a period where she wanted to work in the art department, and then at age twenty directed her first music video. She later moved into advertising, directing commercials for Renault, Clio, and Orange. In 2005 she directed a segment of the anthology film *All the Invisible Children* along with her father, Spike Lee, John Woo, and others who contributed to the project. That same year she directed a three-minute short film for Prada produced by her father. "That was a little odd, but he was great about standing on the sidelines and drinking coffee so I could do what I wanted. I was nervous about working with him and even though we're quite similar, in that we're both strong-willed, stubborn and occasionally have a temper, we understand each other and work well together."[8] Along with their uncle Tony, all three Scott siblings blended their talents as a professional family at Ridley Scott Associates.

6

ELECTRIC LADYLAND

Blade Runner

> Visual directors like Luc Besson (or Terry Gilliam or Ridley Scott) are potentially difficult collaborators because they know exactly what they want; however their commitment to the image means they will always seek to capitalize on what you give them.
>
> *Production designer Dan Weil*

Ridley Scott's third feature, *Blade Runner*, is a science fiction film so influential it sits on a short shelf with *Metropolis* (1927), *Things to Come* (1936), *2001: A Space Odyssey* (1968), and *Star Wars* (1977). The screenplay adaptation is from Philip K. Dick's novel *Do Androids Dream of Electric Sheep?* a title no one thought was appropriate for a movie. Paul M. Sammon has classified *Blade Runner* as a "future noir." The character of Rachael, played by Sean Young, is the femme fatale, and Deckard, portrayed by Harrison Ford, is the doomed antihero. Tyrell, played sardonically by veteran character actor Joe Turkel, is the evil-minded genius/villain. "The neo-noir story has an emotional basis in the cultural past, but the visualization reflects recent trends."[1] A future noir is simply a neo-noir that takes place in the future.

Philip Kindred Dick wrote some of the most noteworthy novels of the science fiction genre: *The Man in the High Castle, Martian Time-Slip, The Three Stigmata of Palmer Eldritch, Ubik,* and *Valis.* He also was a master of the short story. Several of Dick's works were adapted into films, including *Total Recall* (1990), based on *We Can Remember It for You Wholesale,* directed by Paul Verhoeven, and *Minority Report* (2002), directed by Steven Spielberg.

Ridley Scott's involvement as the director of *Blade Runner* began after several circuitous attempts to bring the story to the screen. In 1969 Martin Scorsese and his friend Jay Cocks, screenwriter and film critic, met with Philip K. Dick to discuss the possibility of adapting *Do Androids Dream of Electric Sheep?*; however, they never purchased an option and nothing came of the possibility. In the early 1970s Hampton Fancher became aware of *Do Androids Dream of Electric*

The futuristic architecture of *Blade Runner.*

Sheep? through a friend who thought Hollywood was ready to revive the science fiction genre. Fancher, not a sci-fi aficionado, read the book and didn't care for it that much, but he acknowledged its possible commercial potential. But Fancher couldn't find the mysterious and elusive Philip K. Dick. Eventually, he got his telephone number from science fiction giant Ray Bradbury. Fancher and Dick discussed optioning the novel, but Fancher left empty-handed, perceiving that Dick saw him as a Hollywood hustler and also sensing that Dick did not want *Do Androids Dream of Electric Sheep?* adapted into a movie. Dick later told Paul M. Sammon the problem wasn't Fancher, whom he rather liked, but Hollywood itself. He also revealed that the book had already been optioned by Herb Jaffe Associates. Herb's son Robert was the first person to write a script based on the book. Dick hated the outcome, calling it a comedy spoof.

In 1978 the Jaffe option lapsed. Fancher approached his friend Brian Kelly, a budding producer, and suggested optioning *Do Androids Dream of Electric Sheep?* Kelly purchased the option for only $2,000. Fancher proceeded to write an eight-page treatment that Kelly brought to British producer Michael Deeley (*The Italian Job,* 1969, *The Man Who Fell to Earth,* 1976, *The Deer Hunter,* 1978). Deeley asked Fancher to write a full-length screenplay adaptation. The project was scaled for a low-budget movie. The story took place in one room with a few street scenes. The story of Rachael, the femme fatale who commits suicide, was scrapped.

Fancher's first draft was entitled *Android*. Deeley loved it. The three men made a deal. Deeley proceeded to make the studio rounds and considered a series of directors he thought were rising stars. These included Adrian Lyne, Michael Apted, Bruce Beresford, and Ridley Scott. Scott was aware of Fancher's script while he was shooting *Alien,* but he wasn't particularly interested.

CBS Television was interested in the project for CBS Films, Inc., with a budget of $8 or $9 million. At this time the project was called *Dangerous Days.* Gregory Peck was offered the part of Deckard. He turned it down, although he liked the themes of moral crisis and urban pollution. The filmmakers had a long list for the lead role of Detective Rick Deckard, including Gene Hackman, Sean Connery, Jack Nicholson, Paul Newman, Clint Eastwood, Arnold Schwarzenegger, Al Pacino, Burt Reynolds, Robert Duvall, Peter Falk, and Nick Nolte.

Scott came onto the project late. Because he had already directed a science fiction film, he felt he should move on to other cinematic plateaus; however, Scott knew Michael Deeley and felt they would be compatible, so he changed his mind and signed on February 21, 1980. He was now fixated on the screenplay, which he thought was an extraordinary piece of work with some marvelous design possibilities.

The project was now too expensive for CBS Films. With Scott's name attached to the film, Deeley acquired $12–15 million in backing from Filmways. *Dangerous Days* was green-lighted. The project was renamed *Blade Runner*—Hampton Fancher's idea from the book *Blade Runner: A Movie,* written by beat generation writer William S. Burroughs. Permission from Mr. Burroughs was received, and Deeley bought the title. Unfortunately, no one told Philip K. Dick about the proceedings or asked him to write the screenplay; he found out through someone else. Dick was at first bemused and then it began to agitate him. As Fancher developed a series of rewrites, the narrative moved away from Dick's original story.

Casting, crewing up, and the design process were all under way. Dustin Hoffman was brought into the production. Over three months of negotiations he worked with Ridley Scott and Michael Deeley. Both sides tried to influence each other. Although Hoffman was off type for the character of Rick Deckard, Scott and Deeley believed strongly in Hoffman's acting skills. Eventually, however, they parted ways due to different perceptions of the film.

Actress Barbara Hershey suggested Harrison Ford to Fancher. Like Ridley Scott, Harrison Ford admits he didn't have much of a taste for science fiction. Deeley and Scott jumped on a plane to London, where Steven Spielberg and Ford were working on *Raiders of the Lost Ark.* Scott was impressed that Harrison Ford had acted in two films directed by Francis Ford Coppola, *The Conversation* (1974) and *Apocalypse Now* (1979). Scott found Ford smart and possessed of a dry wit. Ford read the script and had issues with it. He suggested removing the voice-over that was written into Fancher's screenplay and transferring those lines into scenes.

Screen tests were made. Three women were considered for the role of Rachael: Sean Young, Nina Axelrod, and Barbara Hershey. Different camera blocking was used on Sean Young's test. Scott said she was a Vivian Leigh type, acerbic, tough, and smart. Everyone was saying how perfect she was, but Young was depressed and flat-out scared, feeling the weight of the role's responsibility—nevertheless, she got the part.

Ridley Scott envisioned the future in *Blade Runner* as a totalitarian society in a world controlled by a very few major corporations. New building construction in the city would diminish. Everything was old, retrofitted, and needed service. The world of this city is overloaded—things may stop at any moment. There are billboards and electric signs everywhere. The look of the people and their nature reflected Scott's vision of 2019. It would be close to an autocratic state. The Los Angeles of 2019 depicted in *Blade Runner* is predominately an Asian community composed of Chinese, Japanese, and Thai people. The major theme of *Blade Runner* is one that occurs in several Ridley Scott films, particularly *Alien, Hannibal,* and *American Gangster*—what it means to be human, a notion often explored by Philip K. Dick.

Script issues continued, and eventually Fancher was dismissed. To appease him and acknowledge his hard work, Fancher was given an executive producer credit. Then Ridley Scott approached David Webb Peoples (*Unforgiven,* 1992). He was flown to Los Angeles and booked into the Chateau Marmont. Peoples read Fancher's script and told Scott and Deeley he couldn't make it any better. Ridley responded, "*We'll* make it better," and Peoples was brought on board.

Peoples was a good dialogue writer and able to fill in holes in the story. Peoples said he would do what Ridley Scott wanted him to do—and actually did it. Unfortunately, Dick was not informed that Fancher was off the picture and David Webb Peoples was writing drafts, taking his lead from Ridley Scott. Luckily, in the end, Dick was happy with the results when he read Peoples's work. Dick thought Peoples had studied *Do Androids Dream of Electric Sheep?* and transferred the important themes into the screenplay. Peoples is credited as co-screenwriter; eventually the Fancher and Peoples scripts were melded. In reality, the screenwriters did not use *Do Androids Dream of Electric Sheep?* as a reference until after the third draft of the screenplay.

The first budget for *Blade Runner* was $13 million. A start date of January 12, 1981, was established, and a release date of December 1981 was set. After $2.5 million had been spent and a crew was brought on, Filmways pulled out, citing a budget now estimated at $22–30 million as beyond its financial capabilities. A desperate Michael Deeley had very little time to raise $22 million. None of the major studios would agree to cover the outstanding costs.

Principal photography began on March 9, 1981. The money came from several sources. The Ladd Company, through Warner Bros., provided $7.5 million. Tandem Productions, composed of TV moguls Norman Lear, his partner Bud Yorkin, and entrepreneur A. Jerrold Perenchio, put up $7 million for the ancillary rights. They served as bond guarantors for $300,000 if the budget went 10 percent over. Run Run Shaw, the Hong Kong–based Asian producer, put up $7.5 million in exchange for the foreign rights, nearly one-third the budget of *Blade Runner.* Alan Ladd Jr. rushed *Blade Runner* into production. Lear chose not to get involved, which put Bud Yorkin in the lead position.

Ridley Scott was shooting at a painstaking pace. After three days the film was two weeks behind schedule. Harrison Ford grew angry waiting for the schedule to progress. The screenplay gave little information describing the look of *Blade Runner,* but Scott had conceptualized it clearly from the outset. Syd Mead, a visual futurist and industrial designer known for creating a wide-ranging style of vehicles and transportation structures, including the Concorde, created the vehicles and worked on the architecture of *Blade Runner,* also creating mattes and neon lighting in close collaboration with Scott and production designer Lawrence G. Paull.

Many of the buildings in *Blade Runner* are retrofitted, a technical addition to an existing structure. There are electric signs, neon, and billboards everywhere. There was an assumption that the weather pattern had changed radically in this future world, so it rained all the time in formerly sunny LA, as if Philip K. Dick predicted the extent of global warming back in 1968.

Although initially resistant, after scouting various cities, Scott and Deeley concluded that *Blade Runner* should be done on a studio back lot and not on location. The majority of *Blade Runner* was photographed on the New York street set on the Warner Bros. soundstage in Burbank, California. It was at least forty years old. *The Maltese Falcon* (1941) and *The Big Sleep*

(1946) had been shot there. The *Blade Runner* sets were built over the old New York sets.

As an art director/production designer on TV programs and commercials, Ridley Scott as a director is friendly to production design. His talent and skill greatly contributed to the astounding and complex appearance of *Blade Runner*. Historically, the production designer runs the art department. Depending on the director, he or she could take a hands-on approach in working with the production designer and the art department or have minimal or no interaction and let the others do their jobs. On *Blade Runner*, as on all Ridley Scott films, Ridley Scott oversaw the art department. This arrangement is respected in recognition of Scott's art director/production designer training. One of Scott's design strategies for *Blade Runner* was to turn objects and architectural units upside down or around. This would give the setting an entirely new look and create a new fit within the rest of the environment.

The production designer of *Blade Runner*, Lawrence G. Paull, was initially trained as an architect and city planner before designing movies. He joined the art department at 20th Century Fox during the old studio system and apprenticed under master art directors. Before Paull was selected as art director on *Blade Runner*, he had fifteen credits, including *The Last American Hero* (1973), *The Bingo Long Traveling All-Stars and Motor Kings* (1976), and *Blue Collar* (1977). Scott must have been especially intrigued by Paull's background in architecture and city planning because that's exactly what was going to be done on *Blade Runner*—the city would be set in the rather near future, and it would be a Los Angeles transformed into a hellish environment.

Paull or art director David Snyder (*Brainstorm*, 1983, *Pee-Wee's Big Adventure*, 1985) had to be on the set if Scott decided to make changes. Scott personally looked at everything—sets, props, makeup, hair, and costumes—and signed off when he felt it was right. If there were problems, Scott worked them out with a storyboard pad and pencil, creating Ridleygrams to solve current issues or to create a new design element. The crew then readied itself for additional work, and the front office braced for a budget increase.

There were times when an aspect of the set was built while the cast and crew waited, then brought to the set with the paint on the surfaces still wet. Scott would order a new prop, alteration, or addition but give the art department little time to create, complete, and deliver it. "What I had to do as a designer is take everything and build it out to the curbs, really make it narrow and congested and fill it with people, vehicles, and animals and make it alive with signage and very heavy on graphics. . . . I was paying attention to detail to make sure that all the signage and all the lighting was authentic."[2]

The buildings were retrofitted because the middle class had left and the working class, the lower classes, and the homeless populated the city. When something broke they didn't have the means to fix it, so they got rid of it and put in another unit.

Laurence G. Paull's biggest influence was the dean of American architecture, Frank Lloyd Wright, whose Ennis House influenced the design of Deckard's apartment. Poured concrete blocks were utilized, and the result allowed Scott to make a striking use of his greatest cinematic tool—light. Ennis House was designed by Wright in 1923 and built in 1924 for Charles and Mable Ennis. The design was inspired by the symmetrical reliefs of Mayan buildings in Uxmal, Mexico.

Paull explained that costume designer Charles Knode had a unique technique for treating much of the clothing on *Blade Runner*: "It was literally, 'Put it in the washing machine, pour a pound of real strong coffee in, and see what happens.' That's basically it; everything was very browned over, very heavily aged and crusted over."[3]

Paull talks about how the design for Sebastian's apartment came about: "Ridley came into my office, threw a magazine on my desk, and said, 'That's Sebastian's apartment.' Irving Penn was a major American photographer noted for his stark work in fashion. Here was this blonde fashion model that looked like Irving Penn's wife Lisa Fonssagrives wearing a long white gown, and she's standing next to this blue-gray wall with these heavy moldings on the wall panels, and it's all decaying. It looked like someone had gone in and done a sponge painting on a tenement in New York, and the painting is all peeling back. You could almost sense that there were rats running around at her feet . . . that's how the coloration of that set happened."[4]

Edward Hopper's iconic painting *Nighthawks* strongly influenced Ridley Scott, as did the paintings of Jan Vermeer, the Dutch artist whose works often depict domestic scenes of middle-class life, and *Sentinel,* an art book of futuristic works by Syd Mead. The British science fiction artist John Harris, known for his cover art for novels by noted science fiction writers, was an influence for the cityscapes. What Scott was looking for was contrast and deep saturated color, which he saw in Hopper's work. *Nighthawks* especially captures the moody spirit and atmosphere of *Blade Runner.* Painted in 1942, it depicts a coffee shop in a big city at night. It is an exterior view, but through the large curved plate-glass window that surrounds the corner store the viewer sees three people drinking coffee at a counter and a white-jacketed server wearing a white military-style cap. The painting became an important image for the *Blade Runner* art department.

Tyrell's bedroom set was also used as his office and for the Voight-Kampff replicant test for Leon. This machine, which was a form of polygraph, had to be created by members of the art department, who were happy to comply but groaned under their breath when told it was needed in thirty-eight hours.

It was Tony Scott who recommended cinematographer Jordan Cronenweth to his brother. The director of photography's work on the cult gem *Cutter and Bone* (1981), now known as *Cutter's Way*, caught Scott's eye. Cronenweth began in 1957 in the still photography lab at Columbia Pictures, and in 1971 he became camera assistant to Conrad Hall, a young cameraman who was innovative and a risk taker. Cronenweth had eighteen television and feature film credits before he was asked to shoot *Blade Runner*. He was a meticulous craftsman whose distinctive lighting style transformed him into a painter of light. His work includes *Play It as It Lays* (1972), *Rolling Thunder* (1977), and *Altered States* (1980). Cronenweth had his own crew who worked in the Hollywood system. *Blade Runner* was shot with Panavision cameras in anamorphic format. Steven Poster provided additional photography on the movie. Poster would go on to be the director of photography on Ridley Scott's *Someone to Watch over Me*.

Scott was not allowed to operate the camera on *Blade Runner* as he had on *The Duellists* and *Alien* or to work intricately with the director of photography and the camera. Now he was in the US (the first two films had been shot in England), and the American unions wouldn't allow it. At first the camera crew was very hard on Scott, but eventually he gained their respect. Unfortunately, all during production Jordan Cronenweth was in poor health. Originally misdiagnosed and treated for multiple sclerosis, he later learned he was suffering from Parkinson's disease. As the production wore on, Cronenweth became very ill. The disease progressed during the shooting, and for the last month of production he was in a wheelchair.

Scott was painstaking with every detail of *Blade Runner,* even though he was a few weeks behind schedule. The first prop man on the picture left when he put a mug on a desk in a set and Scott questioned the choice. Scott reshot scenes if they were not to his liking.

When Scott approached Douglas Trumbull to work on the special visual effects team, the renowned visual artist, who had worked on Kubrick's *2001: A Space Odyssey* (1968) and *Close Encounters of the Third Kind* (1977), was busy with a directorial project, *Brainstorm* (1983). But when Trumbull was told what Scott had in mind for *Blade Runner,* busy or not, he came on board.

In order to dictate precise camera moves, the *Blade Runner* team had an early form of motion control that allowed the camera to make specific moves over and around a set. Robot cameras were also utilized.

The original special effects budget was $5 million, but was cut down to closer to $2 million. The money just wasn't there. *Blade Runner* is considered the last great in-camera special effects movie. Douglas Trumbull thought that without digital effects—working in analog (on film, shot with film equipment, edited with film opticals)—the production got more for less money and in less time. Regardless of the quality of the footage and the performances, Bud Yorkin was fixated on the possibility of the film going over budget. He and his partners were worried about how many months (years, Yorkin kidded) it would take to finish the film.

Philip K. Dick didn't visit the set, although he was invited. But the making of *Blade Runner* preoccupied the author during the last months of his life. He found dealing with anyone connected to the production troublesome. Dick did see some footage of *Blade Runner* on a television program. On October 11, 1981, he wrote a letter to Jeffrey Walker, in charge of the film's advertising at the Ladd Company, praising Ridley Scott's adaptation of his novel. "I think *Blade Runner* is going to revolutionize our conceptions of what science fiction is, and more, can be."[5]

During production Ridley Scott was short-tempered and loud. The *Blade Runner* set was not a happy one, with lots of anger spewing. Because this was Scott's first American picture he was perceived as the new boy on the block. He was constantly questioned about everything he said or did. He found the large group of cast, crew, and executives around him frustrating. Scott talked about the state of his anger problem during *Blade Runner*: "It's difficult, and it becomes hard on other people and on me, but only temporarily. I find I may get depressed for half an hour, and that's it. If I get into a temper, I'm now trying to just walk away. There are several corridors in Pinewood Studios with holes in the walls!"[6]

Scott's temper explosions on *Blade Runner* came from a lack of total control over the financial aspects, which had an impact on his creativity and work pace. The pressure to make a great follow-up to *Alien* and, since both films were science fiction, the fear of being typed were additional agitating factors. Tandem's constant meddling tried Scott's patience and caused constant stress. Because Ridley Scott so totally dominated the production of *Blade Runner,* the crew dubbed the set Ridleyville. At one point there was so much frustration that the crew began to call the film "Blood Runner." Scott had the smoke machine linked to a fan so the smoke could move through a shot. Because of the presence of beehive smoke on the set, the crew needed to wear gas masks.

Scott wanted the film to feel claustrophobic. Because of the rain effect, the costumes were constantly soaked and had to be cared for. The street environment called for acid rain—a complex sprinkler system was installed overhead. When a downpour was needed, the rapidly spinning sprinklers did the job. The first night the full force of the rain was used on set, all the neon lights went out. The patience of the cast and crowds of extras steadily eroded as the production of *Blade Runner* ground on.

During shooting Ridley Scott sat on the side of the set watching video assist, a system that allows the director to sit in front of monitors that show what each camera is seeing. Scott felt Harrison Ford needed a director on the set where he could always see him. The coldness that developed between them made the experience difficult for director and star; both were under enormous pressure to succeed. Scott gave Harrison Ford less attention than the other players because he considered him a seasoned professional who knew what to do. Ford, on the other hand, was used to having long conversations with his directors as he did with Spielberg. It was Scott's impression that when Harrison Ford worked with Coppola, Spielberg, or Lucas, these directors spent personal time with him talking about his character and motivation. Ridley Scott believed that good casting and acting ability were sufficient; actors knew their job and could be expected to get on with it. Scott believed he didn't need to get in the way of that. Ridley Scott didn't say much to the actors or even the crew—he was concentrating and focusing on the visuals. His relationship with Ford began to sour during production when the actor felt Scott was spending far too much time on the technical and visual aspects, requiring Ford to spend a lot of time waiting to go before the cameras. He did respect Scott's willingness to go over budget and shoot as many takes as necessary for the good of the film. Yet Ford felt there was little of substance to his character and that at times he was there only to give a focal point to the sets.

Ford willingly performed as many stunts as he could on camera. One night he confided to the stunt coordinator that because Ridley Scott did so many takes, maybe he should be compensated for stunt work. The coordinator figured out what would be a fair amount of money for the additional stunt work, and Ford went to the production manager. He was indeed paid the extra fee. This may have been Ford's way of getting "revenge" or consoling himself for his unpleasant experience with Scott, although the rancor passed in time, and in 2014 Harrison Ford agreed to appear in a *Blade Runner* sequel.

The situation involved in shooting the on-screen love affair between Deckard and Rachael also began to deteriorate. The actors just didn't click. The poor chemistry had a negative impact on their scenes, which were more aggressively physical and edged with violence than Scott wanted. In one scene Young's costar pushed her. She cried a lot during the shooting of the scene. To "motivate" Young, Ford mooned her.

Female nudity is rare in a Ridley Scott film unless it is narratively justified. In *Blade Runner* Joanna Cassidy plays Zhora, an exotic snake dancer. Deckard has hunted her down in a sleazy club. He follows her into the dressing room and then says he's on the Committee of Moral Abuses. As Zhora gets ready to shower she finds his questions incredible. Later the camera eye captures her naked breasts, albeit not in an erotically revealing manner. She puts on a futuristic bra and a clear raincoat, then starts a fight with Deckard that leads to a long, involved chase scene in the streets ending with the detective shooting the replicant dead.

During production Ridley Scott was interviewed by the *Guardian,* asked whether he'd rather work with a British or American crew. He answered, "British." The article was taken from his trailer, copied, and distributed to the crew members, who were furious. They made up T-shirts that said, "Yes Guv—MY ASS." At one point a shirt appeared with the words, "Will Rogers never met Ridley Scott." Ridley fired back with a shirt that said, "Xenophobia Sucks." The atmosphere was tense for many days; eventually things got back to normal and the offending T-shirts came off. There were still approximately sixteen weeks left to the shoot.

For the climactic jump between two buildings, two sets on wheels were built to adjust the distance once someone jumped. Rutger Hauer's double jumped but didn't make it. The buildings were moved a foot closer. Harrison Ford volunteered to do the jump and made it in one take. He also performed his own stunts during the sequence in which Deckard and Leon Kowalski fight. During this scene a neon TDK sign can be seen, one of many advertisements shown in *Blade Runner.* The signs forecast a future when advertisements would be omnipresent.

Due to scheduling and financial pressures, Scott and his cast and crew *had* to complete work on the last designated day of shooting. They still had many shots remaining, and so they worked around the clock, until the character Gaff says, "Let's get out of here!" They immediately processed the rushes to make sure everything was alright, then instantly struck the sets—the cast and crew were finished.

Scott hated going over budget and not making the schedule, but he was not going to compromise quality. The pressure was palpable. Ridley Scott would not give in. Nothing Yorkin and his partners could do or say would ever break him. A lot of money had been spent: $20 million. In Ridley Scott's opinion, even a budget of $20 million (which by 2018 standards is $55,951,796) was not enough money to make *Blade Runner*.

Principal photography concluded on June 30, 1981. For the many extras needed in street scenes, Scott had gathered two hundred real punks, one hundred Chinese extras, and one hundred Mexican extras. The shooting had gone on for almost seventeen and a half grueling weeks. A figure even larger than the original—$25 million—was spent shooting on the back lot. There was continual tension on the set, both personal and practical, as the suits constantly gave the impression they might stop production or replace the director. Bud Yorkin was a director, although nowhere near Ridley Scott's league (his credits include *Start the Revolution without Me*, 1970, *Arthur 2: On the Rocks*, 1988, *Love Hurts*, 1990), but there was a distinct notion he wanted to take over as director even though this production was way over his head.

Blade Runner reportedly overspent its budget by $5–11 million. There was a year ahead to edit the film and do special effects work. Tandem held the completion bond on the film when it did go over budget. On July 11, the company's lawyers dropped a bombshell. Ridley Scott and Michael Deeley were fired. Perenchio and Yorkin took over the picture. Bud Yorkin was put in control, but eventually Scott and Deeley were reinstated. Yorkin reminded everyone that by contract he and his partners had the right to edit the now very long film the way they wanted, but this threat didn't go anywhere. The services of Michael Deeley and Ridley Scott were still sorely needed to complete the picture and pave the way for all investors to get their money back and more. Laddie wanted them back.

Scott and Terry Rawlings had from July 13, 1981, to mid-September 1981 to complete editing. Scott closely supervised both the visual effects and editing processes. Jake Scott worked in the editing room doing tasks such as labeling film cans.

In December 1981 Philip K. Dick was invited by Ridley Scott to meet at Douglas Trumbull's company EEG. It is reported that Dick apologized to

Scott for trashing *Alien*. The tone was animated, and apparently Scott was very gracious. Dick did offer some suggestions, and Scott told the writer he would take them—but the mood remained friendly. The contention was over the concept of the replicants. Dick considered them appalling whereas Scott saw them as supermen. On that day Dick was shown twenty minutes from the rough cut. He was impressed with what he saw and was more than delighted with the special effects reel. He told Scott that the effects were just what was in his head when he was writing *Do Androids Dream of Electric Sheep?* Unfortunately, Philip K. Dick died without seeing the completed *Blade Runner* movie. The author assumed that his name would be featured in the credits, but this did not occur. However, at the end of *Blade Runner* it states, "This is dedicated to the memory of Philip K. Dick."

Do Androids Dream of Electric Sheep? was written in the third person. In the many drafts of the script written by Fancher, he introduced narration because he thought the story needed descriptive glue for the rest to make sense. Ridley Scott was totally on board with the idea, which had been his in the first place, although he has made statements about film narration rarely working, a common belief among directors. When David Webb Peoples was brought in, he was given the go-ahead to develop narration by Scott, who closely supervised the entire writing process. When Philip K. Dick learned of the narration device, he made it clear he didn't like it. In February 1981 Peoples and Scott decided to strip out most of the narration. They didn't want the story too dependent on it. They wanted to shoot without narration and decide later if the story was working well without it.

The first two narration recording sessions were supervised by Scott. The material for both sessions was not written by either Peoples or Scott but by Darryl Ponicsan, the novelist who wrote the screenplays for *Cinderella Liberty* (1973), based on his novel, and *Vision Quest* (1985), based on another author's novel. Scott was not happy with Ponicsan's work. Peoples wrote a new draft that combined some of his previously written material along with some of Fancher's earlier work. Harrison Ford didn't like the results of the written material but was obliged contractually to record them. He claimed he hated the material and that Ridley Scott felt the same way. Ford thought it was overkill and disruptive; now Scott wasn't sure the writing could support the filmed script. Tandem screened the results and its reaction was very negative. Scott decided to get rid of the narration idea almost totally. Deeley remembers that after disastrous sneak previews in Dallas and Denver the audience preview cards reflected bafflement about the story line. Next Harrison Ford, Bud Yorkin, and production executive Katy Haber gathered in a Beverly Hills recording studio for a third attempt at the narration. Also there was Roland Kibbe, a television writer and friend of Yorkin's, the prime force behind this go-round of the narration. Yorkin supervised the session. Ford didn't like Kibbe's writing, and it is believed he purposely did a poor job reciting the lines. This is the version that was put into the film for its initial release.

There was a mixed reaction to the finished film. It was screened at MGM for five people including Perenchio, who thought it was a "smash." In-house there were complaints about the grimness of the picture—that it was too atmospheric and fell short of emotion; it was like an art film. It was deemed too dark and existential.

Johnathan Rosenbaum of the *Chicago Reader* said, "The grafting of 40s hard-boiled detective story with SF thriller creates some dysfunctional overlaps, and the movie loses some force whenever violence takes over, yet this remains a truly extraordinary, densely imagined version of both the future and the present, with a look and taste all its own." In the *Hollywood Reporter* Robert Osborne said, "*Blade Runner* is not an easy film to watch comfortably or categorize smoothly. It possesses a size that is awesome, sound and visual accompaniments that blast the senses and a pessimistic attitude that would do justice to the hellish worlds Josef Von Sternberg investigated in his Germanic and Paramount projects in the early 1930s." Janet Maslin of the *New York Times* stated, "The view of the future offered by Ridley Scott's muddled yet mesmerizing *Blade Runner* is as intricately detailed as anything a science fiction film has yet envisioned."

A Tandem executive visited the editing room and suggested that the company was now going to recut the film. This was thwarted by the Directors Guild of America's regulation that the director had total rights to cut the film as he wished without outside interference for a contracted period of time.

For a screening in Denver, Colorado, the last two reels were not available because they were still being worked on, and the music by the New Age artist Vangelis was not yet on the soundtrack. Although there was a lot of negativity toward the picture, it still scored a 44 percent excellent or extremely good rating. At the Dallas sneak preview there was disapproval from the audience members, who felt the film had a pessimistic view. They found the story confusing; in the positive categories the film scored 42 percent.

After a bad preview screening, Tandem demanded a happy ending, which was also shot and edited. Among other things, it depicts Rachael and

Deckard driving away from the city into the country. For the background shots Ridley Scott asked permission from Stanley Kubrick to use some of the outtakes from the opening sequence of *The Shining*. According to Jake Scott, at one point Kubrick sat in the editing room watching the proceedings and drinking beer.

One of the symbolic mysteries of *Blade Runner* is the appearance of the mythical unicorn, usually interpreted as representing purity and grace, appearing as a white horse with a long graceful horn coming from its forehead. In Deckard's apartment the detective plays the piano; there is an intercut to a white unicorn shot in slow motion. The piano was detuned to give it a far-off, dreamlike quality. There also was a unicorn sighting and an origami tinfoil unicorn on the dashboard of the car. The unicorn became a symbol. Members of Tandem didn't understand its presence in the film. Although the image is captivating and beautiful, its placement in the director's cut baffles most moviegoers. For the director the intention was clear: "I'd predetermined that the unicorn scene would be the strongest clue that Deckard, this hunter of replicants, might actually be an artificial human himself," Scott told Trevor Hogg for flickeringmyth.com.[7] The literature on the legend of unicorns doesn't reveal any real connection with Deckard, the story, or replicants. It does connect Deckard, whom the audience believes is human, with Gaff, who makes a unicorn origami figure and gives the impression he may know about Deckard's dream. There is also a small unicorn in the apartment of J. F. Sebastian, who has been involved with the design of replicants. All of this is very oblique, even upon multiple viewings. Harrison Ford felt strongly that Deckard was human because a human was needed in a film filled with so many androids.

The film-noir narration could not have helped the film's initial poor reception. The narration has many detractors and does not appear in the director's cut. There are some noted supporters, like Foster Hirsch, author of *Detours and Lost Highways: A Map of Neo-Noir,* who believes that Ford's narration is "an almost pitch perfect simulation of a high 1940s deadpan monotone" and that it was a loss to remove it from future versions.[8] Another champion is film director Guillermo Del Toro (*Hellboy,* 2004, *Pan's Labyrinth,* 2006, and the Oscar-winning *The Shape of Water,* 2017), who describes it as poetic and lyrical.

On its opening weekend the film premiered in Los Angeles, and audiences liked it. At Westwood there were lines around the block, but the reviews were bad. By Sunday night box office tapered off. *Blade Runner* opened across the county at around 1,290 movie theaters on June 25, 1982, but because *E.T.* and other films of note were also released then, *Blade Runner* was considered a box office failure. Competition included *Poltergeist, Rocky III, Star Trek II: The Wrath of Khan,* and *The Road Warrior,* but it was Spielberg's mega-hit *E.T.* that dominated the box office.

Blade Runner was nominated for Oscars in production design, art direction/set decoration, and visual effects. *Blade Runner* fared very well at the BAFTA awards in England, where Jordan Cronenweth won for Best Cinematography. Michael Kaplan and Charles Knode won for Best Costumes. Cronenweth was also nominated at the British Society of Cinematographers Awards. The World Science Fiction Convention in 1983 voted *Blade Runner* the third most favorite science fiction film of all time. In 1993 the film had the honor of being inducted into the National Registry by the National Film Board of America. In 2002 *Wired* magazine named *Blade Runner* number one of the top twenty science fiction films of all time. Eventually *Blade Runner* found its calling and is currently considered an iconic and influential masterpiece. In a letter to Jeff Walker at the Ladd Company, Philip K. Dick wrote, "The impact of *Blade Runner* is simply going to be overwhelming, both on the public and creative people—and I believe, on science fiction as a field."[9]

In its initial release *Blade Runner* was a financial flop. One problem could have been the noir narration, another that audiences thought they were going to see a Harrison Ford action picture. In time it became a cult film hit.

With the advent of cable television and home video, *Blade Runner* was delivered into viewers' homes, many experiencing the film for the first time. *Blade Runner* became one of the most popular video rentals of all time. After the 1987 release of the Criterion Collection's high-resolution widescreen laser disk, which featured a more violent international cut, interest in *Blade Runner* spiked again. In 1990 a work print of *Blade Runner* was screened at the Fairfax 70mm Film Festival—it was the director's cut.

In 1991 preservationists extraordinaire Ron Haver and Robert A. Harris found another version of *Blade Runner.* It has been screened only in Great Britain at a sneak preview. It is the shortest of all versions, clocking in at 112 minutes. On September 27, 1991, the Santa Monica NuArt Theater and the San Francisco–based Castro Theater began a two-week run of what was called *The Blade Runner Director's Cut.* It received a strong reaction from audiences.

When the director's cut came out in 1992, most reviewers and viewers were pleased to learn the narration was gone. Around 2001 Ridley Scott and his DVD producer Charles De Lauzirika put together a newly edited version of

Blade Runner for theatrical release. With visual and audio adjustments, it was called *Blade Runner: The Final Cut.* Later it was released in a five-disk DVD package that contains every version of the film and includes many extras.

Some believe that *Blade Runner* inspired the creation of the cyberpunk genre and movement. The film was also responsible for influencing countless movies and television shows. Movies include *Brazil, Dark City, The Matrix, Gattaca, eXistenZ, The Fifth Element, The City of Lost Children, Strange Days,* and *Judge Dredd.* Television shows include *Dark Angel* and *Total Recall 2070.*

The director's cut of *Blade Runner* was released initially in fifty-eight theaters nationwide on September 11, 1992. Box office was strong, but critical response was still poor. After five weeks the number of screens was upped to ninety-five, and *Blade Runner* stayed in the top fifty highest-grossing pictures for ten weeks, earning $3.7 million in this period.

There are websites devoted to this film, considered by many to be dystopian and deadly accurate in its prediction for the future of society.

Ridley Scott had not forgotten about H. R. Giger and their strong desire to work together again. In 1988 Scott contacted Giger about a spec script called *Dead Reckoning.* The artist immediately accepted the project because of his artistic faith in Ridley Scott. The screenwriter Jim Uhis, who would go on to write the screenplay to *Fight Club,* created a project that was a concoction of *Alien* and *Blade Runner.* It took place in a future Los Angeles that, as in *Blade Runner,* was overcrowded and degenerating. Here a genetically altered beast was set loose on an underground train. This humanoid had a brain created in a laboratory to be the hard drive in an artificial intelligence project.

From Scott's description of the project over the phone, Giger began concept drawing for the proposed film, which was now called *The Train.* Giger's imagination ran wild. He saw the passengers housed in pods like the hyper sleep chambers in *Alien.* They moved in and out of carriages by a crane mounted on the ceiling. Some of his distinctive and harrowing drawings pictured passengers lying down in larger vessels like cutlery drawers and loaded and unloaded from the train's carriages by truck. Other ideas pictured the train as a bio-mechanical creature. The head was shaped like a skull, and arm-like appendages speared commuters as they waited on the platform for the train. The collection of concept drawings was massive, as the artist worked for nine months between 1988 and 1989. But the short-lived project with Scott was not to be, and ended when the director left Carolco over creative differences. Scott tried to make *The Train* at other studios but without any result.

7

MYTHOLOGY

Legend

Once upon a time . . .

Charles Dickens

In spring 1983 Chiat\Day, the advertising agency for Apple Inc., was looking to make a bold statement for the new Macintosh computer in a TV spot. The message was that computers have to be accessible to the people, not run by the government or mega-corporations. A storyboard was created with an Orwellian *1984* theme. Steve Jobs, co-founder, chairman, and CEO of Apple, gave the go-ahead to shoot the commercial and book air time for the upcoming Super Bowl. Chiat\Day contracted Ridley Scott Associates to shoot and direct a television commercial for the new product. Purportedly, the spot was given a $900,000 budget and was planned as a onetime media event. The ad was to spin off Orwell's cautionary novel *1984* and take a jibe at Apple's powerful competitor IBM. At an Apple shareholders' event in the fall of 1983 the commercial was previewed. A confident and assured Steve Jobs painted giant IBM as a company that made bad choices concerning the mini-computer; Jobs's intention was to dominate the market. The lights dimmed and the commercial aired, but when Apple's board of directors screened the commercial, the majority hated it. The spot was supposed to run during the Super Bowl twice, once in a sixty-second version and once in a thirty-second version. The thirty-second version was cancelled. Despite some executive resistance, on January 22, 1984, in the third quarter of Super Bowl XVIII, the sixty-second spot was broadcast to a whopping 96 million viewers. The reaction was overwhelmingly positive, immediate, and sensational; the media ran with the story, and buzz was enormous. Consequently, a decision was made to show the thirty-second version for weeks in movie theaters before previews. Before the end of the year, the commercial was broadcast at a small television station in Twins Falls, Idaho, and a few other venues so it could qualify for advertising awards. Ultimately, it won over thirty awards, including the Grand Prix at Cannes, and was entered into the Clio Hall of Fame. Estimated costs of the commercial differ, with the *Guinness Book of World Records* citing it as the most expensive television spot ever made at that point, clocking it in at $600,000 for cost and $1,000,000 to broadcast. Apple quoted the sixty-second version cost at $800,000. Ridley Scott, who directed the landmark spot, claims the budget was $350,000. Despite conflicting figures, the obvious common denominator was that the advertisement carried the heftiest price tag in the industry.

The commercial's story is set in the future and starts with a procession of workers with clean-shaven heads trudging through a transit tube into a large auditorium. The opening images are strongly reminiscent of Fritz Lang's silent masterwork *Metropolis* (1927), a film that depicts a bleak, dystopian future society where the workers below ground give energy to the rich and privileged above them. Ridley Scott was an ardent admirer of the film. In the spot the workers join rows and rows of others and all stare at a huge television screen in front of them. On this screen is the face of "Big Brother." His voice drones on about "Information Purification Directives."

Then, in an image that inspires applause, a beautiful blonde, physically fit young woman in athletic garb (played by Anya Major, who in addition to acting was an experienced discus hurdler) runs into the room brandishing an Olympic hammer, chased by storm troopers. She eludes them, stops, screams, and heaves the hammer, shattering the large television screen, which erupts in a barrage of sparks. The commercial concludes with voice and text that says: "On January 24th Apple Computer will introduce Macintosh. And you'll see why 1984 won't be like "*1984.*"

The commercial, commonly referred to as *1984,* was shot in England at Shepperton Studios on the same large stage where the planetoid landscapes for *Alien* had been photographed. Originally Big Brother did not speak, but Scott insisted. The copywriter resisted but moved forward when Scott told him he would write the lines himself. Thus, the final version includes the Big Brother figure communicating to the masses.

Ingeniously, Scott solved the problem of hiring a budget-breaking group of actors for the marching men. He contracted two hundred skinheads who were part of a group known as "the National Front." The amateurs were paid reportedly no more than $125. The extras were rounded up by Jake Scott. Adrian Biddle, who worked with Scott as a focus puller on *Alien* and was director of photography on *Thelma & Louise* and *1492: The Conquest of Paradise,* shot the commercial.

In *Eye of the Storm* Barry Day states: "[It] is one of the most famous commercials made by anybody anywhere in eternity."[1] *1984* has made the list of greatest Super Bowl commercials, according to *Newsday* and the *Huffington Post*, landing in the number one spot on many lists and scoring high on many others even while competing with much more recent ads.

Surprisingly, in the script there was no direct reference to a computer. When Scott read it he thought it was interesting and didn't ask anyone connected with the project about Apple. In the process of directing, he shouted a question to clarify what Apple was and it dawned on him that this was a spot about a computer. The iconic *1984* commercial anointed Ridley Scott as the most influential creator of commercials in the modern era and put his name indelibly on the media map worldwide.

Frustrated that *Tristan and Isolde* had been abandoned, Scott still wanted to explore the fantastical world of fairy tales. Scott sought to find an American writer who could conceive a fairy tale–like story that would be contemporary and understandable to general audiences, including children (among them his own.) He wanted a script without the dark subtextual qualities of ancient European tales.

Scott had read several books by novelist William "Gatz" Hjortsberg (*Symbiography, Fallen Angel*). He contacted Hjortsberg and they met to discuss the project; the principal idea for *Legend* came into being. With a rough outline accomplished, Hjortsberg flew to Los Angeles, where he and Ridley Scott screened Jean Cocteau's *Beauty and the Beast,* which Scott admired as the perfect example of a fantasy that endured as a mysterious and enchanting film. Scott's goal was to reinvent the inner workings of the fantasy genre.

In fairy tale tradition *Legend* begins with the words "Once, long ago . . ." The story takes place in a lush forest populated with mythic creatures and animals, magical godlike unicorns, Lili, a young innocent princess, and her enamored friend Jack, who lives compatibly among the creatures of the forest. Below the earth is Darkness, who is determined to obliterate this ideal, claim Lili as his bride, destroy the woods' protective unicorns, and plunge the fantastical world into darkness. The powers of good and evil, light and dark do battle until good prevails. Lili and Jack live happily ever after.

Ridley Scott concluded that to control the physical environment of the film he would build the forest on a stage in Shepperton Studios—the largest studio in all of Europe—rather than shoot on location. Scott hired highly experienced Assheton Gorton as production designer on the project. Gorton and his team worked diligently for months to create a forest that had live trees, a running brook, a bear, shrubs, small animals, bees, flowers, and a ten-foot-deep pond.

For the role of Darkness, Scott cast Tim Curry after screening *The Rocky Horror Picture Show* (1975). Curry's voice is deep, rich, and full of tantalizing evil. His physical appearance in *Legend* was inspired by the winged and horned demon from the 1940 Disney masterwork of sound and image *Fantasia*. For the role of Lili, Ridley Scott discovered Mia Sara in an English drama school. The seventeen-year-old was screen-tested and cast in her first acting role. Post–*Risky Business* twenty-three-year-old Tom Cruise played Jack. When Cruise arrived at Pinewood Studios, Scott brought him into a screening room to watch François Truffaut's *The Wild Child* (1970), a film about a human boy brought up by animals in a forest. Scott asked Cruise to grow his hair out and make the gestures of a boy/wolf. Growing up, Cruise had constantly practiced back flips and other gymnastic feats—these skills would come in handy in this highly physical role.

Scott wanted the forest to be influenced by Disney animation features, especially *Snow White and the Seven Dwarfs* (1937), *Fantasia* (1940), and *The Jungle Book* (1967). Other influences were French illustrator and wood engraver Gustave Doré, whose work in the 1800s included fairy tales and illustrations of epic poetry. The air on the set was alive, populated with insects, pollen, and flowers. Fans were constantly whirring to simulate a natural breeze moving through the forest.

In *Legend* Scott introduced a complex visual element that was reiterated in future films. Small particles appeared floating in the air. Scott named them "floating fluff," and they became a recurring image in many of his films. The effect was accomplished here by mincing up duck down and blowing it around the set. Scott estimates that a hundredweight of feathers was used to create this mesmerizing effect in *Legend*. The floating fluff creates a magical cinematic mood—visual, dimensional, with texture and movement running through the image, conveying the thought that anything can happen at any time. Depending on the movie, the particles can be snow, rain, dirt, feathers, rocks, or other items built up to fill the screen.

Legend was shot at Pinewood Studios on the very large stage now known in the business as "the Bond stage." It was conceived by production designer Ken Adam for the James Bond film *The Spy Who Loved Me* and officially named "the 007 stage" on December 12, 1976. The 007 stage was later rebuilt and renamed after the legendary producer of the classic Bond films. It was dubbed "the Albert R. Broccoli stage," where Bond's *A View to a Kill* (1985) was produced.

On June 27, tragedy struck: the entire *Legend* set and Bond stage burned to the ground from a flash fire. It was lunchtime and Scott was in the editing room. Someone ran in yelling, "The stage is on fire!" The cause was gas bottles being used on the set to create fire for the fairy dance scene. During the fire all the pigeons flew out. The bottles continued to explode, rippling the stage walls. Most likely a residue of the gas fumes had built up near the ceiling and a spark ignited them. Because it was lunchtime no one was injured as both cast and crew were away from the stage. Once Scott realized everybody was safe and the fire was being extinguished, he left the building. Surprisingly, he went to play a game of tennis. It was his way of dealing with the pressure and tension of the situation. This is just one of many actions that has led observers to perceive Ridley Scott as cold and aloof, especially in the early part of his now long career. Of course, inside were emotions no one could see, penetrate, or interpret. In fact, he was deeply concerned. Amazingly, the company lost only three days of shooting, thanks to Assheton Gorton, who had moved ahead to build other sets. The crew pushed forward, and the shoot was accomplished.

During the preview process Ridley Scott's 113-minute version of *Legend* did poorly with audiences. At the first US preview at the Directors Guild in Los Angeles, there were around four hundred people in the audience. Suddenly someone started to snigger. That person made a rude comment, triggering a torrent of comments throughout the theater. Scott was fuming and livid—and out of these feelings he made a decision to cut down the film radically.

On his own recognizance Ridley Scott and his editor Terry Rawlings cut *Legend* to eighty-nine minutes. The overseas version was slightly longer, at around ninety-four minutes, because he believed Europeans would better understand the nature of the film. This version contained a score by Jerry Goldsmith, whom Scott respected greatly and had brought on for the project.

The other radical surgery on *Legend* was at the behest of Universal Studios mogul Sid Sheinberg: to remove the Jerry Goldsmith score, which Scott loved, and replace it with the music of German New Age band Tangerine Dream. Universal had determined that Goldsmith's score was overly sweet and romantic. The electronic wizards, who had been scoring movies since 1971, including *Thief* (1981) and *The Keep* (1997), had only three weeks to score *Legend*.

From Scott's point of view (although he changed his mind in hindsight), he wanted to do what the audience wanted—cut and change. Unfortunately, the film was still badly received. Because of the radical editing the story and message of *Legend* didn't get to audiences as originally intended.

The film did poorly in America; critics and audiences didn't like the story or the characters. It was out of theaters within two weeks. It did poorly in Europe as well. The whole experience made Ridley Scott believe all the reediting and rescoring was for naught. It made no difference to audiences worldwide. The American box office gross was a slight $15 million, with opening weekend at a paltry $4.2 million.

The critics voiced their dislike of *Legend*. Vincent Canby of the venerable *New York Times* found it to be a mishmash of the Old Testament, King Arthur, *Lord of the Rings* (the book), and comic books. The British fanzine *Starburst* complained about the characters, feeling the film favored the bad guys and didn't care who rescued the unicorns.

Speculative fiction icon Harlan Ellison was most negative toward the film, stating acerbically, "*Legend* is a film made by an astute adult who, when turned loose, when given the power to create any film he desired fled into a throwaway universe of childish irrelevance. *Legend* is, at final resolve, a husk. A lovely, eye-popping vacuum from which a sad breeze blows. Because it finally gives nothing. It steals our breath, captures our eyes, dazzles and sparkles and, like a 4th of July sparkler comes to nothing but gray ash in the end."[2] Roger Ebert stated succinctly, "*Legend* does not work."[3]

In 1986 Ridley and Tony Scott expanded RSA with a new office in New York. In several years they moved their US headquarters to Los Angeles. Eventually RSA had offices in London, New York, Los Angeles, and Hong Kong. RSA's power and authority in commercial ventures was established and as of 2018 continues.

8

NOIR ONE/NOIR TWO

Someone to Watch over Me and Black Rain

I didn't know I was doing film noir, I thought they were detective stories with low lighting!

Marie Windsor

Ridley Scott's fifth motion picture is a neo-noir. He wanted a project he called "normal"—realistic fare. Especially after the anguish and disappointment of working on *Legend,* Scott thought it was time to make a more straightforward, conventional drama with the kind of entertainment values that would evoke a positive audience response. Although Scott's standing in the industry was firm, the failure of *Legend* had shaken him.

Ridley Scott didn't believe in following trends. He made a decision about what to do next based on his own desires, a particular book or script he read or, in this case, a genre he wanted to explore in depth.

The story of *Someone to Watch over Me* was pitched to Scott at a dinner party in 1985 by screenwriter Howard Franklin (*The Name of the Rose,* 1986). Scott really liked it, and the two men started on the project. At the time Scott had been developing *Johnny Utah* at Columbia; this ultimately became *Point Break* (1991) directed by Kathryn Bigelow. Scott had been frustrated by the pace of the development process and decided instead to make *Someone to Watch over Me.* As his career progressed, Scott would option many projects at a time and put writers, producers, and others to work preliminarily so when he was finished with a film he could move onto another with just a bit of time to get up to speed. Thematically, Scott was attracted to the notion of a seemingly unshakeable marriage suddenly rocked by an unexpected affair and the eminent danger of a murderer stalking the female protagonist.

Scott told Paul M. Sammon in *Ridley Scott—Close Up*:

An opinion was brewing around the time I was shooting *Someone to Watch Over Me* that I didn't like working with actors, and that I tended to make the scenery in my films more important than the actors or scripts. That reaction may have started with *Blade Runner* when I said that sometimes the design of a film was just as important as its acting or story. Perhaps I was misunderstood there because I certainly didn't mean *more* important. For instance, I've always tried to attach a reality to what actors create during filming. That's really what my job as a director is, in terms of performance; the actors do it, and I'm there to monitor it. So, ideally, that end of the process should be a partnership, with me as a guidance system. And I've always felt that everything starts with story. In fact, story and performance were two of the reasons I chose to do *Someone to Watch Over Me*—it had a smaller, more contained story that foregrounded the performances.[1]

Ridley Scott was already proving himself to be a filmmaker who couldn't be pinned down in terms of content and subject matter. As far as the bad temper displayed in the past, he was learning he could control it and change the way he interacted with the cast and crew. It would take some time, but eventually he would come close to being in a Zen state of mind while directing a movie.

Scott put together a strong cast. He approached Tom Berenger for the Detective Mike Keegan role. Scott was impressed with Berenger's range, especially in *The Big Chill* (1983) and *Platoon* (1986). Mimi Rogers (*The Rapture*, 1991, *The Mirror Has Two Faces*, 1996), plays Claire, a beautiful rich Manhattan socialite who requires protection after viewing a vicious murder; she is the femme fatale. Andreas Katsulas (*The Sicilian*, 1987, *The Fugitive*, 1993), cast as the archvillain Joey Venza, came through the audition process. Scott liked to look for new faces and found one in Lorraine Bracco (*GoodFellas*, 1990, *The Basketball Diaries*, 1995, *The Sopranos*), who at the time had virtually no motion picture experience. She is cast as Ellie Keegan, the cute, feisty, loyal wife and mother.

Someone to Watch over Me is a romantic/noir/crime thriller that focuses on social class distinctions and the barriers that prevent one from crossing them. Keegan is a newly promoted detective from Queens, a blue-collar family man whose goal is a home in a better neighborhood in the borough. Mike is not very well read, but he has street smarts and is a decent person who is unaware he is about to have his morality tested. His first assignment as a detective is guarding Claire, who is a doyen of the arts and, although she doesn't know it yet, is looking for a real man as opposed to her nerdy and controlling boyfriend Neil. She resides in a stellar townhouse in Manhattan, which transports Mike into an elite environment entirely foreign to him. The contrast between Manhattan and Queens is similar to the disparity between Staten Island and Manhattan in *Working Girl* (1988). In *Working Girl* the Staten Island ferry approaching the Manhattan skyline is the visual metaphor. Here Scott uses the image of the iconic Chrysler Building seen from the borough of Queens. Ridley Scott's visual acuity is clearly evident in *Someone to Watch over Me*. There is beauty and complexity in the production design and photography—the world in the distance is where the protagonist wants to be.

"That opening shot with the Chrysler building still has to be one of the most beautiful shots ever," Mimi Rogers proclaims in *Eye of the Storm.*

> In every New York film that I've seen since then there's some take on that shot, but Ridley created it, it was Ridley's vision. He was going for a somewhat nostalgic feel for the film . . . it is a kind of old fashioned bittersweet romance besides being a thriller. [The fact that Ridley] was an artist prior to becoming a filmmaker really shows in that what I experienced with him in his other films is that he paints with light. It was so beautiful, it really did look like a painting, just an example of how incredibly specific he is about his aesthetic vision. He literally oversaw every piece of my wardrobe. . . . He wanted these Fogal stockings that had the seam up the back with the rhinestones. Ridley is obviously intoxicated by beauty.[2]

In *Eye of the Storm* Jake Scott talks about his father's abilities to create beauty:

> He'll take an object and he'll place it among other objects like a still life and he can make the most simple things look like the most beautiful things. Even at home the way he would arrange pencils in a cup, like Stabilo pencils with the little rubbers on the end. . . . He would just stick them in a pot and they would look beautiful. He's a perfectionist, visually and in his lifestyle, as well as at home, which was basically like being on the set. Well, it's a little like being on a set because everything has its place. It's very neat, it's very tidy, things used to get moved around a lot. . . . He's always trying to evolve his environment so he never has to feel like he is stagnant.

"Maybe I'm OCD, I am organized," Scott told Sean Woods of *Rolling Stone*. "Honestly, life's easier that way then walking around a pile of crap. So if anything stays here long enough, I have to paint it white or throw it out."[3]

Mimi Rogers defines Ridley Scott's manner. "He's completely elusive and very shy and very soft-spoken about his personal life or what goes on deep inside," the actress said in *Eye of the Storm.*

> He's intensely private and I think because so much of the time his energy is consumed by the work, you don't have a lot of opportunity necessarily to hang out with him. . . . There were legendary stories about his temper and behavior during *Blade Runner* which I'm sure was very difficult, but the stories were just screaming and yelling and wild and viscous and angry and horrible, and I remember being a little bit nervous going into the shooting of *Someone to Watch Over Me.* . . . Now we're in the fourteenth week of a fourteen week shoot and I've never heard Ridley raise his voice and all of a sudden, out of the blue in the loudest voice I'd ever heard, Ridley literally roars "Shut the fuck up!" to the whole crew, scared the piss out of me. I almost fell off my chair and this dead silence comes over the set . . . and Ridley said, "For those of you who are curious, that's the way I was every day on *Blade Runner.*"

The film's complex Ellie/Mike/Claire love triangle is threatened by the omnipresent Joey Venza. After he murders one of Claire's friends and realizes she was a witness, he spends the movie trying to kill her and wreak havoc on the Keegan family. At first Mike and Claire have a respectful businesslike relationship, until the beautiful Claire and the posh environment entice Mike and he crosses the line, making love to Claire. When the attractive Ellie finds out through woman's intuition, the dramatic tension is ramped up. The ending involves all the major players and delivers like an old-fashioned movie resolve.

Rita Kempley of the *Washington Post* began her review with a dig at Scott's visualist methods: "With its stunning cityscapes and Chanel-ad surreality, "*Someone to Watch Over Me* shows off director Ridley Scott's extraordinary visual artistry. The sets are so sumptuous, you'll want to move right in. But the haze is so thick, you'll need to bring a defogger. Scott, who directed *Alien* and *Blade Runner,* looks at the world through veils of smog. What with these pictorial pollutants, he loses sight of plot."

Roger Ebert touched upon one of Scott's weak point—sex scenes. "The movie's high-tech sex scenes are done with all the cinematic technical support the director Ridley Scott can muster, but they're dead because they contain only sex not passion. Needless to say, there are no sex scenes in the film between Berenger and Bracco—the man and wife."

Vincent Canby of the *New York Times* belittled the film by attacking the veracity of the script. "Howard Franklin's screenplay plays less like a feature film than like the pilot for a failed television series about New York policemen."

Ridley Scott's next film, *Black Rain,* is also in the neo-noir genre. This one deals with crime gangs and multiculturalism. The story revolves around New York City cops and the Japanese mafia—the Yazuka. It takes place in New York and Japan.

The script had initially been given to Michael Douglas, who had worked with Stanley Jaffe and Sherry Lansing on *Fatal Attraction* (1987) and wanted to work with the pair again. Michael Douglas was excited about working with Ridley Scott. He explains in *Eye of the Storm,* "Ridley loves pressure. He thrives to a certain extent on pressure. He's got a dark sense of humor and it is fun to watch. . . . There is a reserve protection and emotional protection that Ridley has."

Cop Nick Conklin (Michael Douglas) and his partner Charlie Vincent (Andy Garcia) travel to Japan to bring back a murderer involved in Yazuka. When the plane lands Nick and Charlie are met by men they think are Japanese officials who hand over the brutal killer. Moments later they meet another group of officials—this time the real ones. Realizing that Yazuka has the killer, the partners chase the vehicle carrying him. They team up with Masahiro, known as Mas (Ken Takakura), a veteran Japanese cop whose policing methods are entirely different. The friction between people of different cultures was screenwriter Craig Bolotin's metaphor for what he called the zeitgeist of hostile American/Japanese relations in the late 1980s.

Michael Douglas's character in *Black Rain* is conflicted; he has moral flaws that cost him his marriage and the respect of his peers. The two partners are close yet very different—the grizzled seen-it-all veteran and the hotshot newbie love and respect each other.

One of the major themes in *Black Rain* is honor. Nick is a former honorable cop who turned the other way; he becomes honorable again to avenge the death of his partner, who is murdered by the Japanese mob. Ridley Scott has explored the theme of honor in several films including *The Duellists, G.I. Jane,*

Gladiator, 1492: Conquest of Paradise, and *White Squall. Black Rain* is also a "manly man" film that examines the nature and actions of men in stressful situations. What motivates men and their primitive drives? This Conradian theme continues to obsess Ridley Scott and stimulate his imagination.

Black Rain is also about the hostilities between America and Japan. Although it had been many decades since their defeat in World War II, the older generation of Japanese had not forgotten the disgrace of losing the war and the endless pain and destruction caused by President Truman's decision to drop the atomic bomb to end the war. In the late 1980s, when the movie takes place, there is tremendous competition and hostility between the two countries, with Japan's supremacy in consumer electronics and automobiles dominating the American market.

Another theme in *Black Rain* is corruption. Michael was a counterfeit cop when he did his dirty deals. The rival Yazukas value counterfeit money and criminal behavior.

Black Rain is also a buddy movie. The genre presents two male protagonists exploring their friendship, differences, and emotional needs as they investigate an action or event. As Eric Walkuski points out on joblow.com, *Black Rain* is actually a *"two* buddy movie."[4] First there is Nick and his partner Charlie, then, after Charlie is murdered, it becomes a Nick and Mas duo.

At first the city officials of Osaka, Japan, were helpful to the *Black Rain* team. Shooting on *Black Rain* commenced on October 28, 1988. Unexpectedly, on the first day of the schedule, time was severely limited by the Japanese officials, who were very tough on the crew. Cultural and behavioral differences developed right away. During the casting for the Japanese characters, the actors and their managers were highly insulted and angry that they had to audition. This is not the casting method in Japan; actors are selected based on their body of work, the agent is informed, a deal is struck, and the actors show up when it is time to act. Many of the actors were reluctant to see Ridley Scott, but curiosity about the project sparked their imaginations.

Scott wanted the legendary Jackie Chan for the role of the Yakuza villain Sato, but Chan turned the director down out of concern the role would adversely impact the positive image he had built and cultivated so carefully.

Unfortunately, the Japanese officials reneged on the original schedule to shoot the interior of a fish market and insisted the film be shot in far less time. To accomplish this, the crew worked over a weekend for twenty-two hours straight. The original cost to work at this location was $1 million—the producers were able to negotiate.

Then an article was written out of the governor's office in Osaka criticizing the Hollywood filmmakers. The crushing effect had an impact on permits. Officials told the filmmakers exactly where the camera would be positioned and then it could not be moved under any conditions. They could only shoot for fifteen minutes in a given location. There also was resistance to locals having their homes or stores photographed as a Yazuka location, which they felt would have very bad connotations. Ridley Scott also found the Japanese to be xenophobic.

Japanese officials sent watchers to the set to make sure that Ridley Scott and company were adhering to the rules. During one street shoot, Sherry Lansing was watching the proceedings when she began to be harangued and hounded by a man charged with making sure the shooting stayed exactly on time as dictated by Japanese rules. He kept telling Lansing that they were twelve minutes over the allotted time. Lansing did her best to keep the official talking to stall him from shutting them down for the day.

"When I started I had to visit the police station on two or three occasions because . . . they want to talk to the director who they will arrest in the night, if you don't do what you said you were going to do," Scott complained in *Eye of the Storm*. "If the shot was on a doorway they would ask me to mark off the position exactly where my cameras would be in three months' time. . . . In a few months' time these guys were there on the night saying, 'You said here' so I had to put the cameras here and there. . . . It became almost a competition against the bureaucracy, so that's why I started to enjoy it."

The Japanese members of the crew worked two hours more each day, as is the custom in their industry; they worked hard and were dedicated. Scott admired them for their stamina. Scott enjoyed the process of working with Japanese actors on *Black Rain* and respected the high sense of grace and honor they instill—the Japanese officials were another matter.

Kate Capshaw played Joyce, a provider of services with underground connections. Capshaw did her own research by working in a real Japanese club for six-hour shifts. She played a variation on the classical noir femme fatale. Everything was in place except she was not responsible for the undoing of the antihero.

The acting highlight in *Black Rain* is Yûsaku Matsuda, who played the villain Sato, the insane young man who wants to be a Yazuka at any cost, including murder, and he does slaughter several people and decapitates Charlie. Sadly, Matsuda had developed bladder cancer and was very ill during the making of the film, but because of pride and honor, he never told anyone. He died on November 6, 1989, just after the film was released. He was forty years old. He is greatly admired in Japan.

The murder of Charlie Vincent—decapitation by sword—comes around halfway through the film. It is shocking because he was such a likeable and cheerful character, trying to keep Nick on the straight and narrow. For the remainder of *Black Rain* Nick hunts down Charlie's killer with a vengeance and attempts to clean up the mob activity at the same time.

After around six weeks of shooting in Osaka and the Japanese port city of Kobe, it was highly publicized that there was extreme friction between the filmmakers and Japan. Shooting in Japan ended on December 8, 1988. Ridley Scott suggested that the production move back to the US, which it did in January 1989. The producers all agreed that Japan was a strange and hostile environment to make a movie. Moreover, shooting in Japan was so much more expensive than Scott and his producers had originally thought. To make up for the now lost Japanese locations, the team shot in Manhattan, New York's Silvercup Studios in Queens, and parts of Los Angeles as well as other areas in California. One-third of *Black Rain* was shot in the States.

Areas bathed in neon lights were not hard to find in California. Part of the climax of the film was shot in Japan in the winter; then San Francisco's wine country in the Napa Valley was the location for completion. The company found a bleak location and added snow with navy fog machines. A vineyard was converted into a Japanese sake farm and facility where a meeting would play out. The team also built a Japanese temple on the location. The film wrapped on March 14, 1989, in San Francisco.

Black Rain was not as popular with audiences in the United States as it was with Japanese audiences, who responded enthusiastically to Ken Takakura. At one festival in Japan *Black Rain* was nominated for Best Foreign Film.

Black Rain received bad reviews from the critics. One inflamed Michael Douglas by calling the picture "racist." Douglas personally phoned the critic to complain. Rita Kempley of the *Washington Post* found the movie overly violent. "Director Ridley Scott was never one to space the gory details and his Osaka-set 'Black Rain' is no exception. He approaches this prickly action thriller with the gusto of a sushi chef in a fish storm; unfortunately and typically, he loses sight of his story in this barrage of blood and guts. It's a gorgeous erratic movie most definitely not for those with an aversion to cutlery." Roger Ebert insulted the narrative with a jab at the script. "The screenplay seems to have been manufactured out of those Xeroxed outlines they pass out in film school." Peter Travers of *Rolling Stone* found the film stylish but typical. "It's a fish-out-of-water yarn. Another one. Originality is not this thriller's strong suit. Style is. *Black Rain* is exotic, energized entertainment with director Ridley Scott (*Alien, Blade Runner*) nosing his camera into Osaka's dark, unfamiliar corners."

The title phrase *Black Rain* is brought up when a Yazuka kingpin sadly relates to Nick how his family lived underground after the bomb was dropped and what they found when they finally escaped. The chilling words "We forgot who we were" develop the theme of identity. Nick Conklin has forgotten who he once was, but by avenging his partner's assassination he is on the road to redemption.

In 1988 in Los Angeles Jake Scott and Marcus Nispel formed the company Black Dog/Portfolio, later changed to Black Dog Films (referencing Celtic folklore), which became part of the RSA empire. The company was dedicated to the creation of music videos. Later it expanded to supply its talents to musicians, artists, and the fashion world. In 1997 Black Dog opened a shop in London.

During the shooting of *Black Rain,* Ridley Scott's ten-year marriage to Sandy Watson ended in divorce on January 12, 1989.

In 1989 Ridley Scott started directing commercials for the perfume Chanel No. 5. *Eden Roc Chanel No. 5* is a one-minute spot featuring the French actress Carole Bouquet, who had appeared in Buñuel's *That Obscure Object of Desire* (1977), the Bond movie *For Your Eyes Only* (1981), and many French productions. "My Baby Just Cares for Me," sung by Nina Simone, is on the soundtrack as the woman is shown as being irresistible to men. We see her kissing an old man, then enticing a much younger man while he sits in the driver's seat of a red car. Finally, she meets the man of her dreams. The commercial concludes with them kissing and then a fade to black. At the end, in close-up the woman says, "Share the fantasy, Chanel No. 5" while holding the bottle of perfume.

Another spot for Chanel No. 5, again featuring Carole Bouquet, was made in 1990. This one-minute spot takes place on a sunny day by a large swimming pool. As the woman sunbathes, there is a shot of her naked back. A man appears on the far side of the pool. He swims up to her and disappears, as if he is going into her body. The commercial ends with the same line as the other, but in the end cuts to a bottle of the perfume. This commercial is known for its eroticism and magical quality. The music is dreamy and the location is somewhere in our mind's eye.

9

MALE FEMINIST
Thelma & Louise

You rarely get scripts that are about the truth.

Ridley Scott

In spring 1988, thirty-year-old Callie Khouri was driving home from work to her Santa Monica apartment when an idea flashed into her mind—"Two women go on a crime spree," she revealed on sydfield.com.[1] With that one phrase she perceived the characters and saw in her head the movie that would become *Thelma & Louise*. As Khouri developed the screenplay, the two characters emerged as the zany Louise Sawyer and the older, more controlled Thelma Dickinson, who Khouri based on her own personality.

Khouri's longtime friend Pam Tillis, the country music star, may have been the inspiration for the Louise Sawyer character. Two violent real-life events were the genesis for the film's chilling portrayal of the assault on Louise. Khouri was robbed by two young thieves, one with a sawed-off shotgun. In the other incident Khouri and Tillis were jumped from behind by robbers. The screenwriter remembers thinking, "If I'd had a gun, I'd have killed them," Khouri told Sheila Weller of *Vanity Fair*.[2]

It was Khouri's first screenplay. She considered raising the money herself and shooting it as a self-directed low-budget independent film with her friend Amanda Temple, director Julien Temple's wife, as producer. For a cast they had chosen Holly Hunter and Frances McDormand. Khouri placed the film's concept in the genre of a road movie and conceived of an attempted rape that results in a murder. Temple shopped the project but was turned down repeatedly.

In 1980 Ridley and Tony Scott had created Percy Main Productions (named after the town where their father grew up), a development group in Los Angeles. After *Black Rain*, Ridley Scott was looking for material to direct, and Mimi Polk, then executive vice president of the company, was becoming a vital force in Ridley Scott's film project arsenal. After choosing *Thelma & Louise,* Polk became its producer and functioned in various producing capacities on *1492: Conquest of Paradise* and *White Squall.*

Mimi Polk was a friend of Amanda Temple, and Temple gave Polk the *Thelma & Louise* script. Polk liked the running bit of the lewd oil tanker driver who flicks his tongue at the women in a pornographic manner. She had run into such creeps with her college friends on spring breaks. Polk wanted to show the script to Ridley Scott, knowing Scott admired strong, powerful women and would respond to the murderous revenge twist; but there was a question of whether he might produce or direct the project himself.

Scott was looking to accelerate Percy Main so he'd always have material to direct when he finished a movie—a practice that has continued throughout his career to ensure he has more than one script ready to shoot. At that time he was looking for scripts that were character driven and centered on people—not so much on action. Scott met Callie Khouri and read *Thelma & Louise.* He loved it. Scott liked that the women's roles were not stereotypical. Scott wanted to know the entire backstory of the characters Thelma and Louise, from childhood to the opening of the movie. He mined everything he could about their early life. Ridley Scott optioned *Thelma & Louise* for $500,000. Polk told him she didn't think it was something for him to direct, but possibly the company could produce it, so he began interviewing to find someone to direct *Thelma & Louise.* But as his involvement deepened, he decided to direct the project himself.

Scott responded to the ways in which the screenplay put male/female relationships into perspective. He perceived that the eight male characters in *Thelma & Louise* represented pieces of one whole man. He didn't see this screen story as bashing males, but it dealt with issues many women have to cope with, a burden rarely shown in motion pictures. Khouri considered *Thelma & Louise* a straightforward serious drama—for Ridley Scott the story was a seriocomedy. Some critics maintained that all the male characters were painted with the same brush, portrayed as at best insensitive and less than bright, but those who held that point of view were not acknowledging two major roles: Hal, played by Harvey Keitel, a key law enforcement figure who is empathic toward Thelma and Louise and their plight, and Jimmy, Louise's boyfriend, portrayed by Michael Madsen, who assists the women during the police pursuit. Jimmy is clearly sympathetic and respectful, and his love for Louise deepens unconditionally during the evolution of the story. The other males can legitimately be characterized as buffoons, insensitive, manipulating, and menacing—well-known masculine types in society. Ultimately, Ridley Scott committed to the film because he was confident it was truthful and fulfilled a need for insightful films about women in a market where such films were underrepresented.

Initially Scott agreed with Polk; he didn't think *Thelma & Louise* was right for him to direct because he really had yet to make a film that was totally character driven. Khouri also didn't think he would direct it, so he gave her a pitch about being the film's producer. He began interviewing directors, who seemed interested only in why Scott wasn't directing the film. Scott considered his brother, but Tony passed. The feedback from some of the directors he considered was negative. They had problems with the women characters and suggested rewrites. Others had problems with the male characters. Three directors who turned down the project were Richard Donner (*The Omen*, 1976), Bob Rafelson (*Five Easy Pieces*, 1970), and Kevin Reynolds (*Robin Hood: Prince of Thieves*, 1991). While Scott was in search of an appropriate director, he realized that the third major character in *Thelma & Louise* was the physical landscape and that the narrative was a journey—an odyssey of self–revelation for the women. Scott was unaware that while he was conducting these interviews with potential directors he was persuading himself to occupy the director's chair.

Scott confided his uncertainty about directing *Thelma & Louise* to Alan Ladd Jr., who read the script and loved it. Directors' names kept coming up, but Scott would say that they weren't right for the picture. Laddie told his friend straight out that he believed Scott wanted to direct it and was the right director for this project, especially given his positive views on strong women.

Mimi Polk was a cinematic diplomat working both sides. She told Scott that *Thelma & Louise* was a rare gift available to him. With Callie Khouri she worked on making the screenwriter feel that Ridley Scott was the right person to direct her script. Khouri at this point saw Ridley Scott as a man's action film director and was looking for a director with sensitivity toward female characters. Finally, Polk told Scott to come to his senses and direct *Thelma & Louise*. "I was, in a way, a very good choice to do it," Scott told Sheila Weller. "I'd never had trouble letting women tell me what to do. All the years I'd run my company, I'd found that women were the best men for the job. Scott Free L.A. was run by a woman. Scott Free London was run by a woman. I could sit around and analyze the foolishness of men, since men are fundamentally the children in any relationship."

Scott's decision to both produce (along with Polk) and direct the film helped procure funding. Alan Ladd Jr. was again overseeing a Ridley Scott film as an executive for a major studio, this time MGM. A number of Hollywood's top actresses wanted to star in *Thelma & Louise*. Huge selling points were that it was a quality action screenplay and that the women characters carried the whole movie.

Production designer Norris Spencer and Ridley Scott went out on the road and drove the route that Thelma and Louise would travel. On *Thelma & Louise,* he decided, the best visual approach was to make the heartland of America as exotic as he could. As someone familiar with the European sensibility, Ridley Scott found US land and roads vast and expansive. Scott perceived the telegraph pole as a central symbol of that scope, but he had trouble finding telegraph poles; it seemed they had begun to disappear. Finally, he found them in Bakersfield, California, which became a key location.

As usual, Scott used painters as visual references. For *Thelma & Louise* it was the American realist painter John Register, whose subject matter was hotel lobbies and Formica-topped tables in diners. Register's point of view was to make the observer feel isolated. The spaces were devoid of people. Apparently inspired by Edward Hopper, Register was deeply involved with American scenes in which the viewer craves seeing human life. These paintings acted as inspiration for backgrounds in certain scenes. When there is a figure in a Register painting, the lack of personal connection with the environment is emphasized. When Scott first saw the location ultimately chosen for the motel used in critical scenes, he immediately thought of Register. Scott's cinematic reference for *Thelma & Louise* was Terrence Malick's 1973 debut film, *Badlands.* That film captures a stark American landscape and concerned two characters, in this case a man and a woman, on a killing spree.

Spencer and Scott started their journey in Arkansas and drove all the way to the Grand Canyon. Halfway across Texas the director had an epiphany. "It all looks the same to me. We can do this in the valley, and I can go home every night. I can find the Grand Canyon in Utah," Scott says in Weller's *Vanity Fair* article. He realized it wasn't necessary to transport a cast and crew of 149 for three minutes in Texas and four minutes in Arkansas. For Scott the journey in *Thelma & Louise* was an allegory, the last passage for the characters and a vision of the vanishing face of America. Ridley Scott's decisions for the actual shoot were practical and still loyal to the story. Laddie okayed filming in the San Fernando Valley and Bakersfield. The Arkansas houses were all near the Warner Bros. lot.

The casting choices for the roles that were eventually assigned to Susan Sarandon and Geena Davis were originally offered to Jodie Foster and Michelle Pfeiffer, who accepted. While time passed in preproduction the two stars committed to other movies—Foster to *The Silence of the Lambs* and Pfeiffer to *Love Field*.

Meryl Streep and Goldie Hawn asked for a meeting to discuss the film. They read the script and liked both parts, but Meryl Streep felt that one woman should live at the end of the story; Scott disagreed. He wanted a maverick ending where everything doesn't work out.

Meanwhile, Geena Davis, who had just won a Best Supporting Actress Oscar for *The Accidental Tourist* (1988), was pursuing the role. Davis had heard about the script from a friend of her then husband, actor Jeff Goldblum. She instructed her agent to talk to Scott on her behalf about a role in *Thelma & Louise*. That instruction was carried out every week for a full year. Davis was attracted to Khouri's script because she gravitated toward characters in charge of their own fate. She didn't care whether she played Thelma or Louise—she wanted to be in the movie. Meanwhile, Davis's acting coach convinced the actress she should play Louise. In her meeting with Scott, Davis was passionate about the part. At the end of her pitch, Scott asked if she was saying she wouldn't play Thelma, and Davis realized Scott wanted her for that part. The next day Davis was told that Ridley liked her and wanted to cast her, but first he had to see who was playing Louise. More time passed, and Davis was offered a role in another film. Calls went back and forth. Scott finally said that if Davis agreed to play either Thelma or Louise, a contract could be signed that day. Davis told her agent yes, and she was a lock.

Scott had sent Susan Sarandon the screenplay—she hadn't heard about it. She was ten years older than Geena Davis. In Sarandon, Scott saw qualities of Louise's character—hyper-competence, hurt, pain, and cynicism. When she arrived for their meeting, Scott felt Sarandon *was* Louise. Davis was at the meeting, and seeing Sarandon so confident and self-aware, she completely dropped the idea of playing Louise. Before committing to the part, Susan Sarandon made Ridley Scott promise that her character would die in the last scene.

Actor Brad Pitt, who was cast in the role of J.D. (juvenile delinquent) in *Thelma & Louise,* had been in a few movies and some television, but he was not yet a star and was looking for a breakout role. Pitt was a big fan of *Alien* and admired Ridley Scott. The script was light years from what he had been offered so far in his nascent career. Pitt felt that having been born in

Oklahoma and raised in Missouri by Southern Baptist parents, he knew the character. The character, who steals thousands of dollars from Thelma and Louise, spends a scant seven or so minutes on-screen but has a powerful impact. Brad Pitt was not the first choice for J.D.—that was William "Billy" Baldwin of the Baldwin acting clan. There was a delay in the *Thelma & Louise* start date, and Baldwin dropped out of the project and was cast in *Backdraft*. Casting agent Lou DiGiaimo asked Pitt to read and sent him to an audition with Geena Davis. The actress responded well to Pitt, and Scott was kind to him. Unfortunately, Callie Khouri pictured J.D. with a more collegiate look, not the bad-boy type Pitt projected. After the read, there was a group discussion about contenders for the role. The men were discussing everyone but Pitt, and finally Geena Davis put in her choice for the blond one—Pitt. He finally got the role of J.D. and was positioned to create a bit of movie history and launch a superstar career.

Michael Madsen, cast as Louise's loyal love interest, considered himself a hipster and rode a Harley motorcycle. His friends included Harvey Keitel and Dennis Hopper. Ridley Scott saw in Madsen an Elvis vibe and a streak of anger. Originally, Scott wanted to cast Madsen as the rapist, but the actor turned it down, concerned he would be stereotyped as such a despicable character.

Principal photography for *Thelma & Louise* began on June 11, 1990. There were fifty-four locations in *Thelma & Louise* in and around Los Angeles. The coffee shop where Louise works as a waitress was shot in DuPar's Restaurant, a famous local eatery in Thousand Oaks, California. The infamous bar where the women encounter the villain Harlan, Thelma's would-be rapist, played by Timothy Carhart, was filmed at the honky-tonk Silver Bullet Saloon in Long Beach. Gorman, California, was utilized for locations outside Los Angeles. Arches National Park and Canyonlands National Park in Utah were also used. The scenes of the women driving through farmland were filmed in Bakersfield, California. For the scene where a crop-dusting plane buzzes over the turquoise Thunderbird, Ridley Scott and company were on location in the San Joaquin Valley when he spotted the plane dusting crops. He sent an assistant out to ask the pilot if he would work on the film for $200.

The actors searched for a way to collaborate with Scott. Susan Sarandon reported in *Eye of the Storm,* "In trying to communicate with him, it was much more effective to talk about the way things looked than . . . talk about motivation. He just sees what he sees and goes after it. Every day we'd be on the set for hours wondering why we weren't going home and you would see

Ridley and his camera crew racing as the sun was going down. They had to get one last traveling shot of something and my fear was that it was going to be a voice-over with all these fabulous traveling shots."[3]

Scott explains in *Eye of the Storm*,

I'm hopeless with any form of languages. . . . I have a block. But on the visual side, I walk around, I see life . . . in a certain way which I try to emulate in the films and therefore I would see a certain kind of light mood change. . . . If I'm driving in a car, that will go in it, will be remembered and . . . come out in a film to be used at a certain given moment because it evokes something to me. So that's kind of an orchestration of emotions through light. If film is an art form, then lighting is definitely an art form—this certain layer of moviemaking, then there is another layer of moviemaking. So yes, lighting to me should contribute and be a certain statement. I hate it when people say you shouldn't notice the score. That's bullshit! You should notice the score, the score, if it's doing its job, will lift and elevate the movie—lighting also.

Despite Scott's belief that he has limited ability to communicate verbally, film editor Dody Dorn, who worked with him on three films, found him to be very warm and communicative in a reserved way. Ridley Scott respects the professionalism of his actors to memorize their lines, say them on set, and make the characters come alive; he intervenes only if they are not doing something he would like them to do. He sees his job as a listener. The actors know where to stand and when to move to another spot. He wants them to feel he is there for them as their best audience.

Christopher McDonald, who plays Thelma's husband Darryl, was recommended by Geena Davis. The two actors had dated from 1983 to 1984. For the audition McDonald grew a mustache and dressed in polyester and cheap jewelry. He was funny as the character both on- and off-screen, cracking up Harvey Keitel and Ridley Scott on set.

During the first day of shooting, as Darryl comes out of his house, McDonald accidentally slipped and fell on the driveway while yelling at the workman in the yard. The crew broke into raucous laughter. The actor stayed in character, getting into his car and driving off. Scott had kept the camera running and that's what's in the movie; Scott allowed this unplanned humorous moment to remain in the film.

At the Silver Bullet roadhouse bar Scott had expert dancers brought in. During a break in the shooting he saw some of them doing a country line dance. Scott incorporated it into the scene, shooting it without any rehearsal, which made it look just as it would in a real country bar. Two hundred fifty extras captured the joy of that dance. Patrick Swayze's mother Patsy taught Sarandon and Davis how to do the Texas two-step.

When Harlan takes Thelma, drunk and unsuspecting, into the parking lot, he makes unwelcome advances. When she resists, Harlan quickly gets aggressive, manhandling and slapping Thelma hard more than once. No body double was used in the scene. The shots, including a reshoot, that make up this disturbing and pivotal scene had to be performed multiple times, and Geena Davis sustained many real bruises. When Louise comes on the scene brandishing a gun, the audience is relieved that Thelma will be rescued but does not expect what happens next. Sudden and absolute violence punctuates the incident when an arrogant Harlan says to Louise, "I said suck my cock," and in a split second Louise shoots and kills him.

Callie Khouri's first and only choice for the women's car was a Thunderbird. It represented freedom and is considered by many automobile enthusiasts to be the last great American car. The camera car was driven by Sarandon and Davis while scenes were photographed from inside the car. The low tracking shot that starts on the front bumper and travels all the way back to the taillight was shot by Ridley Scott, riding alongside the car from another vehicle. He had to lean out to the road to get the shot—an assistant held onto him by his belt so he wouldn't fall from the moving car. There was an accident with the first car. It was totaled and then caught on fire. At first Susan Sarandon couldn't get her seat belt off, but tragedy was averted by cool heads and swift action.

The motel room scene between Thelma and J.D. required Geena Davis to be naked. The actress told Scott she wouldn't take her clothes off on camera. Switching gears, Scott began to look for a body double. He decided that interviewing Playboy bunnies in his trailer was the way to go. Davis's trailer was next to Scott's. After several hours watching the parade of Playboy bunnies go in and out of her director's trailer, Davis agreed to do the scene herself. The motel scene launched Brad Pitt's career. Scott was very attentive, making sure the young actor had his hair mussed up just right and even personally spraying Evian water on Pitt's abs.

According to Geena Davis, the sex scene was just implied in the script, but Scott wanted to put more of it on the screen. The actress was concerned because it was supposed to be the best sexual experience Thelma had ever had, so she thought the scene had to be great. The proof of her success is on the screen: the scene is sexy, funny, and highly erotic without being particularly graphic.

The scene in question is between the young con man and the woman on the run. While they are leading up to an erotic encounter, their scene is intercut with Sarandon and Madsen saying their good-byes when she tells him he can't come along with her this time. So Scott cleverly "hides" some of the body reveals in between lengthy scenes between the older lovers. Thus Ridley Scott, a director who doesn't especially like nude or sex scenes in his films, manages to put one in this movie—although we never see much.

Originally Scott ended the film on Harvey Keitel's face, but he changed it to focus on Thelma and Louise. With one more day of shooting left, it was a four-day weekend and would have cost the company $600,000 or $700,000. They had to finish. The controversial ending was shot in early August in Moab, Utah. The final scene was saved for the last day and had to be photographed during the magic hour, which occurs at the end of a day and produces a golden quality to the photography.

To make it look on-screen as if the women drive off the cliff, a ramp was built. Three car shells contained dummies of Thelma and Louise. Before a frame was shot, during a test, one of the cameras accidentally went off the cliff at a strange angle. Luckily, the second car took off the cliff perfectly. Next, Sarandon and Davis, in full makeup and costume, climbed into the real car with the camera mounted and aimed at each of them so close-ups could be shot in synch. The one take had to be right—now there were no second chances. Action was called. The women were being chased by a seemingly endless formation of screeching police cars. Thelma tells Louise, "Let's keep going," and Louise gives Thelma a firm kiss on the lips. Meanwhile, Harvey Keitel's Hal Slocumb is running full-out behind them trying to stop them from driving off the cliff. Louise floors the accelerator. The take is perfect— print. The experience was very emotional. Everyone was hugging.

The kiss on the lips between Thelma and Louise has at times been misread. There is nothing romantic about it. It is a bold gesture of sisterhood and a way of saying, "We're going to continue on this trip no matter where it takes us" as they drive off the cliff.

A Thunderbird was stripped of its engine and mounted on a ramp out of camera range near the edge of the cliff. There was a fast-moving river below. There were two dummies inside the car representing Thelma and Louise. A cable was connected to the car, put through a block and tackle. This was hooked to a six-hundred-horsepower Jeep. As the cameras rolled and the Jeep traveled at forty-five miles per hour, the block and tackle system doubled the speed of the cable, which pulled the car over the cliff at ninety mph. The camera was overcranked to produce enough slow motion to make the car appear to fly. This was done to all three cars so Scott could pick from the three takes.

Many viewers think that when Thelma and Louise drive off the cliff it is a double suicide. Callie Khouri believes people have misinterpreted the scene.

> To me the ending was symbolic. . . . We did everything possible to make sure that you didn't see a literal death. That you didn't see the car land, you didn't see a big puff of smoke come up out of the canyon. You were left with the image of them flying. They flew away, out of this world and into the mass unconscious. Women who are completely free from all the shackles that restrain them have no place in this world. The world is not big enough to support them. They will be brought down if they stay here. They weren't going to be brought down. So let them go. I loved that ending and I loved the imagery. After all they went through I didn't want anybody to be able to touch them.[4]

In the official ending the car is stopped in midair by a freeze frame followed by a shot of a Polaroid of the two women and a brief montage of them in happier times, similar to the conclusion of *The Wild Bunch*, which brings back images of the men in good spirits after they have all been killed.

There is also an extended ending that is available on DVD. The car drops into the canyon. From behind we see the Harvey Keitel character running toward the edge of the cliff. This is followed by a full shot of a helicopter flying over the area, then back to the same framing as before, but the helicopter enters and goes down into the canyon and out of sight. Then there is a full shot of the law enforcement men as they get out of their cars, carrying rifles, and begin to walk forward; then there is a cut to another angle of the same action. A medium close-up of Hal looking down into the canyon follows—he is sad and upset that he couldn't prevent this tragedy. He turns and moves toward the men. The final shot is an extreme full shot of Thelma and Louise as they were at the beginning of their journey, driving on a dusty road with a mountain range in the distance, the sky a full blue filled with white fluffy clouds. To Scott this represented the freedom the women were looking for. B. B. King's "Better Not Look Down" is playing on the soundtrack. The film concludes as the car sails out over the canyon. It travels upward, then starts to fall downward. When it reaches the middle of the frame the image dissolves to white.

It is presumed that this extended ending was part of the original director's cut. It prolongs the ending, but the last long take of the women driving away as they did at the beginning of their journey is effective. The montage of the two women alive and happy creates the feeling that their spirit is still with us. The extended ending says the journey continues.

Thelma & Louise opened in the US on May 24, 1991. At some screenings of *Thelma & Louise* audiences cheered when Louise shot Harlan dead; this included the audience at Cannes. Then word of mouth took over, transforming *Thelma & Louise* into more than a movie. It became a phenomenon. *Time* magazine ran a cover story on *Thelma & Louise*. It was a female buddy movie; it was a road film; it was a feminist statement. Many see *Thelma & Louise* as a modern-day feminist western or as *Bonnie and Clyde* with both characters female. *Thelma & Louise* can also accurately be classified as a chick flick, although the movie is a complex member of that genre, as such films are usually targeted for a female audience and deal with the complexities of conventional love. The film may be more related to *Butch Cassidy and the Sundance Kid* than to other chick flicks, but like many great films, it is difficult to pin down.

Peter Travers gave it a rave review in *Rolling Stone.* "Call it a comedy of shocking gravity. *Thelma & Louise* begins like an episode of *I Love Lucy* and ends with the impact of *Easy Rider.* It's a bumpy path between those points, and director Ridley Scott . . . and first-time screenwriter Callie Khouri don't cushion the ride. The film switches moods violently, and sometimes it just jerks your chain. But this is movie dynamite, detonated by award-caliber performances from Geena Davis and Susan Sarandon in the title roles."

Roger Ebert hailed the film's spirit of discovery. "'Thelma & Louise' is in the expansive, visionary tradition of the American road picture. It celebrates the myth of two carefree souls piling into a 1956 T-Bird and driving out of town to have some fun and raise some hell. We know the road better than that, however, and we know the toll it exacts: Before their journey is done, these characters will have undergone a rite of passage, and will have discovered themselves."

Angie Errigo of *Empire* hailed *Thelma & Louise* as a film about gal pals, not guy pals. "This entertaining, giddy tale of two friends who become fugitives is a Big Deal, however, not because it is that original—screenwriter Callie Khouri couldn't have concocted this movie without *Butch Cassidy and The Sundance Kid* and William Goldman's much-copied pattern for an action adventure about comically wisecracking comrades—but because of the astonishing fact that this is the first big-budget Hollywood picture in which the pals are gals."

Thelma & Louise became a cultural milestone. The film grossed $46 million in the US, with a budget of only $16–17 million. *Thelma & Louise* also played strongly in Europe, grossing $4 million in both England and France in the first six weeks of release.

Callie Khouri won the Oscar for Best Screenplay written directly for the screen. Nominations went out to Geena Davis, Susan Sarandon, Adrian Biddle, Thom Noble, and Ridley Scott. The two actresses probably cancelled each other out. Ironically, Jodie Foster, who was originally attached to *Thelma & Louise,* won the Oscar for Best Actress for *The Silence of the Lambs.* When Callie Khouri accepted her Oscar, she said, "For everybody that wanted to see a happy ending for *Thelma & Louise,* this is it."[5]

People were obsessed about the morality of the ending. Scott was always confident that the script's controversial ending was the right one. He saw the women continuing on their journey. He saw the film's themes as choices and freedom.

Thelma & Louise film brought Ridley Scott one of his largest audiences. Buttons with slogans relating to the movie were sold and distributed. The names Thelma and Louise became linked with feminism as well as with any similar spirit or event revolving around outlaw women. The success of *Thelma & Louise* helped widen Ridley Scott's scope as a director. He had been seen as an action director but had now proved he could deftly handle a character-driven movie.

Paul M. Sammon sees *Thelma & Louise* as a multigenre picture comprised of parable, road movie, social commentary, buddy, and comedy. Above all, Callie Khouri's screenplay for *Thelma & Louise* is clearly a feminist work, written by a woman with the state of American women in mind. Louise Sawyer and Thelma Dickinson are victims of male society but come out heroes who, in a tragic and ironic way, take full control of their lives.

10

COLUMBUS DAYS
1492: Conquest of Paradise

Following the light of the sun, we left the old world.
Christopher Columbus

1492: Conquest of Paradise is one of Ridley Scott's most visually beautiful films, containing a detailed history of the birth of America as seen through the eyes of Columbus and his son, who inherited his diary. The film was not widely seen in America or around the world, and critics were not kind, claiming not only that Scott got it wrong, but that he was wrongheaded about a man they didn't feel was worthy of the claims stated in the film.

The year 1992 was the five hundredth anniversary of Columbus's landmark world-changing voyage. In 1991, Ilya and Alexander Salkind of *Superman* fame and Ridley Scott announced upcoming films about Columbus. Some noise was made about this situation at the 1991 Cannes Film Festival, and the Salkinds launched a lawsuit against Scott—which they lost because Scott had proposed his film first. Ironically, the Salkinds had originally asked Scott if he would direct their picture, written by Mario Puzo, best known for *The Godfather* movies. Scott turned them down, and the Salkinds turned to the workmanlike John Glen, director of several James Bond feature films, to helm *Christopher Columbus: The Discovery*, partly financed by the Spanish government's Fifth Centennial Commission. The film received extremely bad reviews. Scott named his film *1492: Conquest of Paradise* so as not to engage any more lawsuits. This production was supported by the Spanish Ministry of Culture.

In 1987 French journalist Roselyne Bosch had traveled to Seville, Spain, where there are extensive archives about Columbus and his journeys. She researched an article about how Spain was to celebrate the five hundredth anniversary of his historic expedition. She was surprised to discover around 40 million parchment documents and scores of letters pertaining to Columbus in the provincial archives in Madrid and Seville. She did thorough research and learned that Columbus was a rebel who pushed to discover lands and pursue new ideas. Bosch became fascinated with the mystery surrounding Christopher Columbus, usually considered more as an icon than a man. She wrote a proposal outlining a script about Columbus's many sea journeys as well as his personal and spiritual ones. It was narrated by one of Columbus's sons. Bosch had a literary agent present her proposal to Alain Goldman, the young president of MKs, a French film distribution company. Goldman was enthusiastic about the project and paid her to write the full screenplay. He became the producer. There was no interest in France because of the massive budget.

A trip to Hollywood was also unsuccessful for the team. Goldman shopped the script around, offering it to Francis Ford Coppola, Roland Joffé, Oliver Stone, and David Puttnam, but no one was interested. The anniversary didn't mean as much to the Hollywood suits as the $45 million price tag, and the fact that it was a period piece was a detriment; they believed the film would have no audience. In 1990 Goldman brought the Bosch script to Ridley Scott, who was intrigued by the opportunity to re-create the fifteenth-century locales. Scott said yes, but only if the production could get Gérard Depardieu in the lead role as Christopher Columbus. Goldman then financed the film himself. He presold the foreign rights.

Scott got his wish for Gérard Depardieu to portray Columbus, with ample support from Armand Assante, Sigourney Weaver, and Frank Langella, plus a phalanx of actors to flesh out both the Spanish and island sequences. Specialized actors and others who spoke the right language and looked the part were needed for the island sequences. As they prepared the film, Bosch and Scott learned how hard and barbaric life was in Columbus's time and that the political powers were the manipulators behind his career and eventual downfall. Scott was interested in the facts, the inner aspects of the man, and the price he paid for being a visionary.

On the first day of shooting, as Depardieu made his entrance, the crew gasped at his performance. The pressure of the grand role had temporarily overwhelmed Depardieu. The actor, whose native language was French, had been concentrating on his English, rehearsing the lines carefully, but when it came time to say his first line what came out of his mouth sounded more French than English. Another gasp came from the crew. Scott, cool under fire, called cut, talked to his actors, and then gave them a break.

Over the years Depardieu had had weight and alcohol problems and struggled with depression. He was still reeling from scurrilous reports that he had a history as a rapist. Depardieu knew this part was a pivotal moment in his illustrious career. Back on the set action was called. Again, Depardieu made his entrance and spoke with accented but clear English. After only three takes Scott called, "Cut and print!"

Shooting began in late 1991 in Seville and Granada, Spain. Because of the endorsement from the Ministry of Culture, Scott and his cast and crew were able to shoot on locations that were centuries old, such as the Alcazar in Seville and the Convent of San Esteban in Salama. To find a place to re-create the New World involved an extensive location scout. Travels took the team to Mexico, the Dominican Republic, Cuba, and Colombia. Finally the decision was made to shoot in Costa Rica, where there was a large population of indigenous inhabitants. One hundred and seventy Indians from four Costa Rican tribes and six tribes of Waunana Indians from Colombia were gathered to play the original inhabitants of that land.

Because of the heightened interest in Columbus and his historic voyage, revisionists were already attacking Columbus on many fronts. Many proclaimed that he wasn't even Italian and blamed the man for much of the evil that developed in America over the centuries.

At first, working with the Indians as actors was difficult for both sides. Communication was hard, as was achieving performances. Assistant director Claudia Gomez, who had worked on *The Mission* (1986), is credited by Scott as helping to solve these problems. On-screen the performances by the Indians are realistic and compelling in their interaction with Columbus and his men.

For the pivotal role of Queen Isabella, Scott wanted Hollywood royalty and selected Anjelica Huston, daughter of actor/director John Huston. Anjelica Huston couldn't quite get herself to commit to the project, so Scott moved on to Sigourney Weaver, with whom Scott had achieved great results on *Alien*. There is much confusing and conflicting evidence about how Weaver felt working with Scott a second time—everything from the two having fought badly to her not liking his method very much to the actress finding the director cold at best—nevertheless, she took the part and gave a strong performance.

The film was an independent production financed by raising $10 million from Paramount for the American rights, $11 million from Gaumont for the French distribution rights, and by preselling the movie on a territory-by-territory basis at the Cannes Film Festival in 1991.

1492: Conquest of Paradise was photographed in four countries on two continents. Some of the interior scenes were shot at Pinewood. Principal photography began on December 2, 1991, outside the Spanish town of Cáceres at a sixteenth-century villa representing the ancient monastery Santa Maria de la Rabida in the film. The film took eighty-two days to shoot, with a company of almost four hundred people.

As for the ships, the *Pinta* and the *Santa Maria* were built when Scott found the proper hulls in a boatyard in Bristol, England. For the *Nina,* production designer Norris Spencer leased a facsimile of the famous ship that had been built by a 1492 society in Brazil.

Other aspects of the locations and the design included re-creating La Isabella, a village Columbus set up on the island of Hispaniola, now known as Haiti and the Dominican Republic. It was built on the Costa Rican coast around a fantastic large tree. It also had a manor house for Columbus, a compound, a Spanish church, a ninety-foot bell tower, and many other elements.

New Age electronic music artist Vangelis created the score. Surprisingly, the studio did not exploit the five hundredth anniversary in its ad campaign.

1492: Conquest of Paradise was released in America on October 2, 1992, for one week over the Columbus Day holiday weekend; it grossed only $7.2 million. Overseas it grossed a more impressive $52 million. The budget was an estimated $44 million, but Hollywood mathematicians say you must earn far, far more to cover the making of prints and advertising to realize a profit.

Roger Ebert liked the film, especially Depardieu's performance, but he found it no more than "satisfactory." The *Guardian* online gave the movie a "D," saying part of it was fake and created a villain with no basis in history. The invented bad guy may be Adrian de Moxica, but there is no evidence he was evil. The *Guardian* claimed the real history is that Columbus was in actuality a poor navigator. The reviewer also accused Scott and his designer of overdressing the island sets. Moreover, according to the review, Columbus was no humanitarian, as he is portrayed in the film. Alex von Tunzelmann's ultimate insult was calling the film a "15th century *Fight Club* with Moxica as Columbus's Tyler Durden."[1]

1492: Conquest of Paradise was photographed in a widescreen format to capture the expansive tableaus planned by Scott. Scott's use of the camera, manned by him and director of photography Adrian Biddle, is sweeping, and each shot is meticulously composed. On any Ridley Scott film lighting is vitally important, and here he again allowed the director of photography as much time as was needed to achieve his vision of perfection. What made the lighting even more complex was that Scott did not want a static camera but one always in motion, either on dollies or cranes. To capture the flow of the violent seas during the voyages, handheld cameras were employed for their roughness. Night scenes in the movie were shot by candlelight and torchlight because of the lack of electricity at the locations chosen for interior scenes. For night exteriors, cherry pickers were utilized to get the moon on the team's side as a lighting fixture. A million feet of film was exposed for the epic.

The scenes aboard the ships put the viewer at sea—able to sense the fear and anticipation of the voyages. The coverage of the New World looks like the company went back in time to capture the arrival of Columbus and his crew and the reaction of the natives. The film is full of compassion for the travelers and those they meet and live with along the way. Once again Ridley Scott took on a project that had myriad possibilities concerning the creation of a fully realized world. *1492* is much more than just a very good period film; it is a movie that allows the viewer to experience the world as Columbus knew it.

Movies are made of scenes and sequences. Many films have memorable scenes or sequences that stay with the viewer and often sum up the spirit of the movie. There are wonderful tableaus in *1492: Conquest of Paradise* containing many people, stimulating action, and visual details, but the most memorable scene in this film, which appears early on, was shot on a beach with Columbus showing his young son the proof he found that the world was not flat, as most believed, but round. He tells the boy to look at a ship far in the distance. After some time passes, Columbus tells him to look again, explaining to his son that less of the ship is seen now, thus proving the world is round—if it were flat the ship would appear the same size. Not only is this instructive, but it also sets up the rest of the movie. There is a real human factor here: the love and respect between father and son.

In 1995 Ridley and Tony Scott were part of a group of investors that purchased Shepperton Studios, which was upgraded under the new management.

11

ADVENTURES NOT IN PARADISE

White Squall

If there are seven characters in a film, I treat the environment as the eighth character—or the first. After all that's the proscenium within which everything will function.

Ridley Scott

White Squall does a remarkably believable job re-creating the 1960s, not the *Easy Rider* 1960s, but an earlier time of honor and respect for the traditional American way of life. A group of thirteen young men sign up for the Ocean Academy—a strict prep school on a ship named the *Albatross* traveling the seas. They take the trip to gain discipline, study English literature, and learn lessons about cooking, health—and life. After gaining those skills from the skipper and his crew, they head home. On the return voyage, they encounter a white squall—a sudden powerful storm of overwhelming wind and rain. The *Albatross* capsizes, then sinks. Four students, two crew members, and the skipper's wife perish. The rest, including the captain, are rescued by another ship, but come home to anger and controversy. The skipper is brought in front of a tribunal where he meets with much hostility and his fitness to be a licensed ship's captain is judged. In the end the boys rally around him.

Screenwriter Todd Robinson was on vacation in Hawaii when he met Chuck Gieg, who told him the thirty-year-old true story of the *Albatross*. Robinson was inspired by *The Last Voyage of the Albatross*, cowritten by Gieg, a survivor of the incident, and wrote his first screenplay. Todd Robinson took his *White Squall* script to producers Rocky Lang and Mimi Polk Gitlin. The co-producers turned down several directors who wanted to alter the script to fit their vision; they were steadfast about maintaining the integrity of the story. Eventually they got the script to Ridley Scott, who acquired it before Christmas 1994. He found the script honest and unsentimental and liked the rite-of-passage aspect of the story. *White Squall* was financed by Buena Vista Pictures, Largo Entertainment, Hollywood Pictures (a subsidiary of Disney), and Scott Free. (Scott Free Productions was formed in 1995 in Los Angeles.) To edit the film, Scott selected the master British film editor Gerry Hambling, who often worked with Scott's friend and associate, director Alan Parker. Hambling, like Parker and Scott, started out in commercials. The real Captain Sheldon and Chuck Gieg were technical advisers on the film.

The film is narrated by Scott Wolf, who plays Charles "Chuck" Gieg. The main female character in the film is Dr. Alice Sheldon (portrayed by Caroline Goodall), the ship's doctor and the wife of the skipper. Dr. Sheldon was the only woman on board the *Albatross* and has the strong attributes of a Ridley Scott female. Captain Christopher "Skipper" Sheldon is brilliantly portrayed by Jeff Bridges. Actors playing the young men include Ryan Philippe, whose character's brother is dead. He carries his brother's photograph with him and acts out wildly until the boys, the captain, and the trip itself calm him.

The vessel utilized in the movie was *Eye of the Wind,* a 110-foot topsail schooner from Germany. Cinematographically, *White Squall* is unique among Ridley Scott films. His earlier films were beautiful, with perfect and complex lighting and framing, while this film is raw and naturalistic. Scott and director of photography Hugh Johnson screened many films for reference, including *Mutiny on the Bounty* (1962) and *Moby Dick* (1956). Scott looked at a lot of documentary footage and studied water patterns to see how they moved and reacted. He did not want to shoot this film in a tank, which was common procedure in Hollywood films, believing that waves do not appear large enough under such circumstances. The perspective is never realistic enough and the relationship of the height of the waves to the movement of the water does not appear as a real experience. Shooting out at sea was difficult, time-consuming, and dangerous, and the constant movement of the ship made the camerawork difficult. Lighting was a challenge. Scott and Johnson wanted a rough look, so handheld cameras were employed.

For the storm and the sinking of the ship, Scott did eventually concede to work in a tank, but he used one in a huge facility located on the Mediterranean island of Malta. Johnson also photographed additional miniature work during the postproduction process. Actually, two tanks were used—one held 6 million gallons of water and was forty feet deep. The other held 3 million gallons of water and was eight feet deep. Also available were tip tanks that held five tons to add water in large amounts. Wave machines were also utilized.

The light was good only from 8:30 or 9:00 a.m. and then from midday until 4:00. At around 6:00 the light began to fall. The in-between hours were difficult to light as it was the hottest time of the day.

The film is set around the time of the 1962 Cuban missile crisis. Tensions between the US and Cuba were at their height. The ship is spotted by a Cuban vessel, which sails right up to the *Albatross*. The men are armed, and the leader demands to come aboard. He is denied by the skipper, but the leader and his men force their way onto the *Albatross*. After inspecting the ship and intimidating everyone on board, the Cubans finally leave the *Albatross*. It is only because cooler heads prevailed with all—the skipper, his crew, and the boys, that no harm takes place.

The storm sequence took a full five days to photograph. The most challenging problem was that the cameras were constantly wet. The actors had to be barraged with water, sometimes up to their necks or even underwater. For the wind effects the standard fans were not good enough for Ridley Scott. He brought in jet engines to do the job.

Hollywood has a long tradition of making movies based on true stories. Rarely do they adhere strictly to the facts. Parts of the story are dropped, parts are amplified, fictional scenes are created, characters are changed, sometimes drastically, and it is common practice to take several real people and make them into one composite character.

What was called the "court of inquiry" sequence at the film's conclusion was shot in Charleston, South Carolina. The courtroom was built as a set in a warehouse. Although this was an effective, dramatic, and emotional ending, in reality there was no tribunal or trial against Captain Sheldon after the disaster at sea. The created scene allowed Ridley Scott to show the anger of the parents toward the skipper, the boys' love and support for him, and the tenacity, courage, and character inherent in the captain. The drama includes placing the skipper's license to sail again in jeopardy. It is filled with dramatic dialogue and actions, concluding with the boys coming to the skipper's rescue so he will be permitted to sail again. The scene is a tearjerker, filled with emotion, and is completely convincing—except it's not the truth. The finale is total artistic license. The dynamics of confrontation make for good cinematic theater, and this one really pays off with the captain's impassioned speech before the tribunal and the demonstration of the boys' solidarity, which ultimately brings the court around. The use of a ringing bell by the boys to bring them all together is particularly effective and dramatic, probably more dramatic than the conclusion of the real story. The danger of invention in a film based on a true story is that the audience feels it now knows the truth. Ultimately, the audience has to ask itself, is it worth it to dramatize a real story and manipulate the facts for the filmmaker's advantage?

Lisa Schwarzbaum of *Entertainment Weekly* admired the director's visualization of *White Squall* but criticized the lack of characterization, "Above all, what Scott—a former student of painting and graphic design—wants to convey is the texture of the sails, the composition of the boys as they swab and batten and unfurl, the movement of the water that tells as much of the story as buttes and canyons describe his *Thelma & Louise*. As a result, *White Squall* is lovely to look at, but frustrating to behold. These boys are fine specimens of American manhood. But they're unreachable, like ships in a bottle."

Some critics compared *White Squall* to the earlier *Dead Poets Society*. Of those, William Thomas of *Empire* still liked it. "Taking a true tragedy—the sinking of the brigantine ship *Albatross* in 1960—director Ridley Scott has fashioned a curiously compulsive drama that for all its inevitable Dead Sailors' Society trappings is still highly entertaining." Barbara Shulgasser of the *San Francisco Examiner* found the narrative slow and pointless. "Although Robinson and director Ridley Scott take forever to get there, the central event is a titanic storm, the white squall of the title, which capsizes the ship and takes the lives of several students and Sheldon's wife. After the survivors are rescued, despite his heroic efforts to save his students and crew, Sheldon is brought up before a tribunal threatening to take his sailing certificate away. The only question I can think of at this point is 'Why?'"

After *White Squall* Mimi Polk Gitlin, Scott's veteran producer, ended their collaboration to become an independent producer.

12

NOT G.I. JOE

G.I. Jane

I'm drawn to strong, intelligent women in real life. Why shouldn't the films reflect that?

Ridley Scott

G.I. Jane (1997) is a feminist/military/war film that follows the journey of Jordan O'Neill, who is persuaded by a high-powered female senator to enter a rigorous, all-male military training program. The United States Navy SEALs are a special-operational outfit employed for counterterrorism, internal defense against foreign aggression, hostage rescue, and other land-based operations. They are an elite group of men, highly trained and in perfect physical condition. Currently, some women have been allowed to participate in parts of the navy SEAL training, often under different conditions than the men, but no woman has ever completed the program and officially joined the ranks as depicted in the film. Refusal to fail, no matter how tough the pressure, is the theme embraced in *G.I. Jane*. So *G.I. Jane* is a "what if" film that has its heart in the right place about the continuing struggle of women to achieve equality and function in what is strictly a man's terrain.

The story and screenplay of *G.I. Jane* was created by Danielle Alexandra, a 20th Century Fox executive, who worked in television as a writer and producer. She became an executive producer on *G.I. Jane*. Alexandra wrote the part of Lieutenant Jordan O'Neill for Demi Moore and convinced the actress to come on board. Alexandra had developed relationships inside the Pentagon and with some congressmen in Washington, DC, and was drawn to the idea of a film about the "women in combat" movement that commenced in the mid-1990s. After Alexandra turned in a first-draft script, David Twohy (*The Chronicles of Riddick*, 2004) was brought in to develop and hone the action elements. Demi Moore approached Ridley Scott with the project, and he agreed to direct it.

Ridley Scott and Demi Moore on the set of *G.I. Jane.*

Scott had met Demi Moore on several occasions; they would swap ideas for a film. Scott thought the provocative and controversial material of *G.I. Jane* would make a great project for Moore, whom he considered one of the best actors around. The Tailhook scandal, in which female naval pilots in training accused their male counterparts of sexual harassment, was around ten months old while *G.I. Jane* was in production. A week before principal photography began, there was another incident in which a young woman encountered resistance after she attempted to enroll in the Citadel—an all-male military academy in South Carolina. These real-life incidents served as a convincing backdrop for the story line.

Prior to shooting, Moore and the male actors went through a rigorous two-week training camp to prepare them for the scenes where the unit is tested by laborious feats on sand and in water. Moore worked with two trainers beginning at 4:00 a.m., so her workout was completed before shooting began. She employed a navy SEAL instructor to help her with the mindset necessary to be a SEAL. Demi Moore did almost everything; a stuntwoman or double was used only a very few times. Nonetheless, the film wasn't taken totally seriously—some felt the premise was too unrealistic and that aspects of it were too focused on the character's physicality.

During the filming Scott fell on the ice and injured his knee. Later, during the shoot in Florida, his knee gave out and production was halted while Scott underwent a fairly serious corrective operation; knee problems continued to plague him in the future. As a necessary relaxation, Scott smoked Cuban cigars, including Montecristo No. 2s.

Although there had been ongoing talks with the navy and the Department of Defense, Scott and his cast and crew were not able to get their cooperation on several points. They insisted on many changes. They told Scott that naval officers didn't curse. They also thought Demi Moore's character would never have cut her hair so short. Although Scott wanted their cooperation to authenticate aspects of the story, he didn't want to execute their list of changes, so he used his own expert team to create locations and obtain equipment through other sources. Demi Moore, who had political connections, tried to persuade President Clinton to use his influence to get them into a real training facility, but even that didn't work.

Scott was able to get real navy craft into the background of the film. Across the way from Scott's camp was the Mayport base, an actual naval facility. While shooting on his base Scott secretly filmed the ships from the Mayport base.

Viggo Mortensen was cast for the pivotal role of Master Chief Urgayle. Mortensen had been in the Tony Scott film *Crimson Tide,* and Ridley liked what Tony had to say about directing him. Urgayle reads poetry in the movie. Scott wanted to portray Urgayle as intelligent as well as tough and macho. Mortensen suggested a poem and was asked to find others. Scott learned later that in addition to other artistic activities, Viggo Mortensen was a published poet. He came up with several poems that he delivered on camera as Urgayle.

To film O'Neill cutting her own hair in the empty base barbershop, Scott used three cameras, one positioned above Moore and one on each side. The scene proceeded smoothly until she had a difficult time reaching to buzz the back. Scott stopped the filming and repositioned the cameras. When they rolled again Moore finished the job.

Ridley Scott has always been reluctant to put a nude scene in a movie unless it is absolutely necessary to the story. In *G.I. Jane* it was. In the scene in which Jordan is taking a shower alone, little is shown because the shots are rather tightly composed. There is one shot that is framed full and reveals the naked Jordan from behind. The master chief enters with an imposing, threatening attitude and continues to turn up the rhetoric as to why he is against women in combat. Then there is a tight composition on Jordan and one shot of selective focus on the master chief where he clearly looks down her body with defiance and a hint of lust. The point of the scene is to demonstrate Jordan's vulnerability, but it is flouted by her determined attitude against his negative spoken views.

There is a scene in which O'Neill is captured and interrogated to prepare her for such a possibility. This procedure was based on actual SEAL training. Scott captured the verbal and physical abuse that could happen by careful camera placement, padding, and sound effects. For the waterboarding scene when Viggo Mortensen holds Demi Moore's head underwater, they worked out a signal for when to pull her up for air. It was Moore tugging on Mortensen's pants. At one point, Mortensen got into the reality of the moment and kept holding her down until Moore yanked frantically on his pants. Finally, he pulled her up out of the water. During the interrogation sequence when O'Neill is fed up with Urgayle and the whole exercise, she yells a classic movie line for *G.I. Jane*—"Suck my dick!" which underscores that O'Neill has earned the right to join her fellow male recruits who will become navy SEALs.

There is a political angle to *G.I. Jane*. O'Neill is being manipulated by Senator DeHaven, forcefully played by Anne Bancroft. The senator has created the whole notion of getting a woman into the navy SEAL program only in order to advance herself politically. Originally Scott wanted to model DeHaven on the colorful Senator Ann Richards of Texas, who is known for famously saying of President George W. Bush, "Stick a fork in him, he's done," but later he decided to let Bancroft create her own interpretation of the DeHaven character.

In the finished film O'Neill goes to Libya, fights in real combat, and rescues Urgayle. To shoot the sequence, Scott wrapped the first unit for around seven weeks and went into editing while he prepped the new scene.

During the seven weeks while the Libyan scenes were being prepped, director of photography Hugh Johnson completed his work and left the film. Scott hired Daniel Mindel to shoot the Libyan scenes with a jittery zoom style. Ridley Scott was operating one of the four cameras. He started experimenting with the zoom lens. The other operators saw his results during playback, and the rough zooms became part of the final battle sequence. Scott wanted a documentary look, and moving the zoom lens with his hands accomplished that.

There is an alternate ending in which O'Neill is shot by a stray bullet and is dying on the floor of the helicopter next to the master chief. The test scores on audiences who screened both endings were practically the same, but Scott decided it was such a negative ending that he went with a Hollywood happy ending in which Jordan lives and Urgayle gives O'Neill his Navy Cross medal.

The editor of *G.I. Jane* was Pietro Scalia, who had cut *Wall Street* (1987) and *JFK* (1991) for Oliver Stone. Scott used Scalia for the first time and found that in addition to Scalia's fine ability to cut for story and performance, he was also very strong visually. Their relationship became an enduring and trusting collaboration. "Usually there are some initial discussions about my reactions to the script and Ridley shares his visual concepts, and ideas about the look of the film," the editor told Norman Hollyn in an interview for *Cinema Editor.* "Ridley and I have worked for a long time so the exchanges are short: 'Yeah, no, absolutely.'" *G.I. Jane* was the first occasion on which Ridley Scott worked with production designer Arthur Max, who has become one of his closest collaborators.

Janet Maslin of the *New York Times* acknowledged the director's ability to render strength on the screen. "Mr. Scott's affinity for the visceral and strenuous, from '*Alien*' to '*Blade Runner*' to '*White Squall*,' is much more central here than the renegade feminism of his '*Thelma and Louise*.' With punishing intensity, he plunges his audience into the maelstrom of the training program and watches Ms. Moore dauntingly do her fair share. Stone-faced and ruggedly fit, she endures the workout from hell with a male supporting cast mostly recruited from triathlon groups and military bases. Mr. Scott finds dark fascination in watching his heroine, for instance, doing brutal push-ups in the surf with a helicopter roaring overhead."

Roger Ebert opined, "The training sequences are as they have to be: incredible rigors, survived by O'Neill. They are good cinema because Ridley Scott, the director, brings a documentary attention to them, and because Demi Moore, having bitten off a great deal here, proves she can chew it. The wrong casting in her role could have tilted the movie toward 'Private Benjamin,' but Moore is serious, focused and effective."

Many reviews took aim at Demi Moore, questioning her abilities. Marcs Savlov of the *Austin Chronicle* wrote,

> Touted for months now as the template for the oft-asked question "Can Demi Moore carry a film on her own?" *G. I. Jane* proves that, yes, despite Hollywood's—and the American moviegoing public's—love-hate relationship with Moore the Superstar, she has the chops down cold. No matter that Scott's film is little more than a run-of-

the-mill crowd-pleaser with a finale that's telegraphed almost from scene one. And no matter, either, that the film carries a muddled message regarding women and power and women *in* power. The number-one question on the suits' minds (certainly in the wake of the *Striptease* and *The Scarlet Letter* disasters) has been: Can she hold her own? She does, and admirably well, to boot.

G.I. Jane wasn't without controversy. The American-Arab Discrimination Committee charged the Walt Disney Company, which distributed *G.I. Jane,* with racial discrimination based on the end sequence where the SEALs are witnessed shooting Arabs. The argument was that Disney, which was accused of distributing a long list of films stereotyping Arabic people, did it again here by portraying the bad guys fought by Jordan and her team as Arabs.

The film was rated R and put into general release on August 22, 1997. *G.I. Jane* is highly entertaining while presenting serious social issues of the day—the operation of the military and the role of women in the military and in society. Ridley Scott has consistently been pro-women during his long career. This is reflected especially in Demi Moore's performance and in a long list of capable female characters in Scott's films: at times vulnerable, they are ultimately in charge of their own destinies.

Also in 1997 Black Dog Films opened offices in London. The unit was quickly as successful as its sister facility in Los Angeles. The company concentrated on creating music videos for visible artists and was successful in winning numerous awards.

In 1999 a TV movie for TNT, *Pirates of Silicon Valley,* told the story of Steve Jobs, Bill Gates, and the making of Ridley Scott's *1984* commercial for Apple. Ridley Scott is an actual character in the film, played by J. G. Hertzler, a brawny, cigar-smoking Scott depicted directing the iconic commercial.

In the late 1990s Ridley and Tony Scott purchased the Mill, a British digital effects house, to service Pinewood/Shepperton Studios, which they had purchased earlier as part of a consortium. Again showing their business acumen, the brothers bought a company that would assist them with postproduction and be a part of a solid growing trend in the moving image industry.

13

RIDLEY SCOTT'S
SPARTACUS
Gladiator

Ridley Scott does very well on controlled chaos.

John Mathieson

Gladiator (2000) is one of Ridley Scott's most popular films and was extremely successful at the box office. *Gladiator* is another war film—a time-trip back to an ancient society where men are primal and rule dangerously.

Screenwriter David Franzoni, who scripted Steven Spielberg's *Amistad* (1997), approached studio executives Walter Parkes and Laurie McDonald with his idea to write a film set in ancient Rome with the Coliseum as its focus. Franzoni had plenty of film history to draw from, with *The Robe* (1953), *Ben Hur* (1959), *Spartacus* (1960), *King of Kings* (1961), and other epics of that era. The first screenplay draft was completed on April 4, 1998. The writer had been inspired by the 1958 novel by Daniel P. Mannix, *Those about to Die*. After reading the *Augustan History,* Franzoni decided to base his story on Commodus—Marcus Aurelius Commodus Antoninus Augustus (161–192), who was Roman emperor from AD 180 to 192 and whose reign attempted to reimagine and transform the Roman Empire in his own image.

Ridley Scott was invited to a meeting by Walter Parkes and Douglas Wick of DreamWorks during which they pitched *Gladiator.* Parkes showed Scott a reproduction of a nineteenth-century painting, *Pollice Verso* (1872), by French artist Jean-Léon Gérôjme. Gérôjme created most of his work in the academicism style and was deeply involved in the historical painting genre. *Pollice Verso* depicts a gladiator in a Roman arena from the sand's perspective: he stands with his weapon over a beaten foe, his foot on the man he is about to put to death. Watchers are in shadow, with strips of light beaming in. The gladiator is looking up at the emperor, waiting for the thumbs-down

Russell Crowe as Maximus fighting for his life in the arena in *Gladiator.*

signal. This classical painting became a major reference for Ridley Scott's *Gladiator. Pollice Verso* popularized the thumbs-up and thumbs-down gesturing in gladiatorial fighting—its title is Latin for "with a turned thumb."

Mel Gibson was approached for the leading role of Maximus but turned it down, believing it was too much like the Academy Award–winning *Braveheart* (1995), which he starred in and directed. Scott then chose actor Russell Crowe, who made a big splash as the volatile Wendell "Bud" White in the popular *L.A. Confidential* (1997). In 1999, he delivered a brilliant performance portraying real-life whistleblower Jeffrey Wigand in *The Insider.*

Russell Ira Crowe was born in New Zealand and lived in Australia for most of his childhood. His parents were both movie set caterers. Crowe's mother's godfather was the producer of *Spyforce* (1971), an Australian television series. When Russell was five or six, he was hired to speak one word of dialogue in an episode opposite series star Jack Thompson, later known as "the Robert Redford of Australia." During the mid-1980s Crowe, under the name Russ Le Roq, had a performing career as a rock 'n' roll revivalist. At twenty-one, after touring as a rock musician, he returned to Australia with plans to apply to the National Institute of Dramatic Art. The head of technical support counseled him not to waste his time at the prestigious school because he already had the skills he would learn there. Russell Crowe spent most of that decade onstage. His breakthrough came on the TV series *Neighbours* and *Living with the Law.* He transitioned to the United States and landed roles in *Virtuosity* (1995) and *The Quick and the Dead* (1995). Crowe won the coveted Best Actor Oscar for *Gladiator* and was nominated for the Ron Howard film *A Beautiful Mind* (2001).

Scott chose John Mathieson as director of photography because of his work on *Plunkett & Macleane* (1999), a period feature directed by Scott's son Jake. Mathieson had a background in commercials and music videos, some for Scott's music video company Black Dog. Scott also liked Mathieson because he was a cinematographer who felt free to experiment.

For reference Scott studied the nineteenth-century painter Sir Lawrence Alma-Tedema, who painted Greek, Roman, and Egyptian environments. His *The Pyrrhic Dance* pictured a Spartan war dance. *The Finding of Moses* was another influential work applied to the look of the *Gladiator* production. This painting captured the grandeur in which a pharaoh's daughter is tended by handmaidens and carried by slaves on her way to bathe in the Nile. Georges de La Tour, a seventeenth-century French painter who created biblical and classical pictures, also influenced the design of *Gladiator.*

Leni Riefenstahl's notorious Nazi epic documentary film *Triumph of the Will* (1935) was screened and studied in detail to better understand the scale of soldiers in relationship to the surrounding architecture.

Scott wanted the gladiators' costumes to mirror their personalities. He did this by suggesting to Janty Yates, head of the costume department, that she borrow ideas from Kabuki theater to create a magical sense to the gladiators' outfits. Yates and Scott have been frequent collaborators on numerous feature films.

Malta stood in for Rome, and a partial set of the Coliseum was built at Fort Riascoli. When possible, set elements were combined with existing building and environments. Proximo's gladiator training facility was built into a ruined fortress in Malta. It took nineteen weeks and a crew of one hundred British workers and two hundred Maltese workers to re-create central Rome and a section of the Coliseum. The London-based company the Mill, owned by the Scotts, supplied the CGI work, providing views of Rome and peopled areas with crowds. To save money, all costumes, props, weapons, and chariots were created by the crew.

The budget for *Gladiator* was $100 million. It was a Universal/Dream-Works production. Scott's vision was to make Rome look crowded and compressed. In view of the camera was architecture that was supposed to be only a year old in the story and next to it was architecture that was eight hundred years old. Arthur Max built a full-scale Coliseum in Malta. The company found an old Napoleonic parade ground surrounded by preexisting Romanesque limestone architecture, saving them around $2 million from the set budget.

Esteemed Croatian film producer Branko Lustig, who had produced *Schindler's List* (1993) for director Steven Spielberg, was one of the producers on *Gladiator* and later worked with Scott on *Black Hawk Down, Kingdom of Heaven, A Good Year,* and *American Gangster.* Pietro Scalia was the editor.

Hans Zimmer, who composed the music, discussed his attraction to working with Ridley Scott: "We kept having meetings in this beautiful tent which was really Marcus Aurelius' tent and Ridley just dumped me right in the middle and we started talking," Zimmer explained to the author in *CinemaEditor* magazine. "He had made it so inevitable what the film was going to be and . . . we were going to move the cutting room to my studio so we could really work closely together. . . . You get to try out dangerous ideas." Zimmer described a mesmerizing image in *Gladiator* that defined Maximus as a complex man torn between family and the call to battle. "The whole opening of the film is a minute of just a hand on the wheat field. Without the music Ridley would never been able to have that shot," Zimmer reflects. "I know Ridley is a poet and I wanted to be able to give him the gift to have a bit of poetry in this movie and to hold on shots that people just might not get without a piece of music behind them."[1]

The poetic image is Maximus's hand touching the wheat as he moves through the field. It is arresting. It mesmerizes the viewer, who now understands that *Gladiator* is not a standard gladiator film. The film's narrative goes into uncharted territory in this established genre. Editor Pietro Scalia was also captivated by the image, telling Edgar Burcksen of *CinemaEditor* magazine:

> It was never scripted that way. It was really shot as part of a dream sequence where he goes to heaven. Instead of just starting with the close-up as was scripted, I wanted to find an image that typified the meaning of the film. And to me that was transcendence, going from being a soldier to being a hero—because Maximus made this journey. What does it mean, is this what he is thinking, is this what he yearns for, is this what he's remembering? When you start with his thoughts and longings, you start inside the man and then you see his shell. It becomes the metaphor for the whole film.[2]

"I call [Pietro Scalia] my co-composer," Zimmer confides about his collaborator. "I will get right into the thick of it in what the film means and what those notes mean and what they should be. We have *passionate* discussions about it. And I so respect and rely on his feel and taste for music—and he will adjust the picture."[3]

Lucilla, the daughter of the Roman emperor, played with strength and complexity by Connie Nielson, is the strong woman of *Gladiator.* She is equal or superior to the men and is very ambitious. Her great beauty creates a mysterious aura, and at times her actions appear to be contradictory, but this is part of her iron will and her method of dealing with strenuous situations in which power and the love of her son are at stake.

Her brother Commodus, portrayed by Joaquin Phoenix, is pure evil. His thirst for power manifests as murder—he smothers and strangles his father Marcus Aurelius, played by Richard Harris. Phoenix gives the role everything he has—jealousy, anger, hatred, unhealthy desires, and a demonstration of how a man can destroy himself, almost everyone around him, the people of Rome, and the great city itself because of unleashed power that has no restraints.

Harris, an actor with a long résumé, inhabits an old frail man close to death trying to get his family and the city's house in order in his last days and hours. He brings a Shakespearean tonality to the character.

To create the large groups of soldiers for the opening battle sequence, VistaVision plates of small groups of soldiers were merged together to form a panorama. Sixteen thousand flaming arrows were fired along with ten thousand nonflaming arrows. Over twenty-five hundred weapons were made for the film. Five hundred gladiator costumes were crafted. Footwear was created in Rome.

For scenes of dismemberment, harnesses were created so actors could attach false limbs that later would be sacrificed to the swift thrust of the sword. During battle sequences collapsing dummies were engaged to give the impression men had fallen.

Arthur Max built the first tier of the Coliseum closely following the actual design on location. The rest of the structure was created by the digital artists. Two thousand extras were on hand for the Coliseum crowd. CGI later expanded that number to around thirty-three thousand. To convince the audience that the illusion was actually real, Scott deployed a Steadicam shot of Maximus and the gladiators entering the arena and then circled 360 degrees. Mathieson was able to create a cathedral-like atmosphere in the Coliseum scenes with a combination of light and sand.

On May 2, 1999, Oliver Reed, who played Proximo, died suddenly of a heart attack in a Maltese pub during production. Some of his scenes were left unfinished. In postproduction computer animation was used to complete his role. Images of Reed in the background of completed shots were taken and put into shots in which he had not appeared. Reed's voice was put together in the editing room from previously recorded dialogue to create proper sentences. A body double was brought in for reverse-angle shots. In some cases, backgrounds from other shots were put into the newly created ones to complete the shot. Ridley Scott dedicated *Gladiator* to Oliver Reed.

Although *Gladiator* is a period movie, Scott and Mathieson collaborated to photograph the film in a modern style; the battle sequences were photographed with handheld cameras. Techniques to heighten the speed of the violence were gathered from studying music videos. In addition, Scott was greatly influenced by Spielberg's *Saving Private Ryan* (1998).

The *Gladiator* team started off with forty special visual effects shots, but ultimately the number more than doubled. Arthur Max built a version of Rome, and it was decided they should go with a scale version of that. A column that had a diameter of eight feet would then be thirty-five or forty feet high. When shooting a wide shot, Scott was able to add an additional eighty feet to the column utilizing digital effects, which revealed the entire upper part of the view with a panorama of the rest of the city. Research told Ridley Scott and his art department that there had been a million people in Rome on seven hills. Scott wanted density so the eye couldn't see the sky. Scott wanted his Rome to be like New York, especially in the palace and Coliseum districts.

Working with tigers, the company found they lay on the ground much of the time, purring or staring at the crew. Six Bengal tigers, around ten feet long and weighing six hundred pounds, were used on the production. The trainer would feed the tiger with his right hand while in his left he held a little handle of a sword with no blade to "stab" the tiger. This was a dangerous situation. If a tiger was lying on the ground swishing its tail, there was a tendency to want to approach the ferocious animal and pet it. Later CGI would drop on a glint of metal going into the fur with blood on it.

Ridley Scott was at the height of his artistic powers, and *Gladiator* was headed for greatness in commercial success and appeal. On the 2015 *Exodus: Gods and Kings* DVD he spoke on a commentary track about his ability to conceive and execute his films.

> When you are making a film, even me, people will stand on the edge and say "Do you really need this?" "Do you really need that?"

and I will say yes because what I have in my head is a word called *vision*. Sounds pretentious, it's not pretentious. I put it right there. I know exactly what I want it to look like. I know exactly what I want it to look like when it gets done.

When I did *Alien,* somebody said, "My god that's gross." I said, "You're paying me to be gross, dude. I want to scare the living shit out of the audience." "The thing comes out of his chest, won't that be funny?" he said. "You sure it won't be funny?" I said, "No," and it wasn't. So I just insist, you have to, it's part of the director's job to insist unless you are being crazily erratic in which case you should be fired—I'm not. I'm usually right on budget and for the most part incredibly cohesive and you are responsible, most of the time."

Todd McCarthy of *Variety* was effusive in his remarks concerning the revisiting of a cinematic era. "After an absence of 35 years, the Roman Empire marks a thrilling return to the big screen in *Gladiator,* a muscular and bloody combat picture, a compelling revenge drama and a truly transporting trip back 2000 years. Ridley Scott's bold epic of imperial intrigue and heroism brings new luster and excitement to a tarnished and often derided genre that nonetheless provided at least one generation of moviegoers with some youthful memories."

The staff of the *Hollywood Reporter* found much to praise in the performances but thought the action sequences tedious. "Although the physically daunting production at times threatens to overwhelm the implausible tale, Crowe and several actors, most notably the late Oliver Reed, Connie Nielsen and, in an extended cameo, Richard Harris, never let the human dimension get lost. . . . The movie is impressive in scope, but like the gladiator games themselves, designed for mindless spectacle to please the multitudes."

Even though *Gladiator* received mostly strong to rave reviews, Elvis Mitchell of the *New York Times* ridiculed the picture, which he found repellant. "Mr. Scott's inhuman, glossy style is fey and terse: postcards from Mount Olympus. At least that's where 'Gladiator' seems to take place—there or some other mythical area, since the Roman Colosseum is roughly the size of the Death Star from 'Star Wars,' thanks to the magic of computer graphics. With each scene composed for an audience's delectation of the constant slaughter, the movie is both pandering and detached. It's like a handsomely designed weapon: you can't take your eyes off it even though you may be repelled by its purpose."

Gladiator became the blockbuster hit Scott had been looking for during the decade of the 1990s. To date, it has grossed a whopping $456 million. It opened on 2,938 screens nationwide. It grossed $103.14 million in the first two weeks of its US release. The film was a great success and put Ridley Scott back on the map as a major film director.

Gladiator scored well at the Oscars. Russell Crowe won for Best Actor. Janty Yates won for Best Costume Design; Tim Burke, Neil Corbould, Rob Harvey, and John Nelson won Best Visual Effects; and Best Picture went to Douglas Wick, Branko Lustig, and David Franzoni. Best Sound went to Bob Beemer, Ken Weston, and Scott Millan. Joaquin Phoenix was nominated for Best Supporting Actor, and David Franzoni, John Logan, and William Nicholson were nominated for Best Screenplay. Arthur Max and Crispian Sallis as well as Pietro Scalia and Hans Zimmer were also nominated. The film was anointed with many other awards and accolades. Although Ridley Scott did not win an Oscar for directing or producing *Gladiator* (he was an uncredited executive producer), his brother Tony celebrated the film's success at the gala by giving his brother a framed still from *Boy and Bicycle* with the inscription "We've come a long way."

Gladiator is a story of slavery, power, class distinction, and the brutality of the Coliseum. It has intelligence similar to *Spartacus* and a heightened sense of the violence inflicted upon the men; their courage and extreme gladiatorial skills used for survival are dramatically expressed. At the center of the film is the story of a dysfunctional family that threatens to bring down Rome.

Russell Crowe gives a fine performance, creating a Maximus who yearns for home and peace and expresses high political intellect. As a gladiator, Maximus is a leader of men, a fighter par excellence driven by his hatred for Commodus. In the dramatic sequences Crowe is emotional and portrays the pain he suffers not being with his family. In the many physically complex action scenes the actor maintains a strong sense of character, a survivor's strength, and the will to defeat the evil emperor and his reign.

The chemistry between the gladiator/slaves Juba (Djimon Hounsou), Hagen (Ralf Moeller), and others on the team is emotionally compelling as they look after each other while desperately fighting against steep odds of being the one sacrificed on a particular day.

The director-actor collaboration of Ridley Scott and Russell Crowe formed in this film and lasted for five motion pictures. Scott told Kenneth Turan how the two worked: "Constant discussion. Constant. From stage one, even when I think I've got a good screenplay, invariably, Russell thinks it's no good; that the screenplay is terrible. So then we've got to sit there and go right through it. And then I realize actually, he means a third of it, or maybe 20 percent, is no good. And the other 80 percent is quite good. And so we talk, talk, talk. It's a build. To get that kind of relationship with an actor is rare."[4]

The acting is superior to most films in the genre where the style is slightly wooden and the speech slanted toward a Shakespearean lilt. The performances in *Gladiator* are fervent and alive, with bodies in motion, and thoughts—some evil, some just—are palpable.

Through the prism of film history, *Gladiator* is a movie out of its time—a genre revised. Scott wisely relied fully on the digital tools not available for films of this genre during its heyday in the 1950s and 1960s. Rather than apply them whole, he and Arthur Max combine the digital with the practical. It is this result, especially in the scenes taking place in the Coliseum, that draws audiences to the film. Scott brought the sand and sandal film back to life—to a new audience.

Ridley Scott continued his relationship with the beautiful Giannina Facio, eighteen years younger than he—she had been born in Costa Rica on September 10, 1955. She has appeared in small roles and cameos in numerous Scott's films—she can be seen in *Gladiator* as Maximus's wife. Giannina Facio is Ridley Scott's constant companion. Her father, Ambassador Gonzalo Facio, served Costa Rica for many terms. His significant and accomplished career first took him to Washington, DC, in the summer of 1956, when he met President Eisenhower. Over the years he had meetings with Presidents Kennedy and Johnson.

After years of their being together, many assumed that Facio and Scott were a married couple, and they finally took that step. Facio is alternately referred to as Scott's wife or partner. She works as a producer on film and television projects with Scott. She's usually at his side in photographs taken at public events. They share several homes together. Ridley Scott and Giannina Facio enjoy a strong and enduring well-rounded relationship.

14

YOU DON'T SAY NO TO "BIG DINO"

Hannibal

Try to touch the past. Try to deal with the past. It's not real. It's just a dream.

Ted Bundy

Hannibal (2001) is a gory horror film, part of a franchise that began with *Manhunter* (1986), directed by Michael Mann and based on the best-selling novel *Red Dragon* by Thomas Harris. Dino De Laurentiis and his wife Martha purchased the rights, but the retitled film adaptation did very poorly at the box office.

In certain circles the legendary producer Dino De Laurentiis was known as "Big Dino," and it was axiomatic that you don't say no to "Big Dino." The list of directors in Italy and worldwide who have worked with Dino De Laurentiis include Federico Fellini, Roberto Rossellini, Luchino Visconti, Ingmar Bergman, King Vidor, John Huston, David Cronenberg, and David Lynch, on such films as *La Strada* (1954), *Serpico* (1972), and *Ragtime* (1981).

When Harris completed the novel *The Silence of the Lambs,* the De Laurentiises did not read it. They owned the rights to the character of Hannibal Lecter, but De Laurentiis felt it was a big mistake that Hannibal Lecter was the center of the story. Harris and director Jonathan Demme approached De Laurentiis about setting the film project up elsewhere, and De Laurentiis lent them the character for free.

In 1991 Jonathan Demme adapted *The Silence of the Lambs,* and it was released on February 14, 1991, and grossed $131 million. It won the Oscar for Best Director (against Ridley Scott for *Thelma & Louise*). It also won awards for Best Picture, Best Actor (Anthony Hopkins), Best Actress (Jodie Foster), and Best Screenplay.

Interest in a sequel grew quickly. Tom Pollack, chairman of Universal Pictures, asked the De Laurentiises to make the sequel at Universal. Bad feelings developed over disputed oral agreements. The De Laurentiises filed a $25 million lawsuit against Universal. The parties later settled, and Universal got the participation it wanted.

Harris, meanwhile, was many years away from finishing the literary sequel to *The Silence of the Lambs*. Harris was a meticulous, secretive, and slow writer, so the De Laurentiises and Jonathan Demme were anxious for him to deliver the manuscript. Demme was looking forward to making the sequel. Finally Harris contacted De Laurentiis with the news that the book was finished, and the Italian movie mogul purchased the screen rights to *Hannibal* for a record $10 million.

Harris's new manuscript was sent to Anthony Hopkins, Jodie Foster, and Jonathan Demme. Martha De Laurentiis flew to New York and began structuring a deal with Demme but to no avail; Demme's agent at CAA, Rick Nicita, called Dino to tell him the deal was off—Demme had changed his mind because he found the material overly violent. It is also speculated that the director was wary of working with Dino De Laurentiis, who had a reputation for not allowing directors full creative control over their work.

Ridley Scott had briefly worked with Dino De Laurentiis on the troubled *Dune*. Scott was in Malta directing *Gladiator* right next to the production of *U-571,* which the De Laurentiises were producing. Over espresso Scott was given the manuscript for *Hannibal.* Scott went off, read the book, and agreed to direct the film.

Scott looked for a screenwriter. Ted Tally, Oscar-winning writer of *The Silence of the Lambs* screenplay, said no. Oscar-winning screenwriter Steve Zaillian, who wrote the screenplay for *Schindler's List* (1993), accepted and prepared a first draft. Scott and De Laurentiis felt the result needed a major revision, and renowned playwright David Mamet wrote another draft of *Hannibal.* Mamet was about to direct *State and Main* (2000), so it was back to Steve Zaillian for further work. Scott talked to Zaillian for hours. The result was a 135-page screenplay. Scott and others were not happy with the original ending in the book, which involved cannibalism, so a summit was held for several days at the Beverley Hills Hotel in Los Angeles. The participants were Steve Zaillian, Ridley Scott, Thomas Harris, and Dino De Laurentiis. They finally came up with what Scott called a postscript.

Having passed on *The Silence of the Lambs,* De Laurentiis didn't have the rights to the character of Agent Clarice Starling—these belonged to MGM, which had acquired Orion's properties when they were dissolved financially. When it was definitive that Jodie Foster wouldn't reprise her part in *Hannibal,* De Laurentiis and Scott moved ahead and compiled a list of actresses they felt could play Clarice Starling, yet another Ridley Scott strong woman. They included Angelina Jolie, Hilary Swank, Cate Blanchett, Ashley Judd, and Julianne Moore, who was interested. Moore met with Scott, who was very impressed with her. Scott asked Anthony Hopkins for his views, and he was excited about the choice, so she was offered the role and accepted. For research Julianne Moore traveled to Quantico, Virginia, and spent time with FBI agents to understand their work. Anthony Hopkins easily moved into the project to reprise Hannibal Lecter and received an $11 million salary.

Jodie Foster had been offered a huge paycheck as well, but strongly defended her decision because she felt the new project betrayed Clarice's values and qualities as a "person." She also had a "go" on a directing project, which undoubtedly influenced her decision. Foster was adamant: "The original movie worked because people believed in Clarice's heroism. I won't play her with negative attributes she would never have."

Ridley Scott didn't think that *Hannibal* picked up where *The Silence of the Lambs* left off. Hannibal Lecter hasn't been heard from in ten years, and the Clarice character is decidedly different. Scott saw the film as a sequel to the characters but not to the story portrayed in *The Silence of the Lambs.* In *Hannibal,* Lecter shows up in Italy, where he destroys Inspector Pazzi. Clarice learns that Lecter is alive and throughout the movie hunts him down while being harassed by corrupt Justice Department agent Paul Krendler. Waiting patiently for Lecter to be captured or killed is Mason Verger, one of Lecter's former victims. The film ends with Lecter eluding law enforcement and escaping into the night.

Everyone had something affirmative to say about Ridley Scott during the shooting of *Hannibal.* Gary Oldman, who played Verger, a character severely and violently disfigured by Lecter, said there were no surprises with Ridley Scott and that he was a total visionary. Julianne Moore found him to be a quiet gentleman, and Dino De Laurentiis paid him the highest compliment, saying Ridley Scott reminded him of Fellini. To Ridley Scott, *Hannibal* was a dark passionate love story of Hannibal's feelings for Clarice.

Roger Ebert thought the film crude and considered that the project misinterpreted the character of Hannibal Lecter's last scene in *The Silence of The Lambs.* "Ridley Scott's '*Hannibal*' is a carnival geek show elevated in the direction of art. It never quite gets there, but it tries with every fiber of its craft to redeem its pulp origins, and we must give it credit for the courage of its depravity; if it proves nothing else, it proves that if a man cutting off his face and feeding it to his dogs doesn't get the NC-17 rating for violence, nothing ever will."

Peter Travers of *Rolling Stone* found the narrative and Moore's performance satisfying. "Credit Scott for transforming narrative tricks, which are used to unite Hannibal and Clarice, into gripping filmmaking. Gone is the novel's tabloid psychology about the roots of Hannibal's psychosis—cannibals ate my sister! . . . Hopkins is perverse perfection, blending mirth and malice with cunning skill. And Moore, in the toughest role, emerges triumphant. Like Foster, she brings out the frightened child in this female warrior. But Moore's Clarice shows newfound maturity and strength. In the contours of Moore's keenly focused and sexually charged performance, Clarice is ready for any predator."

Peter Bradshaw of the *Guardian* praised the collaboration of director Scott and actor Hopkins. "All that can be said of Anthony Hopkins is that he gives a show-stopping turn at the center of the picture. Ridley Scott does an expert job of—well, not directing him as such, but organizing the flash-bang pyrotechnics around his reptilian yet bull-like figure, and just letting Hopkins get on with it."

The New York premiere of *Hannibal* was held on February 5, 2001, at the Ziegfeld Theater on a very snowy night. Ridley and Tony's mother had passed away that week at age ninety-five, so Ridley was not able to attend. Giannina Facio was there on his behalf. Ridley gave his mom an on-screen dedication in *Black Hawk Down,* and Tony did the same in his film *Spy Game.*

Hannibal was a big financial success, grossing around $165 million with a budget of $87 million. *Hannibal* is by far the most bloody and violent film of the series. Some of the highlights include a pregnant woman (who happens to be a very wanted criminal) being shot to death and a flashback that depicts Hannibal Lecter mauling Mason Verger with broken glass, concentrating on his face. Other prime moments are Inspector Pazzi being disemboweled, hanging from a window as many look on, and a thief hired to follow Lecter who, when he gets too close, is stabbed and bleeds to death. Verger is killed when he is attacked in his wheelchair by wild boars, which force him to plunge into a pool after biting him viciously. The most horrific moment comes toward the end and is infamous in film and audience circles. Krendler is sitting in Lecter's kitchen when the serial killer surgically removes the top of Paul's head and then feeds him a piece of his brain. This sequence is truly difficult to watch.

Hannibal is not a great horror film or a great Ridley Scott film. The story is laborious, although the visuals, of course, are superb, especially those taking place in Italy. This really was a director-for-hire job: Dino De Laurentiis was the boss and Ridley Scott the craftsman.

15

THE BURDEN OF MEN
Black Hawk Down

At liftoff, Matt Eversmann said a Hail Mary. He was curled into a seat
between two helicopter crew chiefs, the knees of his long legs up to his
shoulders. Before him, jammed on both sides of the Black Hawk
helicopter was his "chalk," twelve young men in flak vests over tan desert
camouflage fatigues.
                    Mark Bowden, Black Hawk Down: A Story of Modern War

Black Hawk Down (2001) is about the world of men in a fierce and brutal war.
It is a much-admired war film based on a true incident involving US soldiers
in Somalia. The film is epic in scope and detailed in its depiction of warfare.
It is an action picture that stings because of the graphic loss of life. Ridley
Scott handles the events with a bold and swift hand, and it is brilliantly edited
by Pietro Scalia, who won the Oscar with the aid of his director's elaborate
coverage and deft staging. *Black Hawk Down* was also Oscar-nominated for
Best Director and for Slawomir Idziak's cinematography. The film won the
award for Best Sound, acknowledging the sound team of Michael Minkler,
Myron Nettinga, and Chris Munro, who created an atmosphere that seems to
go beyond a movie experience into the documentary world of reality.

   Black Hawk Down fits perfectly into Ridley Scott's attraction to war films in
which men are examined under extreme stress and imminent danger. This film
is adapted from the 1999 best-selling book *Black Hawk Down: A Story of Modern War* by Mark Bowden, which is based on soldiers' accounts of the mission.
Bowden also traveled to Somalia to record eyewitness accounts of the fierce battle. The original notion to make a film from the book came from director Simon
West (*Con Air*, 1997), who persuaded mega-producer Jerry Bruckheimer to buy
the rights and asked Bowden to write the screenplay. West moved on to direct
Lara Croft: Tomb Raider (2001), and Bruckheimer continued to develop the
property; he was pleased with Bowden's screenplay but was considering using
only some of it. He gave that draft to writer Ken Nolan, who worked on another

draft for more than a year. The script went through several other capable hands, including Steve Zaillian's, Steven Gaghan's, and iconic playwright Sam Shepard's. Eric Roth was brought in to focus some of the dialogue between Hoot (Eric Bana) and Eversmann (Josh Hartnett) at the end of the film.

Bruckheimer sent the script to Ridley Scott, who had worked with him on a tire commercial. Scott remembered the tragic events of October 1993, having watched the carnage on the BBC. He agreed to direct the film on one condition—that he could create a combat story that eliminated all information of the actual events with the exception of what went down during the infamous eighteen-hour battle.

Casting *Black Hawk Down* was a challenge similar to finding young actors to play soldiers in *Full Metal Jacket*. The difference is that in the earlier film, the objective was to find good young actors with little screen experience so there would be no star personae. In *Black Hawk Down* some of the actors Scott chose were in that little-known category; others were recognizable and brought the weight of past roles to the forefront. The large ensemble cast includes Josh Hartnett as Eversmann, Ewan McGregor as Grimes, Tom Sizemore (McKnight), Eric Bana (Hoot), William Fitchtner (Sanderson), Ewen Bremner (Nelson), Gabriel Casseus (Kurth), Kim Coates (Wex), Ron Eldard (Durant), Zeljko Ivanek (Harrell), Jeremy Piven (Wolcott), Orlando Bloom (Blackburn), and Ty Burrell (Wilkinson).

The authority figure Garrison is portrayed by the playwright and actor Sam Shepard, who echoes his image of Chuck Yeager in *The Right Stuff* (1983). Shepard's laser intensity and orchestration of the impossible mission centers the film—he is calm and steady in the midst of chaos.

The actual events took place in Somalia in October 1993 during a US military mission. Black Hawk helicopters were ordered by Special Forces to fly into the middle of a Mogadishu marketplace on a busy day. One hundred and twenty-three soldiers were dispatched. The mission was to surprise and capture two lieutenants of the Somali warlord Mohammed Farrah Aidid. What was planned as a quick and decisive action to last around thirty minutes morphed into an eighteen-hour all-out street fight with the Somalis. The result was that two Black Hawk helicopters were shot down, and convoys of troops were ordered to rescue the trapped soldiers and retrieve the bodies of those who had died. Eighteen American soldiers were killed, and seventy-three were injured. Over a thousand Somali casualties were recorded.

Ridley Scott is attracted to characters who are being challenged in some way. He told Jeremy Kagan of the Directors Guild of America: "I like to study people on the edge of some form of event or cutting edge of society, because that's where you see human behavior most stretched and most challenged. It's really my job to take you into a zone that you normally wouldn't experience. I'm going to transport you like a good piece of music. I think more films in the mainstream should provoke discussion and not be simply entertainment."[1]

Ken Nolan was on location during the four-month shoot, adjusting and revising the script and incorporating ideas generated by the actors. *Black Hawk Down* received military support for the production. All the Black Hawk and Little Hawk helicopters were supplied by the 160th Special Operations Aviation Regiment. Many of the pilots in the film were pilots in Somalia in 1993. The Rangers were actual Rangers. There were some complaints. Scott wanted the surname of each man on his helmet. The military advisers said that wasn't realistic, but Scott kept it in so the audience could identify the characters during the complicated mission.

Black Hawk Down was staged and photographed in the Moroccan cities of Rabat, the capital, and the ancient city of Sale, located across the Bou Regreg River from Rabat. This location bore some architectural resemblance to Mogadishu. Some sets were built and others were either retrofitted to existing buildings or the buildings were used as they were. Arthur Max created Mogadishu in Morocco in some of the same locations where *Gladiator* was shot. The area in Sale was used to stage the major action. Digital matte paintings were used to expand the numbers of buildings in a shot and to distress the buildings in Sale. For budgetary and logistical reasons, the production was not able to build a set that extended for blocks, although in the true story the action took place along many streets. Scott, Arthur Max, and his art department found a place to shoot the street scenes. To accommodate the Black Hawk helicopters flying overhead, it was necessary to go door to door to tell residents and ask them to move to a hotel, which was provided for them.

Getting permission to shoot in the area was a four-month process. First the production had to go through the king. The US Defense Department was involved. In order to secure the helicopters, the chain of command went as high as US Secretary of State General Colin Powell and back to the town, the governor, and mayor, all of whom were involved in granting permission.

Casting for the two thousand extras that were needed was done in twenty-four African communities. *Black Hawk Down* was shot in ninety-two days, aided by plenty of military advisers. Production began March 3, 2001, and was completed in early July.

In order to achieve the documentary look Scott wanted, as many as eleven cameras ran simultaneously. In the opening sequence Scott shot one thousand extras; he wanted it to look like eight thousand, so digital faces were rendered on fake figures. Photographs of the extras' faces were used.

In the visual style of the film Scott was influenced by photographs of Somalia taken by photojournalist James Nacthwey, most especially a collection of photos called *Inferno*. These graphic, dramatic, and disturbing pictures were taken in some of the worst war zones of modern times: Romania, Somalia, India, Sudan, Bosnia, Rwanda, Zaire, Chechnya, and Kosovo. The photos, which directly capture the violence and brutality of war, have been called hell on earth, which is why the collection is called *Inferno* and opens with an epigraph from Dante.

Some shots had computer-generated helicopters and crew members. Animatics of helicopters crashing were created at the Mill and sent to Scalia, who cut them into the film for reference. Then the Mill artists proceeded to do detailed animation work. Scott had seen research footage of a helicopter crash he thought was right for the event. To him it appeared as if the helicopter died like a huge beast.

During the gun battle scenes, when both sides are exchanging heavy fire, Ridley Scott was in the middle of it, either operating one of the cameras or checking in with the many operators. At times he was around fifty or sixty feet from the action in a tent with video assist communicating via walkie-talkie to each numbered camera. He would give instructions about shot size and changing lenses. After shooting, the operators walked back to where Scott was positioned to watch a replay from all positions. Then Scott gave them more instructions and notes about the camera speed.

Over the decades there have been analogies drawn between military commanders and film directors. The parallel aptly describes directing a complex war film like *Black Hawk Down*. A man whose family background has drawn him to the military, Ridley Scott has a highly organized mind and knows how to lead actors and crew through complicated sequences. Such planning is similar to the militaristic preparation before an approaching battle. In both situations the ability to improvise as the situation requires is paramount.

Because of the nature of the story and the action that occurs, Scott couldn't shoot in a conventional manner; he estimated that would have taken twenty-five weeks. There was a pending Screen Actors Guild strike, so he had to shoot in fifteen weeks. The actors kept asking what their motivation was in a scene. Scott's response was merely to describe the situation the characters were in. They knew where their marks were; Scott was ready to barrage them with special effect gunfire and explosions. When, he called, "Action!" he just wanted the actors to get on with it.

Before the finished film was released in the United States, Ridley Scott showed *Black Hawk Down* to selected audiences at US military bases. Their reactions were extremely positive, which gave Scott reason to believe he had gotten it right. Critics and others were not so happy. The commander of Malaysian forces in Somalia during that time, the retired brigadier general Abdul Latiff Ahmad, was angry that the film gave the impression the battle was fought by US forces alone, without acknowledging the role his troops had played in the event. The BBC's Yusuf Hassan of the Somali service believed that in the real story the Somalis were not actually fighting the Americans; rather, they were neighborhood people trying to defend their homes, thinking they were under attack. Scott believed that the invasion was to remove the fascist dictator Aidid and bring relief to the starving population.

James Chapman, author of *War and Film*, critically analyzed the political intentions of *Black Hawk Down*: "The pro-interventionist narrative of *Black Hawk Down* [was] in production before 9/11 but [the fact that it was] hurried to completion [takes] on an even greater significance in the context of the 'War on Terror.' [It suggests] that intervention in trouble spots such as Somalia and Vietnam is justified: there is no room for questioning US foreign policy. One commentator described *Black Hawk Down* for example as 'an astonishing glorification of slaughter that makes the tragedy look like a majestic triumph for the brotherhood of man, rather than a humbling defeat for the United States.'"[2]

Disney would not distribute the film because it had an R rating. Joe Roth, a former Disney studio chairman, agreed to distribute it under his Revolution Studios production/distribution company.

Black Hawk Down went into limited release on December 28, 2001, so it could be eligible for that year's Oscars. It earned $179,823 in the first weekend, an average of $44,956 per theater. The budget was $90 million. By April 2002 *Black Hawk Down* had recouped its cost on the US box office receipts alone.

Like most war films, *Black Hawk Down* is principally about battle and action, although there are vivid characterizations by a stellar male cast within the framework of the narrow narrative. There is nail-biting dramatic tension produced by the choreography and orchestration of the tumultuous fighting, from the point of the helicopter being shot out of the sky to the raid and continuing to the film's conclusion. The emotional pressure causes hearts and nerves to pound, but most of the screen time is devoted to explosions, constant gun battles, and the movement of the helicopters. The composition and staging are masterful. The film has tenacity and constant drive; however, on balance, *Black Hawk Down* is overshot, overedited, oversounded, and over-orchestrated by Hans Zimmer. *Black Hawk Down* is awesome in cinematic excitement, but Scott would be criticized for presenting too much showmanship and not enough content.

Black Hawk Down is dedicated to Ridley Scott's mother: "For my mum, Elizabeth Jean Scott 1906–2001."

In 2002 Ridley Scott won an Emmy for *The Gathering Storm,* a biopic of Winston Churchill and his wife Clementine depicting Churchill's personal and psychological troubles prior to World War II. The ninety-six-minute film was produced by HBO Films in association with Scott Free. Ridley Scott and Tony Scott were among the producers. Albert Finney played Churchill and Vanessa Redgrave his wife Clemmie. Scott was inspired to make the film because of memories of his dad talking about seeing Churchill arrive at the Mulberry Harbour where the elder Scott worked. Albert Finney won an Emmy for his performance as Winston Churchill, and the film received strong positive reviews.

16

CON JOB

Matchstick Men

I was the realization of their dreams. The idol. The hero. The master and arbiter of their lives.

Charles Ponzi

This film is based on the 2002 book *Matchstick Men* by Eric Garcia. The motion picture rights were quickly picked up by Warner Bros. The screenplay was written by brothers Nicholas Griffin and Ted Griffin, and Ted Griffin was one of the film's producers.

The first director slated to direct *Matchstick Men* was Robert Zemeckis, but down the line he passed, and the project was offered to Ridley Scott. Scott was interested in *Matchstick Men* because he had not done anything quite like it. Giannina Facio had met the Griffins at a cocktail party; she was one of the co-producers of the film.

Ridley Scott has a peculiar perception as to whether material is dramatic or comedic. His first reaction to the *Thelma & Louise* script was that it was a comedy. He also identified *Matchstick Men* as a comedy, although the writers didn't at first see the humor in their work.

Scott had the time for the *Matchstick Men* project while he prepped a spec script that, at the time, was to be his next film—*Crusades,* written by William Monahan. Monahan also had a script called *Tripoli* he had brought to Scott. Monahan would go on to work with Ridley *Scott* on *Kingdom of Heaven* and *Body of Lies.* These projects involved a clash of cultures that lead to armed conflict. Based on Monahan's book *Light House: A Trifle, Tripoli* was never made. Scott talked to Monahan about creating a film about knights. Monahan suggested a movie about the Crusades, telling Scott that many desirable plots were available for such an idea. Scott instructed the president of Scott Free, Liza Ellzey, that a search for a story and script for a knight movie was high priority. Ultimately, this became *Kingdom of Heaven.*

Ridley Scott directs *Matchstick Men*.

Scott read the *Matchstick Men* screenplay and loved it, but had concerns as to whether it was his kind of project. Scott asked Ted Griffin if he could move the locations from Philadelphia to the Valley in California. When he engaged the writers in discussion he was impressed and became attached to the film.

The story follows con artist Roy Waller (Nicolas Cage), a character with multiple psychological issues and many pronounced facial tics. Roy and his partner Frank Mercer (Sam Rockwell) rip people off with a fake lottery scam that involves a pricey water-filtration system. When Roy has a seismic panic attack, Frank suggests he visit a psychiatrist. He has a session with Dr. Harris Klein (Bruce Altman), who medicates him. In the session Roy talks about his ex-wife Heather (Melora Walters), who was pregnant at the time of their divorce. Klein is asked to call Heather and reports back that Roy has a fourteen-year-old daughter, Angela (Alison Lohman). Father and daughter meet, and after much prodding Roy persuades Angela to join the con game; she proves a natural. Later she convinces him to engage in a long con with Frank involving a patsy—Chuck Frechette (Bruce McGill). The con involves tons of cash in a suitcase that is switched out at the last moment; the con will result in Frank and Roy sharing the riches. It unravels. Chuck, the patsy, figures out the scheme and goes after the con artists. When Roy and Angela return home from dinner, they find Chuck has badly beaten Frank.

Angela gets Roy's gun and shoots Chuck. Roy sends Frank and Angela away. After they leave Chuck comes back to life and knocks Roy out with a sharp fist blow.

Roy finds himself in a hospital guarded by two police officers, who tell him that Chuck is dead and Frank and Angela have disappeared. Roy provides Dr. Klein with the password to his bank account, telling him to give Angela the money.

Later, when Roy goes to Klein's office, he finds it stripped bare—and all Roy's money is gone. Frank has pulled a long con on him. Roy goes to see his ex-wife Heather and learns that back in the day she had a miscarriage and that there is no daughter Angela.

A year passes. Roy is now a carpet salesman. Angela, looking a lot older than she pretended to be before, walks in with her boyfriend looking to buy a carpet. She asks Roy to forgive her. Roy tells Angela that he enjoys being an honest man. Roy goes home to his new wife Kathy (Sheila Kelley), who was a checker at his local supermarket. She is pregnant—a happy ending.

Nicolas Cage, an actor known for playing quirky and distinctive characters, was perfect as the neurotic, phobic con artist. Especially for this role he needed a director who would be there as the character developed and became the victim of a complex con. "Ridley, of course, was a director that I admired and wanted to work with," he told Rebecca Murray of About.com. "His connection to actors is a good one. He helps you to be free as an actor. His rehearsal is an important process for him. We had two or three weeks where we could work out and map out the characters together, so that everyone was on the same page."[1]

Alison Lohman went even further when she talked to Murray. "Without even saying anything, just his eyes . . . it's not like he forces you to do it, but the power that he has, and it's something in his spirit. The power that he has, it's almost like intangible and kind of magical. He has an energy that kind of lifts you. Any doubt that you had is just gone. You just do it—it's really simple. It was so easy to work with him."

Ultimately, Scott saw the film as a dramedy. He wanted to keep the narrative funny. He thought there was a fine line to maintain in handling Roy's mental state. Under another director this could have been an edgy, dark film, but Scott and Cage treat the neurosis lightly with a deft comic touch so the film never becomes a serious story about mental illness; the neurosis is part of the character and a plot point that allows the long con to take place. The lively pace also rescues the film from a heavy result.

For the style of *Matchstick Men* Ridley Scott wanted a 1950s/early 1960s look, but one that was not specific or noticeable. Roy's house needed a retro feel because Roy lives in the past.

Nicolas Cage is an excellent driver, so he did his own stunts and other elements of the driving sequences in the film; there is a high-octane chase in a parking garage, and Roy drives his car in crowded traffic to the bank in one of the last shots of the movie.

Scott's regular editor Pietro Scalia was not available to edit *Matchstick Men*. The producers were familiar with Dody Dorn, who had cut the structurally complex *Memento* (2000). She would go on to edit *Kingdom of Heaven* (2005) and *A Good Year* (2006) for Ridley Scott.

It was decided between Dorn and Scott that jump cuts would be used to visually represent Roy's mental state. In addition to the jump cuts, slow motion and high-speed motion were used for Roy's POV when he is in a highly anxious state. One particular segment involving sunlight coming into Roy's sensitive eyes plays like an avant-garde experimental film created by Stan Brakhage (*Dog Star Man*, 1961–1964).

During postproduction there was a question about the Hans Zimmer score and the use of Nino Rota's previously recorded music. Nino Rota was famous for his work with Fellini and for the creation of *The Godfather* music. The Rota themes are at times repetitive to support Roy's mania, such as closing a door a certain amount of times. It also recalls the 1950s and 1960s, eras in which Roy is stuck. Roy also listens to retro music in his house—Frank Sinatra and Herb Albert and the Tijuana Brass.

Before the final fadeout, while Roy is hugging the stomach of his pregnant wife, he has one last eye tic. It is the perfect touch to go out on for this particular movie.

Matchstick Men was released in the United States on September 12, 2003, and a week later in Europe. The critical reviews were mixed, but audiences responded well. By December 2003, the film had grossed $36 million in the United States and $65 million worldwide.

Peter Bradshaw of the *Guardian* ended his review on a critical note: "The movie is watchable, attractively sited in a breezy, sunny LA, and only Scott could have thought of using George Formby's 'I'm Leaning on a Lamp-post' on the soundtrack. He orchestrates his principals adroitly, though Rockwell's part is a little underwritten. But Scott is saddled with a final, saccharine sentimental scene between Cage and his ex-wife which has almost certainly been added as a result of a test-screening: a reassuring little sugary moment to take away the cynical taste. So the movie's not as flavorsome as it could have been."

At age sixty-five, Ridley Scott became Sir Ridley Scott when he was knighted by Queen Elizabeth II for his "service to the British Film Industry," joining the ranks of Alfred Hitchcock and his idol David Lean. To commemorate the occasion Tony Scott gave his brother a 1940s letter opener in the shape of a sword. The honor was presented by the queen during a ceremony at Bucking-ham Palace. His response was, "As a boy growing up in South Shields, I could never have imagined that I would receive such a special recognition."[2]

17

CRUSADES AND ROMANTIC COMEDY

Kingdom of Heaven and A Good Year

> The lessons of history don't suit our wishes: if they did, they would be a
> fairy story.
>
> *Clive James*

In 2005 Ridley Scott directed *Jonathan,* a film his daughter Jordan had written for the omnibus film *All the Invisible Children,* which consisted of seven
short films. The enterprise was supported by UNICEF. Scott's segment concerns a disillusioned war photojournalist, played by David Thewlis, who
returns to the life he lived as a child. On his journey, he encounters children
who inspire him to embrace life again.

Also in 2005 Ridley Scott, Tony Scott, and others became executive producers on the US television series *Numb3rs,* broadcast on CBS from January
23, 2005, to March 12, 2010. The successful show starred Rob Morrow. For the
show, law enforcement used mathematics to solve crimes.

Ridley Scott made it known to 20th Century Fox that he wanted to create a
film concerning knights. He was interested in what he called "right action"—
the knight's ability to do absolute right in any situation. Scott wanted to
set his tale in the Holy Land during the Crusades and explore the eternal
struggle between European and Middle Eastern cultures. The resulting film,
Kingdom of Heaven (2005), depicts the ancient conflicts as opposing forces
fighting for Jerusalem, but it also reflects the recent history of conflicts in
Afghanistan and Pakistan and the back history of terrorism in the era of 9/11.

Scott's paradigm for style and aesthetics was David Lean's masterpiece
Lawrence of Arabia (1962). He was also inspired by Andrei Tarkovsky's *Andrei
Rublev* (1966), a chronicle of the real-life Russian hero who defended his

country against relentless attacks by the Tartars, and by Ingmar Bergman's 1957 masterpiece *The Seventh Seal*, which takes place in the fourteenth century. There is a knight in that film, and the driving force is the concept of service for the glory of God.

The beginning of the film includes the Scott Free logo. It is a painterly colorful animation and was designed to simulate a moment from the Sir Carol Reed masterwork, *The Third Man*. It is unusual when compared to corporate film studio logos. The logo was created by Gianluigi Toccafondo, who was born in San Marino and studied art in Urbina, Italy. Fittingly for directors Ridley and Tony Scott, who paint, the animated logo was created in paint. The image begins on a black background, where a white flash appears at the top corner of the screen. A man inspired by Orson Welles enters and a burst of red flame appears. He runs, transforming into an eagle as the text "Scott Free" is presented in an offbeat font.

The practice of an opening crawl was prevalent in Hollywood films during the 1940s, 1950s, and into the 1960s, but eventually became passé in light of new cinematic storytelling techniques. Growing up, Ridley Scott had seen films that used this convention. Scott's reference to this technique as "Irving the Explainer" would seem to suggest negative feelings about it, but he has used it in many of his films. The practice is generally used when a film deals with complex real or invented history. Some audience members may like to be brought up to speed, but more are probably bored and want to get on with the picture.

Kingdom of Heaven is set in the twelfth century at the time of the Crusades. Balian (Orlando Bloom) is a French blacksmith heartbroken by his wife's recent suicide. When Crusaders come to his village on their way to Jerusalem, one of them, Baron Godfrey de Ibelin (Liam Neeson), reveals to the young man that he is his father. Balian leaves his village and joins his father to travel to the Holy Land. En route they battle enemies, and Godfrey is fatally wounded. Before dying, Godfrey knights Balian and orders his son to protect all those who need help and to serve the king of Jerusalem. On his way to the Holy Land, Balian has an altercation with a Muslim. They resolve their conflict and create a strong bond. The Muslim leads him to Jerusalem. Balian becomes involved with King Baldwin IV (Edward Norton), a leper. Tiberias (Jeremy Irons) is the marshal of Jerusalem who wants peace; the king's sister is Sibylla (Eva Green). Her husband, Guy de Lusignan (Marton Csokas), is a supporter of the anti-Muslim activities of the brutal Knights Templar faction. Guy's plan is to become king after Baldwin, get rid of the Muslims entirely, and claim the kingdom for the Christians.

Guy and his cohort Reynald de Chatillon (Brendon Gleeson) provoke Saladin (Ghassan Massoud), leader of the Muslim forces, to attack the Christian kingdom. Although they are outnumbered, Balian and his knights are forced to move forward against Saladin's cavalry. A fierce battle takes place. Saladin's forces are superior, but he saves Balian, knowing the knight is righteous. As the Christians lose the battle, King Baldwin intervenes and despite his severe ill health leads his army and imprisons a defeated Reynald.

When Baldwin dies, Sibylla takes the crown and reluctantly names Guy king of Jerusalem, despite her love for Balian. Guy releases Reynald from prison and instructs him to instigate a war against the Muslims. Reynald kills Saladin's sister (Giannina Facio). A ferocious battle between the Christians and the Muslims ensues for the people and soul of Jerusalem. Balian says, "This is our door into Jerusalem. . . . Before I lose it, I will burn it to the ground." After enormous carnage Balian surrenders and Saladin discusses terms. Saladin promises that no people of Jerusalem, regardless of religion, will be harmed. Balian asks him: "What is Jerusalem worth?" and Saladin reflects, "Nothing." After a contemplative pause he adds, "Everything!"

Balian returns to France and his village to resume his life as a blacksmith. English knights come looking for Balian, who tells them he is merely a blacksmith and does not reveal that he was a leader of the Crusade in Jerusalem. The leader of the men is King Richard the Lionhearted (Iain Glen), who initiates a new three-year Crusade to retake Jerusalem. Balian is reunited with Sibylla when she relinquishes her crown and joins him in France. They ride past Balian's wife's grave toward a new life together.

Kingdom of Heaven is a violent movie. The violence is blunt and realistic and can be unsettling to some viewers—here killing is the path to heaven. Scott often used multiple cameras during the filming. Flaming arrows whizzing through the skies produce a potent image in *Kingdom of Heaven*. Parts of the war are presented in montage style. At times, when there is a weapon projectile, the camera shakes to visually express the impact.

In the scene where Balian meets Sibylla, actor Orlando Bloom focused on Eva Green's body from head to toe while the camera was running. In postproduction, using CGI, the digital artists were able to steady his eyes, allowing the moment to appear more discreet, as if he were mainly looking at her face.

146

Ridley Scott perceives of himself as a dramatist as well as an entertainer. Balancing those two aspects of filmmaking is complicated and not always received as delivered to critics and audiences. A year of editing led to a May 2005 opening, but a struggle between Tom Rothman, head of 20th Century Fox, and director/producer Ridley Scott ensued about the length of the director's cut—a whopping 194 minutes. *Kingdom of Heaven* was reedited to 145 minutes. In 2006, the 194-minute director's cut was released on DVD as *Kingdom of Heaven: The Director's Cut,* which restored subplots, expanded some of the roles, and reinstated other details Scott originally felt were crucial. He added back what he believed was a critical 17-minute section that explains the death of Sibylla's son.

During production and into its theatrical run, *Kingdom of Heaven* was mired in controversy over religious, ethnic, and political issues. Morocco's king had to offer a thousand soldiers to protect the company and guard a set located in the Sahara after a volley of death threats. There was an angry perception that the film was American propaganda against the Arab people, creating the view that they were all bloodthirsty terrorists. The *New York Times* had given the script to Islamic and other academics—their reactions were swift and full of fury toward Scott and his film. They denounced the film because it showed Saladin in a positive light, believing it supported the view of Saddam Hussein and Osama bin Laden. Many American critics found the film filled with political rhetoric. Scott's unsophisticated conflicting statements only made the controversy worse. Once he said the film supported a Boy Scout ethic. On another occasion, he called the knights cowboys who were fair, chivalrous, and full of religious faith.

Historians accused *Kingdom of Heaven* of distorting the history and characters it purported to depict. There were liberties taken concerning the siege of Jerusalem, among other historical facts. Scott dismissed most of these criticisms because the scholars were basing their data on a fifteenth-century French source written by a priest hundreds of years after the events. Scott maintained that history is conjecture, a statement that may contain some truth in certain circumstances.

Kingdom of Heaven was released to the kind of mixed reviews Scott was used to receiving in response to some of his projects. Roger Ebert liked the film. "What Scott seems to be suggesting, I think, is that most Christians and Muslims might be able to coexist peacefully if it were not for the extremists on both sides. This may explain why the movie has displeased the very sorts of Muslims and Christians who will take moderation as an affront. Most ordinary moviegoers, I suspect, will not care much about the movie's reasonable politics, and will be absorbed in those staples of all historical epics, battle and romance." Jonathan Riley-Smith, Dixie Professor of Ecclesiastical History at Cambridge University, was quoted by the *Daily Telegraph* as saying that *Kingdom of Heaven* was "dangerous to Arab relations" and that the film was Osama bin Laden's version of the Crusade and would "fuel Islamic fundamentalists." He also said that it would perpetuate long-standing myths and that it "relied on the romanticized view of the Crusades propagated by Sir Walter Scott in his book *The Talisman* published in 1825 and now discredited by academics."[1] Thomas F. Madden, director of Saint Louis University's Center for Medieval and Renaissance Studies, said, "Given events in the modern world it is lamentable that there is so large a gulf between what professional historians know about the Crusades and what the general population believes. This movie only widens that gulf. The shame of it is that dozens of distinguished historians across the globe would have been only too happy to help Scott and Monahan get it right."[2]

While historical accuracy was a big issue for the critics and some audience members, Scott and company got some things right and, of course, some things wrong. Here is a partial list: Balian de Ibelin was a nobleman, not a blacksmith; there was no romantic connection between Balian and Sibylla; Reynald did not capture Saladin's sister. Scott knew at the outset that the love connection between Balian and Sibylla was not historically correct. William Monahan has stated that the fireballs that appear in the battle scene might not be historically correct.

Scott hoped the film would provide background relating to current Middle East conflicts. Whether audiences are able to see a connection between then and now is questionable. There is no evidence of a parallel that indicates the movie is truly about the present-day situation between the Arab countries and the State of Israel. One assumes that Ridley Scott would like to think he made a film that offers insight; if we can recognize the message of performing right actions, then perhaps Scott did achieve his purpose for the film. Still, *Kingdom of Heaven* is too long and tedious to be successful.

A Good Year, Scott's next film, released in 2006, is a romantic comedy about a London financial trader, Max Skinner (Russell Crowe), who inherits his Uncle Henry's (Albert Finney) estate and winery in France. In numerous flashbacks we see the uncle with his nephew as a child, played by Freddie Highmore. As an adult, the nephew meets a beautiful Frenchwoman, Fanny

Chenal (Marion Cotillard), through happenstance—an incident involving his car and her bicycle. After some feuding they fall in love.

The film's secret is that, unbeknownst to them, the lovers have met before, as children. Young Uncle Henry, a womanizer, had an affair with Fanny's mother, played by Catherine Vinatier. While the adults make love upstairs, the children are left on opposite sides of a swimming pool. In flashback the two children stare at each other for a while, then the girl plunges into the pool, swims to the boy, kisses him directly on the lips, and whispers in his ear, "Forgive my lips, they find joy in the most unusual places." The pivotal moment in *A Good Year* occurs when the trader realizes the Frenchwoman is the little girl from his childhood. The adults consummate their love and presumably live happily ever after.

There are side plots and characters to support the main plot, such as Max's trader's tricks and the troubles he faces back home. Key in these sequences is Gemma, played in high style by Archie Panjabi (known for her TV role in *The Good Wife,* on which Scott was executive producer) as Max's savvy and mischievous London executive assistant who manipulates him while he is in France. The performances by Marion Cotillard and Albert Finney are solid. The negative exception is Russell Crowe, who is not funny or very romantic.

This is Ridley Scott's first flat-out romantic comedy. Scott actually announced to the public that he saw himself as a good director of comedy and wanted to direct a film with some fun. But the film was not well received in the US or France. Reviews everywhere were largely negative. Audiences all but stayed away.

Stephen Holden of the *New York Times* managed to find some worth in the film. "*A Good Year,* an innocuous, feel-good movie that reunites Russell Crowe with the director Ridley Scott, is a far cry from the triumphant metallic stomp of 'Gladiator,' their previous collaboration. A sun-dappled romantic diversion, which one British critic has already dismissed as 'tourist gastroporn,' *A Good Year* is a three-P movie: pleasant, pretty and predictable. One might add piddling."

Dan Jolin of *Empire* gave *A Good Year* the benefit of the doubt. "Quite simply, Crowe and Scott are just too heavyweight. There is some novelty value in seeing Crowe squeezing his burly frame into the kind of role usually reserved for Hugh Grant or Colin Firth but it soon wears off. The film does at least *look* great—who better than Ridley Scott to shoot the villages and sun-snogged vistas of Bouche-du-Rhone?"

Paul Arendt of BBC Homepage represents the distaste most critics had for the film. "Ridley Scott's sun-dappled tale of wine-making in the wilds of Provence slips down easily enough but leaves a nasty residue on the palate. Russell Crowe begins the story as a deeply unpleasant stockbroker and completes it as a deeply unpleasant vintner with a palatial estate and a pretty girl on his arm. A wish-fulfilment fantasy aimed squarely at middle-aged men, *A Good Year* might be forgivable if it wasn't so perilously short on jokes."

18

CRIME STORY
American Gangster

In truth, Frank Lucas has probably destroyed more black lives than the
K.K.K. could ever dream of.

Richie Roberts

American Gangster, released in 2007, is a bold epic crime film that weaves
together many themes and motifs. Ridley Scott calls *American Gangster,*
based on a true story, his most ambitious filmmaking adventure; it allowed
him to create and explore two worlds—the flashy world of drug lord Frank
Lucas (Denzel Washington), who built his empire on an almost pure grade of
heroin product he named Blue Magic, and the down-market domain of
Detective Richie Roberts (Russell Crowe), a rough cop studying to be a lawyer who combs the streets for drugs and dealers and ultimately becomes
obsessed with bringing Lucas to justice.

The film opens in Harlem at Thanksgiving time, 1968. Old-school gangster kingpin Bumpy Johnson (an uncredited Clarence Williams III) gives out
free turkeys to the local residents, who adore him. Later, after Johnson dies of
a heart attack and Frank Lucas rises to power to fill the void, Lucas continues
the tradition of distributing the turkeys.

Family is a potent theme in *American Gangster.* Frank enlists his large
family to work for him in the drug business. The Thanksgiving theme is
extended as Lucas presides over Thanksgiving dinner, carving the bird while
all the family members anticipate the luscious traditional meal. The image
recalls an iconic painting by Norman Rockwell, *Freedom from Want.* Frank
and his family appear to be a prototypical wholesome American family.
Nothing could be further from the truth. These men are killers and dope
dealers responsible for much deadly misery. They are thankful only for their
own profit and are filled with greed.

American Gangster was based in large part on the *New York* magazine
article "The Return of Superfly" by Mark Jacobson, published on August 14,

Ridley Scott and producer Brian Grazer on location for *American Gangster*.

2000. Jacobson apparently borrowed the title from the 1990 movie *The Return of Superfly*, the sequel to the 1972 blaxploitation hit *Superfly*. The article contains quotes from an interview with Lucas and is an overview of the drug kingpin's life. Steve Zaillian was asked to create a screenplay based on the life of Frank Lucas.

As Zaillian was writing his screenplay adaption, producer Brian Grazer, long associated with Ron Howard (the two were co-founders of Imagine Entertainment), purchased the rights to the project.

Antoine Fuqua, a successful music video director and director of the feature film *Training Day* (2001), starring Denzel Washington, who won the Academy Award for Best Actor, was scheduled to direct *American Gangster* in 2004 with Washington as Frank Lucas and Benicio Del Toro as Richie

Roberts. The title was *Tru Blu,* referencing a type of heroin product in 1970s Harlem. Universal Studios had just joined with General Electric, now its corporate parent. Universal claimed that production plans were in chaos. According to Universal and Imagine, Fuqua lost control of the project. He didn't respond to demands to cut specific scenes for budgetary reasons, he hadn't completed casting and scouting locations, and he did not meet with the director of photography to plan shots. Fuqua addressed the allegations, and he and his agent Jeff Berg considered a lawsuit.

Then Universal Pictures became concerned with the budget, which had climbed to nearly $100 million, and canceled the project. Del Toro had a play-or-pay contract and received $5 million. Denzel Washington, who was furious with the studio for not telling him in advance they were considering firing Fuqua, had the same proviso, with $20 million coming to him, but he deferred his option and ultimately applied the salary to Scott's production.

Peter Berg (*Friday Night Lights,* 2004) was next going to direct the film, but Universal realized there was still much to prep before the rapidly approaching original start date, so the studio canceled the film. One year passed, and then writer and director Terry George (*Hotel Rwanda,* 2004) was commissioned to do a rewrite on the Zaillian draft. His objective was to reduce the project's scope—and, more important, its cost. Terry George wanted to reunite with his *Hotel Rwanda* star Don Cheadle to bring Frank Lucas's story to the screen. Again the project stalled. Grazer was not willing to give up; he decided to bring back Steve Zaillian and ask him to write another draft. Then Grazer decided to approach Ridley Scott to direct. The persistent Grazer, still full of energy and desire to make the film, brought Zaillian's script to Scott as many as eight times. On each occasion the timing was not right for the always-busy director. By the ninth or tenth time—Grazer lost track—Scott said yes.

Ridley Scott first became interested in *American Gangster* while he was in production on *Kingdom of Heaven.* He read the 165-page script and liked it very much. While working on *A Good Year* he began to discuss the project with Russell Crowe, thinking he would make a fine Richie Roberts; their talks led them both to sign onto the production.

Denzel Washington was a bit wary about the film's fate but was very interested in working with Ridley Scott. Washington had acted in several films directed by Tony Scott, who gave Washington glowing marks.

Famed crime writer Nicholas Pileggi and Steve Zaillian met the real Frank Lucas and Richie Roberts at the Regency Hotel. (Ridley Scott did not attend this meeting but later met with Frank Lucas for five hours.) Zaillian

Ridley Scott directs Denzel Washington in *American Gangster.*

ended up with fifty hours of taped interviews with Lucas and about the same for Richie Roberts. Zaillian transcribed the interview tapes, then wrote a story outline. Because of the parallel stories, Zaillian decided to write two screenplays, one focusing on each man. Then he created a master version and interwove their stories.

Ridley Scott's concept for the film was to show how gradually, over the course of the two hours and thirty-seven minutes of the epic, the two men come together. Zaillian was told the script was too long, so he cut it. After eighteen months the final screenplay was around 135 pages—there were 350 scenes. During production Scott shot all of it, believing in Zaillian's talent; he had an intense working relationship with him during the writing process.

Ridley Scott was familiar with New York City from his time there in the 1960s. Scott remembered old Harlem well. By the late 1990s Harlem had gone through gentrification. It was challenging to re-create an authentic-looking 1970s Harlem; Scott and production designer Arthur Max searched the exterior buildings and streets and through meticulous selections put the Harlem of the 1970s on the screen. Frank Lucas was a consultant on the film, and he and Richie Roberts occasionally appeared on set.

It is believed that Frank Lucas was the first person to travel to the source of the drug chain in Asia. He saw the poppy fields himself and dealt with the local powers. Not even the Mafia had done that. To create a massive field of poppies, Ridley Scott and his art department turned to the visual effects experts, who created the image digitally. To portray Lucas's visits to procure large shipments of drugs in Vietnam, northern Thailand was selected to stage and shoot the sequences.

The total shooting schedule lasted four months and had an enormous number of locations, rumored to be between 180 and as high as 360. Shooting took place in all five of New York's boroughs. Upstate New York and suburban areas of Long Island were utilized. These were all practical locations, not sets. Scott was maintaining an astonishing fifty setups a day. He would do two takes of a shot and be ready to move on. Sometimes Denzel Washington or Russell Crowe asked for one more, and the director would comply.

Because of the film's realistic nature, instead of referencing paintings, Ridley Scott and his director of photography, Harris Savides (*Elephant,* 2003, *Zodiac,* 2007, *Milk,* 2008) examined photographs. Savides was an experienced fashion photographer and cinematographer on music videos and had shot such stars as Madonna and Michael Jackson; he also photographed commercials.

In addition to Denzel Washington, there is a large ensemble cast of black actors in *American Gangster,* including Chiwetel Ejiofor (Huey Lucas), Roger Guenveur Smith (Nate), RZA (Moses Jones), Malcolm Goodwin (Jimmy Zee), Cuba Gooding Jr. (Nicky Barnes), Joe Morton (Charlie Williams), Bari K. Willeford (Joe Louis), Idris Elba (Tango), Anthony Hamilton (funk band singer), Lil Chuuch (playing a drug dealer) and, in a superb portrayal of Lucas's mother, Ruby Dee, who was nominated for an Academy Award for Best Supporting Actress. Another major mob figure, Dominic Cattano, head of the Lucchese crime family, is portrayed elegantly but with menace by Armand Assante. This character may have been partly based on Carmine Tramuti, the actual boss of the Lucchese crime family.

The use of score and selected songs in *American Gangster* is highly effective and at the elevated level of a Martin Scorsese picture. Composer Marc Streitenfeld, music supervisor Kathy Nelson, and rap artist Hank Shocklee made musical choices that speak to the action and nature of the characters and to the period in both conventional and unconventional ways. Scott credits Nelson and Shocklee, who remixed and produced music and other feats of audio magic, with finding records from the period that people in the audience might not have known but that depicted the times and mood perfectly. Some of the older songs in *American Gangster* are "Why Don't We Do It in the Road," "Hold On, I'm Comin'," "Good Lovin'," "I'll Take You There," "Across 110th Street," and "Only the Lonely."

In a pivotal scene, Frank Lucas has front-row seats at Madison Square Garden for the Muhammad Ali/Joe Frazier fight. Allegedly Richie was there taking surveillance pictures, but because of the enormity of the venue he and Lucas didn't make any sort of contact. Of the 1,000 "extras" used to re-create this scene, only 650 were real people; the rest were inflatable dummies. Also in the crowd were lookalike actors posing as Sammy Davis Jr., Frank Sinatra, Joe Louis, and other notables. Madison Square Garden wanted an exorbitant amount of money to allow filming, so Scott shot the scene in one day at an ice hockey arena. Scott deemed the fight irrelevant—he was there to show Richie taking a photo of Lucas in an outrageous chinchilla coat and matching hat, a present from his adored wife. Lucas's over-the-top outfit was his downfall—it made the elusive drug lord instantly recognizable to law enforcement.

The use of television imagery throughout *American Gangster* grounds the film in the reality of its time. The march on Saigon is shown on color television. One clip of Nixon from 1973 shows the soon-to-be disgraced president announcing the withdrawal of US troops from Vietnam. These clips were all written into the script by Zaillian.

American Gangster tested very high with preview audiences—92 or 94 percent favorable. British reviews were also mostly enthusiastic. The movie grossed $265 million worldwide and $130 million in the US. The budget was estimated at $100 million.

The statement posted at the beginning of the film is "Based on a true story"—the operative word is "based." Many events and actions depicted in the movie are true, but much has been invented or changed, sometimes drastically. Filmmakers of many motion pictures based on true stories tend to stray from the truth to satisfy their artistic visions.

In the film Richie Roberts is in a tough custody battle with his wife—this never happened. Other scenes are also fictional. For example, although Roberts didn't have a son, one of Richie's best friends from the old neighborhood, now a mob member, is the boy's godfather.

Frank Lucas's plan to import the deadly heroin from Vietnam was an idea of evil genius; he reportedly had pure dope shipped back to Harlem in the military coffins of US soldiers who had fought in the war. In Scott's movie the drugs are actually in the coffins along with the bodies, but the real-life Lucas claims that he used twenty-eight replicas of official government coffins made by a North Carolina carpenter who was married to one of his cousins.

The decoy units had false bottoms to carry between six and eight kilos of heroin. Nonetheless, in the DVD documentary, *Fallen Empire: Making* American Gangster, Lucas talks about the dope being smuggled in the real coffins of dead servicemen. Perhaps it can be concluded that Frank Lucas, a key source for this film, is not totally reliable.

During the early minutes of *American Gangster,* we witness Bumpy Johnson die of a heart attack in an appliance store. But the real Bumpy Johnson died in Wells Restaurant, famous for its chicken and waffles. Scott chose to alter the setting for dramatic reasons. Frank Lucas says he was at the restaurant that day, which means he was aware the filmmakers were altering reality for dramatic purposes. Mayme Johnson, Bumpy's wife, reports that Bumpy died in the restaurant and that Frank Lucas was not there. Johnson, she says, died in the arms of his childhood friend, Junie Byrd. Mayme Johnson also disputes Lucas's statement that he was Bumpy's driver for fifteen years. She has reported that Lucas may have driven her husband a few times, but he was more likely someone who might have carried Bumpy's coat—they were not in a close mentoring relationship as portrayed in the movie.

Ron Chepesiuk, author of *Superfly: The True, Untold Story of Frank Lucas,* *American Gangster,* states that Richie Roberts was actually "a minor figure in the Lucas investigation." Roberts spoke directly to this claim, explaining there was a squad of law enforcement figures who brought Lucas down. He confirmed that his character on-screen was a composite, a technique often used by Hollywood in "based on a true story" films. Other composites in *American Gangster* are Detective Trupo, played by Josh Brolin, and Dominic Cattano.

In reality, when the authorities finally apprehended Frank Lucas, he was not on the steps of his mother's church. This scene is quite theatrical and very effective visually and in content. It is Frank and Richie's first meeting. Scott optimizes his mise-en-scène with shots from behind Lucas on Richie and reverse angles to show Richie's POV. The compositions are epic and powerful. At a critical point the camera is behind Lucas on the steps for quite a few beats, then it jogs just a bit to reveal Richie with his gun drawn. In the actual apprehension authorities launched a surprise raid on Lucas's home in Teaneck, New Jersey, on January 28, 1975. His wife Julie panicked and threw suitcases with $584,000 out the window. This would also have made for a dramatic movie scene, but Scott and company obviously couldn't resist the dramatic confrontation between drug lord and detective after Richie's long screen hunt.

In early 2008 three retired Drug Enforcement Agency agents filed a $50 million libel case against Universal Pictures on the grounds that their character and integrity has been sullied by the makers of the movie. Their argument was that they were libeled by their portrayal during the surprise raid on Lucas's mansion looking for drugs, money, or anything that would incriminate him. They were angry that one of the officers was portrayed as shooting Lucas's beloved dog and beating up his wife. Universal denied the charges, and the case was dismissed on February 15, 2008, but it is significant that the judge believed that Universal and the filmmakers got the facts of the real story wrong. It should be noted, however, that successful films often get served with high-dollar lawsuits.

The night Frank burned his chinchilla coat, which became a key element leading to his capture, may not have been the night of the Ali/Frazier fight, but his wedding night, dispelling a key plot point in *American Gangster*. The list of discrepancies may seem troubling, but it is common practice in movies and television to manipulate material. For history, search out a book on Frank Lucas—for a taut and intense drama, see *American Gangster*.

The surprise of 2007 came at the Venice Film Festival, which hosted a special screening of *Blade Runner* with Ridley Scott in attendance. In the past Scott has made it clear, actually before he made *Alien* and *Blade Runner*, that he doesn't like science fiction. Of course, that didn't stop him from directing two of his greatest films in the genre. In a speech given at the festival Scott proclaimed that science fiction was dead, gone the way of the western. He must have had a change of mind before the 2012 release of *Prometheus*.

19

I SPY

Body of Lies

Here's the thing about being a spy; sometimes all you have are your lies. They protect your cover and keep your secrets, and right then I needed to believe that it was true even when all the facts said otherwise.

Ally Carter, United We Spy

In *Body of Lies* Ridley Scott continues to explore the ongoing clashes of ideological, religious, and ethnic differences that have been the cause of so much hatred and bloodshed. *Body of Lies* (2008) is an unconventional spy movie that pits a CIA operative against his control man. It was only a modest success even though it featured the stellar pairing of Leonardo DiCaprio and Russell Crowe. It contains heart-pounding action that embraces Scott's themes of adventure (with deadly results here) and the conflicts of confrontation between protagonists.

The story, set in a hot spot in the Middle East, concerns Al-Saleem (Alon Aboutboul), an extremist/terrorist who believes his cause is righteous. He is bent on murdering CIA case officer Roger Ferris (DiCaprio). Al-Saleem believes Ferris has mortally sinned by murdering and torturing Muslims. Ferris's supervisor is Ed Hoffman, played by Russell Crowe. Hoffman orchestrates deceit, double-crossing, and violence via telecommunications. Hoffman tells his superiors that the terrorist today can best be fought by an operative like Ferris. The CIA has high technology but lacks the human intelligence to properly fight terrorism in the Middle East. Hoffman constantly reminds Ferris that regardless of his risk and sacrifices, the CIA is a results-driven organization.

The espionage film is filled with twists and turns as Ferris navigates through treacherous terrain dealing with dangerous people—many of them terrorists. Hoffman, it turns out, has his own agenda, using Ferris to advance his own plotting. The two men spend the great majority of the film communicating by phone and other technology. There is some intercutting, but the

Ridley Scott flanked by two cameras during the production of *Body of Lies*.

camera spends most of the time with Ferris. Eventually they have a face-to-face interaction, but Ferris is most familiar with receiving orders via a voice in his ear or electronically. Hoffman is portrayed as a family man who tends to his children while on the phone doing CIA business. It is a chilling juxtaposition to see him express paternal tenderness as he conducts deadly spy operations. Hoffman is a devious individual whose behavior sheds light on the duplicitous lives of those in the intelligence agency.

There is a romantic angle. Ferris is injured during one of his violent confrontations and is taken to the hospital. He meets a nurse, Aisha, played by Golshifteh Farahani, and a romance ensues. Aisha is a strong and beautiful woman who is sure of her feelings for Ferris, although her sister is suspicious of the American. Al-Saleem orchestrates Ferris's capture, and Aisha is the subject of a faked abduction. Ferris is tortured and loses two fingers and the will to fight in this "war." Ferris goes off the undercover grid and sees Aisha again. It is assumed they will have a happy off-screen ending, but in an environment of violence and polar-opposite ideologies, the outcome is questionable.

Body of Lies began in March 2006 when Warner Bros. hired William Monahan to adapt David Ignatius's novel *Penetration*. Ignatius had covered the CIA and the Middle East for the *Wall Street Journal*. The book was a quasi-documentary view of life on the front lines in the Middle East during the "war on terror." It was a thriller about deception and what it takes to infiltrate a culture and the enemy. Later the screenplay was revised by Steven Zaillian, who deleted many of the subplots Monahan had created.

By April 2007 Leonardo DiCaprio had been cast in the lead role. DiCaprio's interest was generated by his admiration for 1970s political films such as *The Parallax View* (1974) and *Three Days of the Condor* (1975). For the role DiCaprio dyed his blond hair brown and was fitted with brown contact lenses over his blue/green eyes. Russell Crowe formally signed on after Monahan's script was revised by Zaillian. Crowe gained 63 pounds for the Ed Hoffman part, weighing in at 257 pounds. "It just felt right for the character and it's what Ridley wanted as well," Russell Crowe told Nancy O'Dell of *Access Hollywood*. "He wanted the image of Ed to feel like a retired football player whose knees didn't allow him to train anymore or something like that. . . . And he wanted to show that this is a guy that actually spends most of his time sitting down."[1]

Principal photography began on September 5, 2007, in Washington, DC, at the Eastern Market. Practical locations were used throughout the film. Scott yearned to shoot in Dubai in the United Arab Emirates but was denied access because of the project's sensitive political nature. Scenes taking place in Jordan and ten different countries were shot in Morocco, a location with excellent film-production capabilities that Scott uses frequently.

Leonardo DiCaprio talked to Sheila Roberts about Ridley Scott's work method:

He's like a human editing bay. He's constantly saying to himself, "Do I believe this? Do I not believe this? Do I believe the people I've surrounded the main character with? Do I believe what they are saying? Do I believe what I am seeing through this screen?" He's this filter, this bullsh—t filter and he trusts his own instincts on such a gut level. It's great to work with somebody who will come in and say, "Okay, this entire scene is wrong. Get rid of three pages of dialogue or let's move it outside. Whatever it is, I'm not believing it. . . . Or, I am believing it. Push it to an even more extreme."[2]

Director of photography Alexander Witt worked on six Ridley Scott films, starting as a second unit cameraman on *Black Rain. Body of Lies* was shot in Super 35mm, which offered much flexibility. There were three cameras shooting simultaneously. Mark Schmidt, part of the operating team, praised Scott to Patricia Thompson of *American Cinematographer*: "Ridley will stand at the monitors and tell you what he's looking for—he'll look at four monitors and say, 'I'm cutting from this to this to this.' He knows exactly how he will cut it."[3]

Practical light sources were used on practical locations. In the torture sequence that concludes the film, the only light was provided by torches held by the torturers. Three cameras were utilized—bounce cards directed the light onto the actors' faces. Once again Scott used smoke to create atmosphere. The scene was difficult and challenging for DiCaprio, who actually fell ill for three days after the scene. The tremendous intensity the actor put into the scene drained him.

Body of Lies is an old-fashioned spy thriller that purports to present the modern-day world situation, especially in the Middle East. There is little chemistry between DiCaprio and Crowe—lots of action but not as much content, lots of weapons, explosions, and wheeling and dealing, but not enough character development or a cogent plot. It fits on Ridley Scott's résumé as something different that he wanted to do, but does not stand out as the worst or the best he has created as a film director. In general, it was a movie audiences didn't want to see.

In the film DiCaprio is vibrant and electric at times. He is full of life, but except for the romance, he is caught up in situations with which he can barely cope. Spies like James Bond have all the latest gadgets, but Ferris has little assistance and is basically on his own, a stranger in a strange land. DiCaprio is as handsome as ever, charismatic and intelligent; although presumably, DiCaprio's legion of female fans couldn't have been very satisfied with the brown-haired, brown-eyed character when they were used to a blond, baby blue–eyed male god. The men are men in this picture. They are strong and lust for violence and adventure. Each character has distinct characteristics, and there is an established tension.

This is an unconventional war film. There is a turf war, and men who appear to be military leaders. It is a contemporary war that can't be won. The movie has a curious blend of high and low technology; there are conventional weapons and ultra-modern communication tools.

Critical reaction was mixed at best. Roger Ebert found the performances convincing and appreciated the realistic locations and tight dialogue. He did, however, question the believability of the story, finding much of it implausible. In the *New York Post* critic Lou Lumenick said there was nothing in *Body of Lies* that he hadn't seen before. Lisa Kennedy of the *Denver Post* called it an

"A" project with a "B" outcome. David Denby in the *New Yorker* praised Scott's direction but found the movie too similar to other films in the genre. *Variety*'s Todd McCarthy liked the setup and plot, but thought the film was formulaic and had a corny ending. A. O. Scott, writing in the *New York Times*, found Ridley Scott to be as professional as ever, but thought the film lacked conviction. Joe Neumaier complained in the *New York Daily News* that *Body of Lies* tried to be contemporary, but was more of the same old thing. Scott and others think that films on this subject do poorly because of the intense public anger toward "the war on terror."

20

REVISIONIST ROBIN

Robin Hood

I must only warn you of one thing. You have become a different person in the course of these years. For this is what the art of archery means: a profound and far-reaching contest of the archer with himself.

Eugen Herrigel, Zen in the Art of Archery

Ridley Scott continued to develop his visualist tendencies and take criticism for stressing the image in order to express the narratives of his films. In a June 3, 1991, review of *Thelma & Louise* published in the *New Yorker* and later in the book *The Thing Happens: Ten Years of Writing about the Movies,* film critic Terrence Rafferty discusses Scott's craft:

The director's entranced gaze slows down the rhythm of the narrative; quite a lot happens in this movie, but it has a leisurely, expansive air. Scott . . . is known for his striking, overpowering, visual style: the compositions in his films are meticulous, shiny, and elaborately textured. They frequently look too good to be true, and Scott has sometimes been seen as just another member of a school of filmmakers who developed a slick, manipulative craft in the British advertising industry—directors like Alan Parker . . . Adrian Lyne . . . and Ridley's brother Tony Scott. . . . Ridley Scott isn't really that kind of filmmaker, though. He has never been a cynical manipulator of audience reactions. Here is a romantic, and a rather innocent and credulous one, at that, investing everything he works on with the passion and enthusiasm of an imaginative child. His images have a true believer's intensity, and if they're not always persuasive, it's because Scott isn't terribly selective about what he believes in.[1]

In 2009 Jordan Scott directed *Cracks* with Eva Green. The novel *Cracks* was written by Sheila Kohler. The screenwriters were Ben Court, Caroline Ip,

Ridley Scott directs Russell Crowe and Cate Blanchett in *Robin Hood.*

and Jordan Scott. This independent psychological period drama, executive-produced by her father Ridley Scott and uncle Tony Scott, bears resemblance in some of its aspects to several films directed by Ridley Scott, such as the compositional framing and lighting utilized by Stanley Kubrick, in which a center person(s) or object(s) is counterbalanced by person(s) or object(s) on the far right and left; a tracking shot following action, a feature of both Ridley Scott and Kubrick; both directors' mastery of cinematic lighting; a judicious use of slow motion photography; a love of beauty and landscape shots; and strong capable women.

Legal dramas are nothing new to television—*Perry Mason, The Defenders, The Practice, L.A. Law* are all solid examples of the genre for the medium. Coming up with a new or different twist is a challenge. Ridley and Tony Scott, working with other producers, came up with such a show, *The Good Wife,* which first aired on September 22, 2009. The show ran for a decade and was extremely popular with viewers. It is Scott's most successful venture in the network television arena. The hit program was financed by Scott Free. The cast included Julianna Margulies, Christine Baranski, Archie Panjabi (who worked with Ridley Scott on *A Good Year*), Matt Czuchry, Alan Cumming, and Josh Charles. Chris Noth is featured in a recurring role. *The Good Wife* garnered consistently good reviews and a strong continuing viewership and has been highly decorated with many honors, including a Peabody Award.

Ridley Scott's eighteenth feature film, *Robin Hood,* released in 2010, is an adventure epic about a legendary character known in England, Ireland, Scotland, and America as the man in green who, accompanied by his Merry Men, robbed from the rich and gave to the poor—Robin Hood. The legend of Robin Hood, which evolved in many forms, harkens back to the thirteenth century. In America, the best-known cinematic Robin Hood is Errol Flynn (in what looked like hand-painted, frame-by-frame color but was really glorious Technicolor) in the 1938 Hollywood production *The Adventures of Robin Hood,* directed by Michael Curtiz and William Keighley. There are other versions, of course, among them the Mel Brooks comedy spoof *Robin Hood: Men in Tights* (1993) and Richard Lester's more romantic production *Robin and Marian* (1976) starring Sean Connery and Audrey Hepburn.

Scott became obsessed with archery and archers. This fascination lit the creative spark and became integrated into his visual storytelling. At the time Scott made it crystal clear that he did not like previous film versions of Robin Hood, including the one with Errol Flynn. The exception was the Mel Brooks version, *Men in Tights,* for its comedic virtues.

Ridley Scott's *Robin Hood* investigates the tale of Robin Longstride, a freelance archer who is sort of a hit man for the king. Upon the murder of the gallant but flawed King Richard, played by Danny Huston, Russell Crowe as Robin travels on horseback to France with his newly assembled crew of Merry Men. During their journey they are ambushed, and Robin accepts the duty of returning the sword of a dying soldier, bringing it to Nottingham, a village suffering from excessive taxation. Here Robin meets the dead warrior's wife, Marian Loxley, portrayed by Cate Blanchett. They scuffle both in word and deed, with some intervention from the departed's blind father, played by Max Von Sydow (an actor closely associated with Ingmar Bergman, a director Ridley Scott reveres). Marian and Robin fall in love and in the end understand the importance of home and family.

Issues of class is a British concern, and this theme is woven throughout *Robin Hood.* The king is a greedy cretin, but Robin and his men go off to war for him because he is what stands between England and the condescending French. The corrupting force of power, a theme in many of Scott's films, is certainly prevalent in *Robin Hood.*

Initially actress Sienna Miller was cast as Maid Marian but talk of tensions between Russell Crowe and the rest of the *Robin Hood* team most likely caused her to quit. A source suggested that originally the film focused on a love triangle between Robin, Marian, and the sheriff of Nottingam, but more than forty script pages were redone to be specifically devoted to Robin, apparently due to Crowe's rising ego, which was an issue in past performances. During his finest performance in a Ridley Scott film, on *Gladiator,* Russell Crowe so detested the climactic line "And I will have my vengeance, in this life or the next" that he improvised an alternative. Eventually Ridley Scott was able to persuade Crowe to do the line as written in the screenplay. Again the ego took over as he told his director, "I'm the greatest actor in the world and I can make even shit sound good."[2]

Concerning Ridley Scott's work ethic and filmmaking knowledge, Crowe told *New York Times* writer David Carr:

> He comes prepared to work. He can tell you exactly how many horses he has, how many severed heads he has on hand in the props department, how many cameras he needs for a shot. He is the boss, and by having that command of infrastructure, he is able to create entire other worlds. . . . We were at Fresh Water beach in England, filming a massive scene where the French army was landing and the tide was coming in furiously. We are setting and resetting and there are, I don't know, fourteen barges and 500 extras as French infantry, and one of the backs of the boats kept swinging into the frame where it wasn't supposed to be. And Ridley jumped into the waves and grabbed this 15-ton barge with both hands, bum knee and all, and starts to put it out of the shot. When it was clear he was not going to win his lone battle with the barge, he looked back at the beach and the hundreds of extras and said, "Well, what are you waiting for?" That's leadership.[3]

Throughout film history there have been many productive and legendary director/actor pairings: Federico Fellini and Marcello Mastroianni, Martin Scorsese and Robert De Niro, Tim Burton and Johnny Depp. Ridley Scott and Russell Crowe collaborated five times; *Robin Hood* was their last cinematic dance. When asked about their partnership, Scott replied, "He's angry all the time and I'm angry all the time as well. We don't mean to be irritable but we don't suffer fools gladly."[4]

Sources close to the *Robin Hood* set claimed Crowe blamed Scott for the negative reception their last collaboration, *Body of Lies,* had received. (Crowe is known to be hotheaded. In 2005 he faced criminal charges for hurling a telephone at a hotel concierge.) There were also rumors that Crowe was pressuring George Freeman of William Morris, who represented both Crowe and Scott, to have Ridley Scott replaced on the *Robin Hood* project. Both Freeman and producer Brian Grazer deny this allegation. Still, the pairing of Scott and Crowe will stand the test of film history. There were two other films that Scott wanted to make with Russell Crowe: *Black Hawk Down,* which the actor turned down because he had recently done a film involving helicopters, and *Kingdom of Heaven,* which Crowe couldn't take on because he was working on another film and wouldn't be available for a year. Scott was not interested in waiting.

Robin Hood opened the Cannes Film Festival on May 12, 2010. Russell Crowe made the television circuit to publicize the movie. Known as an actor who speaks his mind, Crowe outdid himself and shook up a few talk-show hosts by ripping into the past Robin Hood films and performers. This tirade included ridiculing Kevin Costner's poufy hair in *Robin Hood: Prince of Thieves* (1991), the Disney animated musical *Robin Hood,* released in 1973, and the silliness of the Mel Brooks satire. But Crowe went over the top when he took on the classic *The Adventures of Robin Hood.* Crowe lashed out at Errol Flynn's performance and insisted that it was not Flynn's performance but his own that captured the essence of Robin Hood. Crowe declared he would be remembered as the man who gave the definitive performance. Appearing on the popular morning show *Live with Regis and Kelly,* Crowe also made it very clear that the film was a fresh look at an old legend. "What it's about—is throw out the comic books, super powers, clichés, and start from scratch."[5]

New York Times critic A. O. Scott, who tends to take a literary approach to film criticism, reviewed Scott's *Robin Hood* on Friday, May 14, 2010, headlined in the Weekend Arts Section as "Rob the Rich? Give to the Poor? Oh, Puh-*Leeze!*"

> [Robin Hood] . . . has been played most memorably by Errol Flynn, most forgettably by Kevin Costner and now, least merrily by Russell Crowe.
>
> If only the story were leaner and more nimble—but then again this is a Ridley Scott film, so you go in expecting bombast and bloat

in the service of leaden themes. You also expect skill and precision in the orchestration of large-scale action sequences, and there are enough of those . . . to keep you alert and fitfully engaged.

As it crashes and bellows towards its sanguinary end, *Robin Hood* makes a hash of the historical record, and also of its own hero's biography, the truth of which is revealed through a series of preposterous and unsatisfying flashbacks. Who was Robin Hood? After more than two hours of flaming arrows, loud music and defiant sloganeering, it's oddly hard to tell. He's for liberty though—the English kind, by the way—so if you have anything bad to say about him, you'd better say it in French.[6]

In the online edition of *Rolling Stone,* Peter Travers opined:

Any resemblance to the Oscar-winning *Gladiator* is purely not coincidental.

Scott is striving for Shakespearean rather than swashbuckling—right down to Robin getting a "Prince Harry" style speech—but despite Crowe's physicality . . . the characters all lack weight. Instead of trying to show what really makes Robin tick, the script writers spread the subplots on thick . . . all vying for screen time—of which, as per usual where Scott is concerned, there is an unhealthy amount. . . . Crowe has clearly been spending rather too much time listening to Scott, since his northern accent has a distinct (and unnatural) Geordie twang in places.[7]

Ridley Scott had every intention of making the definitive Robin Hood film. Cate Blanchett is perfect as Maid Marian, a strong Ridley Scott woman who can stand up to any man. If the Michael Curtiz film with Errol Flynn is the gold standard, then Scott's film falls short. It's too grubby and too violent and contains too much battling. Although robbing the rich to give to the poor is still there, it is less noble and satisfying. The film is too long, with too much money spent on its creation.

The film fared well worldwide, grossing an estimated $322 million. It did less well in America, with an estimated weekend opening of $36 million and an estimated to-date gross of $105 million.

This is certainly another manly man movie. Robin has a solid love for his men and is a brilliant leader and tactician. The Merry Men are virile, strong, tough, and loyal. Ridley Scott's *Robin Hood* takes its place in the cinematic pantheon of films on the man, myth, and legend of Robin Hood. As far as putting his distinctive stamp on the subject, the film may be more realistic than audiences wanted, compared to past versions. The most exciting aspect of the film is the staging and photography of the many bow and arrow sequences. In the air they seem to fly endlessly, but eventually hit their target. The overall look is nothing special for Ridley Scott.

Always one to keep all his options open, Scott said he would consider creating further Robin Hood films.

In 2010 Jake Scott directed *Welcome to the Rileys* with James Gandolfini and Kristen Stewart. *Welcome to the Rileys* was produced by Jake's father and his uncle Tony. The craft and storytelling are capable. The style is not like his dad's visualist kind but more straightforward and direct. The performances are strong, but the reviews were mixed.

YouTube announced the start of another Ridley Scott project, *Life in a Day*, an experimental documentary to incorporate footage shot on July 24, 2010, by contributors from around the world. The results were premiered at Sundance on January 27, 2011. One of the project's purposes was to stand as a historical record for future generations concerning what life was like on that particular day. It has been called a time capsule. The mission was to support storytellers from around the world and provide a platform for expression and experimentation and to engage the YouTube community with something new and unexpected. So far two other films in what has now become a series have arrived—*Britain in a Day* and *Japan in a Day*, joint openers at the Tokyo International Film Festival in 2012.

Prophets of Science Fiction, a documentary television series hosted and executive-produced by Ridley Scott, premiered on the Science Channel on November 9, 2011. The concept was to cover the life and work of leading science fiction authors and how they predicted and influenced the development and creation of scientific advancements. The format utilized documentary film clips, reenactments, illustrations, and interviews. The first season of eight hour-long programs covered Mary Shelley, Philip K. Dick, H. G. Wells, Arthur C. Clarke, Isaac Asimov, Jules Verne, Robert Heinlein, and George Lucas.

Prophets of Science Fiction received mixed reviews. The concept of intercutting scientific research and biography was criticized for emphasizing exaggeration over substantive content. Just some of the far-fetched links included bringing together Mary Shelley's *Frankenstein* with heart transplants, supercomputers, and DNA. In the opening, Scott as narrator intones a lofty speech of prophecy and accomplishment, then is shown at a table writing in a book.

Ridley Scott's frequent tennis playing wore him down to the point that he needed knee-replacement surgery. "I had bone on bone for the last ten years." Scott's stiff upper lip guided his judgment as he continued to play almost every day. "It hurts a bit, you take ibuprofen. You've got to have a ball to pursue. You must."[8] He didn't take the recovery period well, cursing his doctor to Steve "Frosty" Weintraub of *Collider*. "He said two and a half [weeks]—he's a liar. It's about—this is now the seventh week—sixth week." He described the surgical procedure in graphic terms, making it seem most unmedical, although it certainly was. He concluded that his tennis playing was over. "And tennis is great, but it's disastrous for your knees. The hard courts, you see? So I don't think I'm gonna go back to—I don't wanna do this again."[9]

21

PREQUEL?

Prometheus

We tell enough but not too much.

Ridley Scott

After a number of sequels in the *Alien* saga were released, Ridley Scott, who had not been involved with the franchise for many years, decided in 2002 to develop a prequel to the original *Alien*. Scott was interested in exploring the origins of the *Alien* antagonists as well as the Space Jockey, the extraterrestrial who appears briefly in *Alien* as the dead pilot of a derelict spacecraft.

"I always wondered when they did 2, 3, and 4 why they hadn't touched upon that. . . . Whatever happened to the space station and the pioneers that were on it? That was all logical at the time, and yet they missed one of the biggest questions of all which is: who's the big guy? Who's flying the ship, basically? And where were they going? And with what? Why that cargo? There's all kind of questions," Scott told *Empire* magazine.[1] "I'm really intrigued by those eternal questions of creation and belief and faith. I don't care who you are, it's what we all think about. It's in the back of all our minds," Scott said in an interview with *Esquire*.[2] Originally on *Alien* the studio did not want the Space Jockey in the film for budgetary reasons, but Scott was able to convince them.

In 2009 Ridley Scott once again showed specific interest in a prequel to his 1979 film. Fox announced the project was a go, calling it an untitled prequel to *Alien*. Development came to a halt in June 2009 when Fox argued with Ridley Scott (who would be the producer) about his choice of Carl Erik Rinsch as director. Rinsch was a former television commercial director who had been part of the RSA team. To this point he had directed only short films (in 2013 he directed the feature *47 Ronin*). Fox wanted Ridley Scott to direct the film, and by July Scott was contracted to direct. A prequel script was written by Jon Spaihts, whose task was to engage in the mysteries from *Alien* like the Space Jockey, all of which he thought were extraterrestrial in nature. To get the viewer to care about all this, he developed a path from the alien mysteries to the past and future of humankind. He found it hard to write some of the visual concepts Scott had created into script form. "I would go and write my draft, and then Ridley and I would sit for weeks, wrestling the story into shape," reported Spaihts to the *Hollywood Reporter* in May 2012. "He has a fascination with uglier forms of parasitism, dark examples of anatomy from subterranean creatures with staring eyes and jaws." Scott revealed his dark interest in parasitic creatures in *Alien* and his fascination with the subhuman forms created by artist H. R. Giger. A man who reveres beauty in paintings and movies, Scott has a dark place, his "black dog" mentality. Many of the extreme distortions of human life seem to come from the artist Francis Bacon, and the art of William Blake also appears to open the door to the imagery Scott was looking for in creating *Prometheus.*

In June 2010 Scott announced that the script was complete and preproduction would begin. The film was to start shooting in January 2011. Fox pushed to develop the project into an original work, so by July, Damon Lindelof was brought onto the project to rewrite Spaihts's script. Scott had called Lindelof about a top-secret project and asked him to read a screenplay that would be hand-delivered to his home in Studio City. When the writer received the script it had no cover and no title, but reading it he quickly realized it was a prequel to the legendary *Alien,* of which he was a massive fan. Later Scott took Lindelof to a building opposite Scott's Los Angeles offices: "Ridley walked me up a stairwell," Lindelof told the *Hollywood Reporter,* "and there was a great big metallic vault door. It was a foot thick with some kind of locking apparatus, and he opened it carefully." Once inside he saw people working diligently. "He introduced me to production designer Arthur Max and four twenty-year olds sitting at computers designing stuff. . . . All around the walls was conceptual art work. I got to step behind the curtain."[3]

In October 2010 the screenplay, rewritten by Lindelof, was officially submitted to Fox. Scott asked for a $250 million budget. He also specified that he wanted the film to be aimed at an adult audience, not children. Fox said no to the money and wanted a lower age rating to broaden the pool of potential viewers.

In December 2010 journalists learned that the film, previously called *Prometheus,* would now be called *Paradise* after Milton's blank-verse epic poem *Paradise Lost,* originally published in ten volumes in 1667. The poem is about Adam and Eve's expulsion from the Garden of Eden. Scott was rather concerned that this title would reveal too much information about his film. It was Fox CEO Tom Rothman who put forth the title *Prometheus,* after the Greek mythological figure, and this was the confirmed title in January 2011.

In a statement concerning *Prometheus* and *Alien,* Ridley Scott proclaimed that by the final act the audience would recognize the DNA of *Alien* but not of any of the other films in the franchise. He made it clear that *Alien* was indeed the starting point for this current project, although the creative process would bring mythological influences into the universe of the new work. Scott and his production team started a campaign to distance *Prometheus* from *Alien.* They were also vague about the connections, believing this would build worldwide audience curiosity for *Prometheus.*

Scott stressed that the ideas in the film would be on a grand scale. He wanted the film to pose big ideas such as how the human race began; the implication was that aliens were part of the creation of humankind. To separate the film even further from *Alien,* the character of Elizabeth Shaw, to be played by Noomi Rapace, would be differentiated from Ripley, played by Sigourney Weaver in the *Alien* films.

Many factors went into the selection of Noomi Rapace, the principal one her stunning performance in *The Girl with the Dragon Tattoo* in the Swedish production. In *Prometheus* she is luminous, with porcelain skin, futuristic looks, and a strong but vulnerable presence.

Rapace had a strong collaborative relationship with Scott, as she told Sean O'Connell of Cinemablend.com:

> He loves actors. I remember that I said to him, "I don't want to be this perfect action heroine, I don't want make up. I don't want to look beautiful and sexy and all of those stupid things. I want it to be real. . . ." I think that's the problem with many big action movies. The women get caught up trying to look good. . . . That becomes their main purpose. . . . He was like "No, absolutely not, no makeup, no mascara, more sweat!" And I love him for that. And he is so precise with the details. . . . He's so observant. Sometimes I wonder how his brain works. How can he be looking at seven monitors with seven cameras going and still care about that blood on my cheekbone?

Rapace also talked about Ridley Scott's vision for a film and his collaborative spirit. "I think what is so fantastic with Ridley is that he is the master of finding and building new worlds. And he knows exactly what he wants. . . . He wants our opinions. He has asked many times, 'What do you think, Noomi? How would you do this?' And I had a lot of ideas and things I wanted to try. I actually had a few scenes that I wanted to add. He thought about it, and came back and said, 'Brilliant. You know what? I think you're right. We need that.'"[4]

Michael Fassbender as David, an android that monitors the flight and mission, is convincing as a machine because he brings human vulnerability to the role. Swedish great Max Von Sydow was originally cast to play Peter Weyland, the billionaire founder of Weyland Corp. supporting the initiative who has a God complex, but the decision was made to hire Guy Pearce so that he could play Weyland both young and old. His performance is mesmerizing and maniacal at times. Charlize Theron plays a Weyland employee who oversees the space project. The stunningly beautiful model-turned-actress seems to be here strictly for her perfect looks, as she gives a relatively wooden one-note performance. Idris Elba plays Janek, the captain of the *Prometheus*—his strong persona and specific actions are centered when the ship is mired in confusion.

Preproduction on *Prometheus* began on April 2010. Scott was able to convince Fox to spend millions of dollars to employ scientists and conceptual artists to create a vision of the late twenty-first century.

Scott demanded the highest degree of secrecy concerning the film's story. The cast members could read the script only under tight supervision and only in the film's production office. They were all required to sign agreements that they wouldn't talk about the script. One actor, who was outside the United States, got the script from a courier who stood guard while he read the script. Scott took precautions to prevent the script from leaking to the digital, broadcast, and print media. He thought that if the public found out about the story it would spoil the experience. Also, there was the possibility that the original screenplay would get into hands of other filmmakers, who could crib it and come out with a competitive film.

As always, Scott storyboarded the entire film. In the car assigned to drive him to the studio he had a drawing setup and a fax machine. During the daily forty-five minute ride, he created Ridleygrams that shaped the entire film in detail. Scott's extensive experience as a camera operator gave him the gift of "seeing" the entire film. He just had to draw what he "saw." The next step was to begin editing from the images on the boards. Scott has a great gift of memory and is able to storyboard a location he saw three months before.

As Scott got more deeply entrenched in the material, he involved others in his vision. He conferred with Arthur Max and top digital artists, who drew for months while the screenplay was being polished and the budgeting process was developing. For Scott the drawings were like photographs that documented the design process as it evolved.

For the *Prometheus* spaceship Arthur Max built a two-level structure. A wraparound windscreen was created for the front of the ship. The garage for the ship was built on the back lot at Pinewood. The vehicles held inside were constructed in eleven weeks and were designed to look futuristic and able to travel on treacherous terrain. The alien world contained a large pyramid structure. The interior was connected by chambers, corridors, and tunnels. The structure was so large that some members of the film crew got lost in it. In postproduction the pyramid was increased in size via CGI. The chamber where the humanoid head statue is found was created to look like the interior of a cathedral. The murals inside were created by H. R. Giger, who was an influential creator in *Alien* and all its sequels.

The descent to the alien moon was created by visual effects art director Steven Messing, who referenced NASA imagery and vortex cloud structures. NASA also provided concepts for what the alien worlds would look like. Aerial photos of locations in Iceland and Wadi Rum were shot by visual effects supervisor Richard Stammers and his team. Other references include the Martian mountain Olympus Mons and other large mountain structures.

The alien creatures were created by Neal Scanlan and Conor O'Sullivan. Carlos Huante was a creature designer on the film. Huante referenced Giger, national monuments, large sculptures, and the Crazy Horse Memorial statue. In designing the Engineers, Scott and Huante referenced William Blake, J. M. W. Turner, and classical sculptures. Scott wanted the Engineers to look like Greco-Roman gods. He asked designer Neville Page to reference the Statue of Liberty, Michelangelo's *David,* and Elvis Presley.

The Humanoid Engineers, which stood eight feet tall, were achieved by using body prosthetics. The snakelike alien called the Hammerpede was created with a blend of CGI and a practical puppet whose wires were later digitally removed. For a decapitation scene, the visual effects artists digitally animated the creature and put in the spontaneous growth of a replacement head. Ridley Scott personally controlled the wires. He deliberately did not tell actress Kate Dickie, who played Ford, what was going to happen in the scene, so her reaction of screaming at the top of her voice was real. Part of the inspiration for the design came from studying sea creatures that have visible arteries and other internal parts.

To realize Shaw's tentacle offspring called Trilobite, the early designs were inspired by an octopus or squid. Designer Neville Page took this concept and made the creature into an embryo with tentacles that would gradually split, creating new ones. This was a practical creature, an animatronic that was remote controlled. It was covered in a silicone skin.

An important scene involving a large 3D hologram star map called the Orrery was inspired by the 1776 Joseph Wright painting *A Philosopher Lecturing on the Orrery* in which a scientist shows a mechanical planetarium by candlelight. The scene is reported to have been shot to a playback of Pink Floyd's landmark "Dark Side of the Moon."

Although science fiction films historically rely heavily on computer-generated imaging, Scott, who has long disliked the use of a green screen, complaining that it takes up too much time and therefore is too expensive, built most things rather than have a computer realize it.

Scott and his designers fashioned an innovative helmet for the space suits of 2083. The interior of the helmets had nine working video screens, internal lighting, and an air supply delivered by two fans and battery packs concealed within a backpack. The exterior of the helmet sported a working light source and high-definition video cameras with a transmitter and recorder.

Marc Streitenfeld wrote the music backward on the sheet music and the orchestra played the music backward; once recorded, it was digitally flipped. The effect produced an ethereal atmospheric sound.

Scott promised 20th Century Fox he would deliver a PG-13 version if the studio requested it. During the filming the director was careful to shoot both R-rated material and PG-13 material. If necessary, the more adult material could be cut and replaced by the PG-13 scenes. Scott proceeded to create the most explicit cut of the film he could. The issue was not so much blood and violence but complex ideas. Tom Rothman of Fox stated he would not force Scott to cut the film to avoid an R rating. On May 7, 2012, *Prometheus* did receive an R from the ratings board, and Fox announced the film would be released as an R without any cuts. Apparently it was one scene that prompted the harder rating of R, the one in which Shaw surgically removes her alien offspring. The scene would have had to be deleted in its entirety to earn a PG-13 rating. On his own Scott did shorten a scene of Shaw wounding an Engineer.

Prometheus received its fair share of good reviews. The majority of critics were taken with the visuals but disappointed by the script and the story, which they felt didn't come together. The running total gross for *Prometheus* is an estimated $404 million worldwide and $126 million in the US.

Scott announced at the March 17, 2012, WonderCon convention that many of the unanswered questions presented by *Prometheus* would be answered in a sequel. There are probably only a few people who understand what *Prometheus* is about, and Lindelof isn't one of them. Those who claim they do totally understand the film have viewed it twice or more—a necessary practice for a film with ambitions as extensive as *Prometheus*'s. The big questions posed, such as "Where do we come from?" are so very big that the mind of the viewer can't grasp them; there are few answers here. Although a box office success, *Prometheus* largely fails to answer any of the questions it raises. Instead it succeeds in confusing many viewers. Ridley Scott's first science fiction film in decades was hotly anticipated. People trusted him, but many left the theater scratching their heads. The 3D is spectacular but the content is not—what is the narrative about? Unfortunately, *Prometheus* is not a great film like *Alien* and *Blade Runner*—it leaves many wanting more, forced to wait for the sequel for answers to the questions it poses.

Damon Lindelof, one of those responsible for the confusion in *Prometheus,* has announced that due to other commitments, he will not be writing or contributing to *Prometheus 2,* but there are conflicting reports. Scott has said the second film most likely will move even further away from the beginning of the original *Alien.*

In 2012 Ridley Scott shot a commercial for singer/performance artist Lady Gaga for her perfume, Fame. The spot clearly has the Ridley Scott touch while capturing the spirit of Lady Gaga. Its influences seem to be a combination of *Alien* and Scott's *1984* commercial. The collaboration between director and performer resulted in a seamless visual commercial that represents the avant-garde sexuality of the artist and the futuristic vision of the filmmaker.

Sadly, on October 9, 2012, Ridley Scott experienced the loss of one of his collaborators, Harris Savides, the director of photography on *American Gangster* and many outstanding films. He died of brain cancer at age fifty-five.

22

AT LAW
The Counselor

This is a film about people who get involved in something they should have stayed out of.

Cormac McCarthy

The Counselor is Cormac McCarthy's first original screenplay. McCarthy is considered a modern-day William Faulkner by many in the literary community. He is the author of *Sutree, Blood Meridian, The Crossing,* and other works. Three of his novels were adapted into motion pictures: *All the Pretty Horses* (Billy Bob Thornton, 2000), *No Country for Old Men* (the Coen Brothers, 2007), which was heavily nominated for Academy Awards and won four, including the Oscar for Best Motion Picture, and *The Road* (John Hillcoat, 2009).

On January 18, 2012, it was revealed that Cormac McCarthy had sold his first spec script to Nick Wechsler, Paula Mae Schwartz, and Steve Schwartz, who had produced the screen adaptation of McCarthy's novel *The Road*. Ridley Scott was attracted to Cormac McCarthy's work. For some time he had been interested in making a movie of *Blood Meridian*. He talked about the difficulties involved to Helen O'Hara of *Empire* online in November 2008:

> I think it's a very tricky one, and maybe it's something that should be left as a novel. If you're going to do *Blood Meridian* you've got to go the whole nine yards into the bloodbath, and there's no answer to the bloodbath, that's part of the story, just the way it is and the way it was. When you start to scalp Mexican wedding parties, that'll draw the line. One scalp of coarse black hair is pretty well either Mexican or Indian, and there was no difference to the scalp hunters in Arizona at the time who didn't draw the line.[1]

The level of violence in a movie can be a personal perception of what is acceptable and what isn't, what is necessary to a story and what is not. Scott talks about the scalping in *Blood Meridian* as over the line for him, yet in *The Counselor* he puts in McCarthy's ultra-violent scene of a man having his head cut off with a deadly bolo device. Scott very much wanted to work with McCarthy, whom he considered one of the greatest living novelists; that perhaps convinced him to include a scene comparably violent to the one he found unacceptable in *Blood Meridian*.

The opportunity to collaborate with McCarthy came suddenly. "Somebody called me and they said, 'There's a script coming from Cormac McCarthy,' and I said 'Who? Cormac McCarthy! Wow!'" Scott explains in an interview on YouTube.

> I took it very seriously. I stopped everything that morning and read. It was in the form of a novella, not a film script. It read like a book. It took me about an hour and a half to read. . . . It makes you feel uncomfortable, but you have to read on. . . . I think it was a Friday. . . . So I flew to Albuquerque. I met him on a Monday and by Monday afternoon we had shaken on it—it was that simple—we just shook on it and that was the deal. . . . With Cormac it's all about tone, he's a master dramatic engine.[2]

The Counselor is the story of an unnamed lawyer, played by Michael Fassbender, who is in over his head when he gets involved in drug trafficking. The rest of the impressive cast includes Brad Pitt (Westray), Javier Bardem (Reiner), Cameron Diaz (Malkina), Penélope Cruz (Laura), Rosie Perez (Ruth), Bruno Ganz (diamond dealer), and Rubén Blades (Jefe). Production designer Arthur Max has a cameo as a cartel man.

Principal photography was launched on July 27, 2012, in London. On August 19, 2012, while Ridley Scott was in his home in France's Luberon Valley, he received a phone call from Tony Scott's wife Donna, who was in California. Panicked and frightened, she said Tony was missing. That began what Ridley Scott has called "the worst weekend of my life."[3] Tragically, at around 12:30 in the afternoon on August 19, Tony Scott, sixty-eight, committed suicide in San Pedro, Los Angeles, by jumping off the Vincent Thomas Bridge. He left two notes, one in the car he'd driven to the bridge and the other at his office. Officials later stated that neither note mentioned any reason why he decided to take his life. The coroner's report revealed that Tony Scott did not have any serious underlying medical conditions and was not suffering from inoperable brain cancer, as had been reported by the ABC news organization. The ABC report was also denied by his wife. Some antidepressants and a sleep aid were found in Scott's system but at low amounts, considered a therapeutic level.

Production on *The Counselor* was halted as soon as Ridley Scott heard the news. Shooting was canceled for a week as he flew to Los Angeles to be with Tony's family. Donna Wilson, who met Tony Scott on his film *Days of Thunder*, was his third wife. Their twin sons, Frank and Max, were born in 2000.

In both Quentin Tarantino's *Django Unchained* (2012) and *The Counselor*, there are on-screen tributes to Tony Scott. In the past Tarantino has given Tony Scott a special thanks credit. Tarantino called *Days of Thunder* (1990), a film he loves, "a Sergio Leone race-car movie" in Jeff Dawson's book *Quentin Tarantino: The Cinema of Cool*. Tony Scott directed *True Romance* (1993) with a script by Tarantino. Tony Scott had asked Tarantino for something of his to read, and the latter sent him *True Romance*. Tony liked the script and told Tarantino he wished "there was something we could do about it." Tarantino immediately said, "I want *you* to do it." "I had met Tony through a mutual friend and I was a big fan of Tony's *Revenge* (1990)," Tarantino said. "I think along with *Revenge* this [*True Romance*] is his best movie."[4] Tarantino also did a polish on dialogue for the script to *Crimson Tide*, which Tony Scott directed in 1995.

Nicole Kidman, who acted in *Days of Thunder*, greatly admired Tony Scott. As she told Pamela McClintock of the *Hollywood Reporter*:

Tony was a visionary. Somehow he was able to translate story and character into visceral consuming images and sounds. There was a musicality to everything he did; an intensity, but also an elegance. And yet for all his talent and innovation there was nothing pretentious about Tony or his movies—he had an instant connection with an audience, he spoke their language. I feel so lucky to have been directed by him. As an actor, it's a rare thing to feel such trust and confidence, to know you are a part of something special. Tony was a master filmmaker, but he was also a gentle spirit, someone whose sensitivity and generosity could be obscured by the scope of his work. He was a great supporter of other artists. Filmmakers loved working with him as I recently found on a film called *Stoker* (2013), which Tony produced. His appreciation for and curiosity about making movies permeated everything he did. I think it is that side of Tony that made him so great. The passion of his work and personality; the emotion within it, was consistent. Tony's loss is a complete shock. I feel blessed to have known him. I am deeply sad that he is gone.[5]

In 1985 Don Simpson and Jerry Bruckheimer, both among the minority of admirers of Tony Scott's first film *The Hunger,* asked Tony Scott to direct *Top Gun* (1986), which raked in $176 million in the US alone. Tony Scott's career was launched. He became associated with entertaining action films that audiences wanted to see, such as *Days of Thunder; Crimson Tide* (1995), which grossed $157 million worldwide; *Man on Fire* (2004), grossing $106 million worldwide and starring Denzel Washington, with whom Tony Scott collaborated on five films; *Déjà Vu* (2006), which brought in $175 million worldwide; *The Taking of Pelham 123* (2009), which grossed $149 million worldwide; and *Unstoppable* (2010), which made $169 million at the world-wide box office. In the domestic market alone, Tony Scott's movies have earned more than $1 billion.

Tony Scott's directorial style has been called "hyper-kinetic." Historically, action films move quickly, but the editing in a Tony Scott film is distinctive for its high-octane energy. Working long and hard in commercials like his brother Ridley, Tony adapted the rapid pace of a thirty-second spot and applied it to entertaining and engrossing picture and sound stories that audiences responded to in big numbers.

Tony Scott's films were known for their high testosterone levels, and he lived that life himself. He collected Harleys and Ferraris and loved to drive them. He went on long runs every day and slept only three hours a night. He climbed three-thousand-foot mountains and breakfasted on black coffee and cigars. His invariable lunch was a tuna fish sandwich.

A generous man, Tony Scott shared his great success with those who contributed to his films, showering them with expensive gifts like Il Bisonte luggage or overflowing bouquets of flowers. He had Churchill cigars shipped to him from London and delighted in sharing them with colleagues. He always wore his faded pink baseball cap, a pink T-shirt, and pink shorts with mountain boots. On the last day of shooting on one of his pictures, his loyal crew jokingly dressed up in the same outfit.

In an interview with Ariel Leve of the *Sunday Times* magazine, Tony Scott defined what he saw as the differences between his films and those of his brother's. "Ridley makes films for posterity. His films will be around for a long time. I think my films are more rock 'n' roll. I experiment more. Rid was always very classical, whether it was paintings or film."[6]

The Scott brothers were totally united as brothers, film directors, and in co-running RSA. "I will sometimes have a cut of the film and will show it to him saying, what do you think?" Ridley explained to the *Daily Beast*. "And I'll immediately get 36 pages of notes. And he never asks *me* to do that for him."[7]

Ridley Scott was a mentor to his younger brother; they were as close as can be and savored their relationship. Throughout their lives they spoke to each other either on the phone or in person at least once a day.

For over two years Ridley Scott was silent in public and to the media about the tragic loss of his brother. All over the world, fans of the Scott brothers mourned and wondered in disbelief why this vibrant man who made exciting and thrilling films had taken his own life. As Ridley Scott grieved in silence, one could only imagine the pain he endured, losing someone with whom he was inseparable, so close and so dear to him.

For the November 25, 2014, edition of the venerable *Variety*, Scott sat down with journalist Scott Foundas and publicly talked about the tragedy for the very first time. Tony Scott had been in a long struggle with cancer. The family chose to keep the illness private while he was enduring treatment and after his death. Tony was his second brother to die of cancer, older brother Frank having died in 1980 at age forty-five of skin cancer. Nonetheless, Ridley Scott called his brother's suicide "inexplicable." "Tony had been very unwell, actually, and that's the moment I realized I had to get very close to him again, though we were always close. I miss a friend. I'd go to him even when he was doing recovery, and I'd say, 'F—— the chemo, have a vodka martini,' and he and I would go out."[8]

The Counselor, the first episode of *Coma,* the first episode of season 4 of *The Good Wife,* and *Exodus: Gods and Kings* are all dedicated to Tony Scott.

Production on *The Counselor* resumed as a grief-stricken Ridley Scott returned to London on September 3.

Ridley Scott has worked closely with most screenwriters, often into the shooting phase—but no screenwriter as prestigious as Cormac McCarthy. Scott thought the author would be on set for about a week, but McCarthy remained for the entire shoot. Scott found the writer extremely bright and listened to his opinions. At times Ridley Scott found his presence irritating, but the final results of the film were pleasing to both men, and that made it worth it.

Penélope Cruz spoke on YouTube about working with Ridley Scott:

> I knew him before because I'm friends with his wife and we hung
> out together a few times before and we talked about making other
> projects together, but it didn't happen. With this one I was so
> excited to finally work with him and I admire him so much. He's
> done some masterpieces and it's really great to see him get there in
> the morning and set up a shot with four or five cameras. It's like he
> has 100 eyes everywhere. He gets into the room and it's really
> beautiful to see him work. I see him like a choreographer in a way.
> It's very impressive to see.[9]

Although the film opens with a sex scene between the Counselor and
Laura and there is the infamous sex-with-a-car sequence featuring Malkina,
both are eclipsed by a highly erotic scene staged at a pool with Laura and
Malkina lying on lounges with white towels loosely draped around their
naked bodies. Throughout the film many of the characters talk about sex; it is
usually connected to power, drugs, greed, and death.

The car sex scene is more silly than erotic, although it is intended to stimulate Reiner, who is watching Malkina's sexual machinations from inside the
car. Malkina is stretched out undulating on top of the outside windshield.
Scott uses high angles to exploit the situation and probably to avoid an NC-17
rating. Also it appears that a female double was used; her figure doesn't quite
match Cameron Diaz's body.

Scott talked to Lynn Barber of the *Guardian* about the rare depiction of
nudity or sex in his films. "I find sex scenes actually, embarrassing. I think it's
possibly a bit prudish. I was brought up at a time where parents didn't talk
about it, they just assumed you'd find out. . . . When I watch sex scenes in
films, it's like ho-hum or it's flapping curtains and gauzy pictures, which is
kind of boring."[10]

The Counselor does not fit easily into Ridley Scott's oeuvre. It is darker in
content and deals with sex and gratuitous violence on a subterranean level.
Scott and McCarthy have balanced the two female characters. Malkina is
stunning, and Laura is very beautiful and sweet, possessing a sort of innocence. In Malkina Scott presents a major female character who is strong but
deeply evil.

A fine, intelligent, and perceptive actor, Javier Bardem understood
McCarthy's intentions in the work: "What the movie talks about . . . is the

statement of this world we're living in. . . . When we are being naïve and we don't want to see things that blind us or [are] going to create a lot of pain and harm too many people. So that . . . the lack of glamour in the violence made me feel that was something I wanted to say in a movie," the actor said on YouTube.[11]

There are many fine performances in *The Counselor,* but Javier Bardem practically steals the picture with his acting skills, his outrageous wardrobe (provided by Versace), and his spiky haircut that looks like the one sported by Brian Grazer.

Cameron Diaz, who gives a chilling performance, understood McCarthy's intent and Scott's purpose. She felt they were in the darkest world, revealing what people are truly capable of doing to each other. Because of the characters' actions they will have to pay a dear price. So the clear message is to be careful what you do.

Rubén Blades plays Jefe. He talks to the Counselor only by phone. If it were in person the chieftain would have killed the Counselor on the spot, as happened with all the others caught in the cartel web. Jefe is the essence of McCarthy's literary voice. He speaks in phrases that are poetic statements from a wise person. This is not the "advice" the Counselor is expecting, but it is clear that he is doomed and will be killed in a matter of time. Cormac McCarthy sees the Counselor as a classic tragic figure, a good person who decides once to go the wrong way and that is enough.

McCarthy's film script has all the characteristics of this legendary American author's books—his dark view of humanity and a deep investment in exploring the base nature of the species, reminding us how relentlessly greedy and ultra-violent we are. Most of the sparse dialogue is good, but some of it falls flat or seems out of date.

All the characters in the cast are basically on one note, without real human complexity. The major flaw of *The Counselor* is an unclear understanding of who the Counselor really is, what is his back history before the film begins. Michael Fassbender, a fine actor, is unable to totally communicate his character to the audience.

The most violent scene in a film filled with violence is the murder of the Brad Pitt character, Westray. While walking down the street in London, he is brutally slaughtered when an assailant runs up behind him and wraps a bolo-like device around his neck; it spins and spins as blood pours out of his neck. He can't get it off, and he dies. The scene is relentless, providing no real cutaways—we watch this man die a horrible and very bloody death. It is the kind of scene that is difficult to look at, and some may turn their heads until it's over.

There is a moment of off-screen violence that is worse than any on-screen scene because one's imagination is more vivid than a movie image. It is revealed earlier in the movie that snuff films are part of the cartel culture; Westray tells the Counselor about them. When Laura is abducted, she is wearing a bright red dress signifying blood. The audience is meant to realize she will meet a horrendous end. Toward the movie's conclusion, the Counselor is hiding out in a grubby room when he receives a package from a small boy. When he opens it he finds a DVD in a plain jewel case. He turns the disc over and the word "HOLA!" is written on it. It is a snuff film. Now we know for sure what has happened to his beloved Laura.

The Counselor is still alive when the movie ends. It is to be assumed that the cartel is saving him for last and probably has planned his death to be the most excruciating of all. It's a good choice for McCarthy and Scott not to show his inevitable demise on screen.

The Counselor is rated R, not NC-17. Perhaps it should have received the NC-17 strictly because of the Westray murder scene. The Counselor received largely negative reviews. Audiences were not interested in viewing Ridley Scott's latest film. The budget was an estimated $25 million. Opening weekend in the States earned a paltry $7.8 million. The number one movie in the country at the time was *Jackass Presents: Bad Grandpa*, which pulled in $32 million. American gross to date is only $17 million, with worldwide sales at $36 million.

Among a long list of very poor reviews there was a positive viewpoint expressed by the chief film critic of the well-respected, industry-trusted *Variety*. Scott Foundas actually liked the film:

> *The Counselor* is not *Blade Runner,* but it is bold and thrilling in ways
> that mainstream American movies rarely are, and its rejection
> suggests what little appetite there is for real daring at the multiplex
> nowadays. . . . *The Counselor* is a ravishing object—a triumph of
> mood and style as an expression of content, and dialogue that finds a
> kind of apocalyptic comedy in this charnel-house existence. . . . *The
> Counselor* is one of the best films Ridley Scott has made in a career
> that is not often enough credited for just how remarkable it has been.[12]

When asked on YouTube what he would like audiences to understand about *The Counselor,* Scott stated, "Not a life-long lesson. I hope they're entertained.

I hope they're stressed. I hope they've been aggressed because that's what it is—it's a very challenging film."[13]

In 2013 *Springsteen and I* was produced by Ridley Scott and others. The documentary of the iconic rocker was created using an approach similar to Scott's unconventional *Life in a Day.* Fans of Springsteen all over the world were asked to make their own short film about the Boss and what he meant to them. Black Dog Films and Scott Free London were behind the production.

During 2013 Jake Scott made an endearing and well-received commercial for Budweiser that telecast during the Super Bowl; it involved a baby Clydesdale and its trainer. More traditional than the other commercials aired that day, it won the hearts of viewers. Like his father, Jake referenced classic movies for his inspiration: Robert Bresson's *Au Hasard Baltazar* (1966) and *White Mane* (1953) by Albert Lamorissel.

The Vatican was the first television pilot directed by Ridley Scott. Kyle Chandler starred in the show, a thriller about the machinations and politics in the Vatican. The showrunner and writer was Paul Attanasio. The original idea came from Sony Pictures co-chairman Amy Pascal. After seeing the pilot, which aired in 2013, Attanasio left the project. Reshoots were ordered but were found problematic. David Zucker was a co–executive producer. Although there were high expectations, the show never made it to the air.

23

NOT OTTO PREMINGER'S
EXODUS

Exodus: Gods and Kings

> And I will take you to me for a people, and I will be to you a God: and ye shall know that I am the LORD your God, which bringeth you out from under the burdens of the Egyptians.
>
> *Exodus 6:7*

Throughout his life Ridley Scott had identified himself as an atheist, but after directing his next motion picture, *Exodus: Gods and Kings,* he said he preferred the designation agnostic, a term that leaves the door open for the possible existence of God. He relates to the film's rendition of Moses as a reluctant hero, a nonbeliever who slowly begins to accept his destiny. Scott tries to put Moses in a historical context, a man who sees God in front of a burning bush, but the movie clichés of thunderous clouds and lightning are avoided. "If you believe, you believe; if you're faithful, you're faithful. I don't care what your religion is. The same if you're agnostic. That should be accepted too," he told *Variety's* Scott Foundas. Scott admitted to knowing very little about the Old Testament of the Bible, only what he learned in Sunday school as a boy.

Exodus: *Gods and Kings* is the director's take on Moses and the book of Exodus. Originally, the project was named *Exodus,* causing confusion about whether it was a remake of the 1960 Otto Preminger epic production of the same title concerning the founding of the modern state of Israel. Finally, to dispel confusion it was retitled *Exodus: Gods and Kings.*

Scott pledged that *Exodus: Gods and Kings* would not be a Hollywood epic and that it would avoid the conventions of earlier religious epics. The film was based in part on the story of how the Israelites, numbering up to four hundred thousand, leave Egypt, where they have been enslaved for hundreds of years. They are led by Moses through the wilderness to Mount Sinai, where they are offered Canaan, the Promised Land, in return for their faithfulness.

At the beginning of production, on March 15, 2013, Scott made it known he wanted the talented Christian Bale as Moses, and Joel Edgerton, the Australian actor who had appeared in *The Great Gatsby* (2013) and *Zero Dark Thirty* (2012), was cast to play Ramses, the powerful third pharaoh of the Nineteenth Dynasty of Egypt. Aaron Paul of TV's *Breaking Bad* fame was hired to play Joshua, who assisted Moses and led the Israelite tribe after his death.

The most well-known screen Moses was Charlton Heston, whose portrayal featured heroism and action in Cecil B. DeMille's *The Ten Commandments* (1956), in which Yul Brynner played a one-dimensional, vindictive Ramses. In *Exodus: Gods and Kings,* Moses, Ramses, and the other characters are examined in more psychological and emotional complexity.

The large scope of *Exodus: Gods and Kings* visualizes throngs of people, so three to four thousand extras were cast in Spain in Almeira and Pechina, one to two thousand in Quteventura, and another one to two thousand in Fueteventura.

Scott's decision to cast the lead roles with white European and Australian actors garnered a fervent outcry from critics and religious groups. His response was that it was a practical business decision. It would be hard if not impossible to get a big-budget film that is relying on tax rebates financed if he cast the film in a racially correct manner for the time and place. His approach is part of a long tradition of using either big-name actors or those audiences are familiar with.

Christian Bale used the word *kinetic* to describe his director to Scott Foundas, who was writing a cover piece for the November 25, 2014, issue of *Variety.* At the advanced age of seventy-five, Ridley Scott was still perceived by those decades younger as fueled by an energy that kept him in constant motion. "I'm absolutely sure he springs out of bed at ten times the speed that I do," the forty-year-old Bale said.

The *Exodus* project was put into motion when Peter Chernin, past head of 20th Century Fox, sent Ridley Scott a script by Adam Cooper and Bill Collage for what became *Exodus: Gods and Kings.* Scott's first reaction was that he would never do the film because of his ambivalent feelings about God and religion, but out of respect for Chernin he read the script and was surprised and intrigued by the complexity of Moses's character. As he often does with a first draft, Scott brought in another writer to shape the story. He was an admirer of *The Constant Gardener,* written by Jeffrey Caine, so when Scott learned the writer was deeply versed in Moses's journey, he brought him on. Caine's draft extracted the importance of Moses to Jews, Muslims, and Christians alike. When Scott determined Caine had gone as far as he could in developing the script, he brought in a tried-and-true collaborator—Steve Zaillian. The screenwriter considered himself an atheist and felt strongly that he was not right for the project. Scott ultimately convinced Zaillian he was the right person for the necessary revision because he was a nonbeliever who would provide objectivity and clarity. Partly serious and partly joking, Scott told the writer, "Maybe you'll be an agnostic by the time you finish the screenwriting," as he related to the *San Francisco Examiner.*[1]

Scott's version of biblical events, such as the plagues of frogs, flies, boils, and locusts that invade Egypt and the parting of the Red Sea, are explained scientifically. What is presented as an act of God is when, during Passover, Hebrew children are saved when the doors of their houses are painted with the blood of lambs while Egyptian children die. "I couldn't honestly devise anything else. I have to deal with it. I have to believe it. I think it's the first time I let it go into what you can put under the heading of magic," Scott also told the *San Francisco Examiner.*

A radical choice was made to image God as a young boy who talks to Moses. Scott eschewed past presentations of God's deep and resonant voice coming from the sky as light beams shine through the clouds. He suggested to the writers the inclusion of a character named Malak, which is Hebrew for "angel" or "messenger," played by eleven-year-old British actor Isaac Andrews. Throughout the history of religious genre, filmmakers had to choose their own visual depiction. "Malak exudes innocence and purity, and the two qualities are extremely powerful," Scott told the *Hollywood Reporter.*[2] The boy appears repeatedly to Moses, who eventually realizes the child is speaking as God.

Although Ridley Scott continued to ridicule films past and present that begin with a text card or crawl to tell the audience what happened before the film and provide background, he used the device, which he flippantly refers to as "Irving the Explainer," to begin *Exodus.* Irving may represent a nerd who feels compelled to update the audience. Scott seems to be using Irving as a very intelligent person chosen for the task of getting viewers up to speed before the formal start of the movie.

Ridley Scott continued to practice what he calls "the school of everything," referenced in the Scott Foundas *Variety* profiles, a total vision of a film in which the director is completely involved with the moviemaking process.

In talking about his heroes Lean, Kubrick, and Welles, he said, "Everything was important, not just the script and the story and the actors, but everything on the screen was suited to the subject."[3]

The estimated budget of *Exodus: Gods and Kings* was $140 million, but it ballooned closer to $200 million before European tax credits. The epic format translated to a running time of two and a half hours, not unusual for a religious-themed film, and was photographed and presented in 3D. It was considered an event movie. It was shot in only seventy-four days. Scott shot with four cameras and did only two or three takes on a shot, constantly working himself and the cast and crew hard.

The most famous scene in *The Ten Commandments* is the parting of the Red Sea, which shocked and awed audience when the film was first released in the 1950s. In that movie the event is depicted as an act of God. Scott's rendition of the iconic sequence is to explain it as a massive tsunami caused by an underwater earthquake off the coast of Italy around 3000 BC, which has been evidenced historically.

Don Steinberg reported that the film's visual effects supervisor Peter Chiang said,

> Ridley wanted to convey the sense that everything could be natural phenomenon, like an eclipse or tsunami, not just someone waving a stick in the sea. More than 1,500 visual effects shots were created to digitally enhance the number of Hebrews and to make plagues of hail, locusts and frogs look authentic, but 400 real life frogs were used on the set. Thirty to forty real people were with Bale while crossing the Red Sea, everyone else was computer generated as well as a 180 foot wave, the horses and chariots. A total of 400,000 humans were depicted. For the hailstorm sequence the effects team built custom made thirty cannons that fired polymer balls that would bounce and shatter just like real ice balls. Distant hail was created by computer simulation. Of the many fires in the film, three were real, the rest digital.[4]

Justin Chang of *Variety* gave the film a good review, also discussing Scott's point of view as an agnostic, saying Scott turns

> his own skepticism into a potent source of moral and psychological conflict. . . . If this estimable account of how God delivered his

people out of Egypt feels like a movie for a decidedly secular age, its serious-minded, non-doctrinaire approach arguably gets far closer to penetrating the mystery of religious belief than a more reverent approach might have managed. . . . The final hour of *Exodus: Gods and Kings* is a sensationally entertaining yet beautifully modulated stream of visual wonders and terrors that at once honors and eclipses the showmanship of Cecil B. DeMille's 1956 masterpiece *The Ten Commandments* and makes it all but impossible to tear one's eyes from the screen. . . . A self-professed agnostic whose films have nonetheless betrayed a restless spiritual dimension, Scott seems to have accepted his distance from the material and worked with it, finding a point of identification with a hero who never stops questioning himself or the higher power that guides his every step. . . . Bale's Moses emerges a painfully flawed, embattled leader whose direct line to the Almighty turns out to be as much of a burden as it is a blessing.[5]

Veteran film critic Richard Corliss wrote a scathing negative review that insults the project with ridicule. The headline, "Don't Let Your People Go See *Exodus: Gods and Kings*," is just the beginning of the rebuke. "*Exodus* is a stolid mess, bleakly laughable without being an entertaining hoot like De Mille's camp classic. On the plus side there are some vividly depicted plagues—alligators turning the Nile red, locusts, hailstones, a toad torrent (the frog of war), boils for the soulless, helpless Egyptians—and, in the parting of the Red Sea, the snazziest 'enormous wall of water' since . . . well, since *Interstellar* last month. On the minus side is everything else."[6]

Christy Lemire wrote on the Roger Ebert website, "A numbing and soulless spectacle of 3-D, computer-generated imagery run amok, Ridley Scott's 'Exodus: Gods and Kings' presents an enduring tale by pummeling us over the head with it." One of her many criticisms is that Ridley Scott comes off impersonal behind this film and doesn't present a emotional point of view toward the characters and story. *Exodus: Gods and Kings* opened on December 12, 2014, in the United States. The box office take, according to Box Office Mojo, was $65,014,413.

In some parts of the world this film was banned. In Egypt it was seen as Zionist and often historically inaccurate. The United Arab Emirates banned the film because of mistakes they found concerning Islam and other religions. Kuwait was another place *Exodus: Gods and Kings* was banned.

Controversy began before the film was released with Scott's statement that the parting of the Red Sea was possibly caused by a tsunami. Equally controversial were statements by Christian Bale about Moses reported in the *Christian Post*. "I think the man was likely schizophrenic and was one of the most barbaric individuals I ever read about in my life." The casting of the four white actors (Bale, Edgerton, Sigourney Weaver, and Paul) irritated many who followed their Holy Bible. It made things worse when Ridley Scott told Scott Foundas for his *Variety* profile on the director that he couldn't have made the film without big-name stars: "I can't mount a film of this budget . . . and say that my lead actor is Mohammad so-and-so from such-and-such. . . . I'm just not going to get financed."

Aside from the long list of inaccuracies cited by religious communities, there were complaints that some scenes in the movie are entirely fictional. There were many calls for viewers to boycott the movie. In the end, the general consensus was that the film did not satisfy either religious or secular audiences.

Exodus: Gods and Kings features the dedication "For my Brother Tony Scott."

On March 29, 2015, the National Geographic channel aired *Killing Jesus*, based on the best-selling book written by the controversial conservative former talk-show host of *The O'Reilly Factor*, Bill O'Reilly, with collaborator Martin Dugard. Scott Free Productions was responsible for the program, and Ridley Scott was one of the producers. The show, like the book, focuses on the life of Jesus Christ and details the circumstances that led to his Crucifixion.

24

RED
The Martian

When we see the shadow on our images, are we seeing the time 11 minutes ago on Mars? Or are we seeing the time on Mars as observed from Earth now? It's like time travel problems in science fiction. When is now? When was then?

Bill Nye

In the 1990s, Andy Weir began writing science fiction, which he made available on his website. He received strong responses to his stories and developed an internet following. Weir came up with an idea for a long-form work set in the near future in which a NASA astronaut becomes stranded alone on Mars. He used Google to research orbital mechanics, conditions on Mars, and the history of manned spaceflights. As the installments moved forward, some of his followers suggested that Weir publish the complete story as a Kindle book. *The Martian* rose high on the Kindle charts. Next Weir sold the book to Crown Publishers, and it was published in 2011. It was a best seller. NASA admired the book, believing that it portrayed the organization in a good light and was accurate in its descriptions of NASA's plans to send a team to Mars. Weir was invited to the Johnson Space Center and the Jet Prolusion Lab.

In 2013 20th Century Fox optioned *The Martian*. Drew Goddard, a staff teleplay writer for *Buffy the Vampire Slayer, Angel, Lost, Alias,* and the feature film *The Cabin in the Woods,* read it and was highly enthusiastic. He began writing an adaptation and was slated to direct *The Martian* based on his own screenplay. Matt Damon signed to play Mark Watney, the astronaut/botanist stranded on Mars. The actor got along well with Goddard. Damon told the director he wanted *The Martian* to be a love letter to NASA. *The Martian* posed an intriguing acting challenge. For a sizeable portion of the film, Damon would be on-screen by himself; Damon was interested in the opportunity to experiment with this character's dilemma. The book was heavy on Watney's dialogue, offering many prospects for the actor to apply a broad range of emotions as he spoke lengthy stretches of voice-over. Damon had ample room in the stellar vehicle, so the character could move physically and relate to his environment. The Watney character has a keen sense of humor that he readily expresses even in his dire circumstances.

For a crew to reach the stranded astronaut on Mars would take four years. To stay alive Watney has to grow food in soil where nothing has been able to grow before. As the botanist considers and eventually solves the problem, Watney delivers lines destined for the annals of great movie one-liners—"I'm going to have to science the *shit* out of this" and "In your face, Neil Armstrong!"

While in preproduction, two other projects came Drew Goddard's way. One was *The Sinister Six,* a *Spiderman* spin-off, and the other a *Daredevil* series for Netflix. Goddard wanted to do these projects, but the studio was not willing to wait for him, so he left the director's chair for *The Martian.* Ultimately, *The Sinister Six* was canceled by Sony. Then Goddard dropped out of *Daredevil* for creative reasons, but by then it was too late for him to go back to *The Martian.*

To replace Goddard, the studio wanted a director who would be compatible with Matt Damon. Damon thought about worthy directors with whom he had collaborated—Terry Gilliam, Gus Van Sant, Steven Soderbergh—and even considered directing *The Martian* himself. Finally he decided to ask Ridley Scott.

When Ridley Scott read the script, he set aside what he was doing and committed to the project within four hours. Damon is a self-assured star. He and Scott admired each other and were a good match. Scott likes actors who know their job and are collaborative. When Scott and Damon finally met the conversation was short. Ridley Scott told Damon he liked the script a lot, and Damon concurred. Scott responded with something to the effect of "Well, why the fuck aren't we doing it, then?" Both men laughed. Negotiations were over and the deal was set. They would make the movie.

Scott saw the story as a tale of shipwreck. Moreover, what both he and Damon liked about *The Martian* novel and screenplay was the real science involved and the fact that NASA could be part of the project. Because the story took place in the near future, it was believable that a human crew could be sent to Mars to create a colony there.

Ridley Scott contacted NASA and secured complete cooperation. During production, Jim Green, NASA's director of planetary sciences, visited the set of *The Martian* and told Scott the production was capturing all the right details. For the agency the movie would be an opportunity to tell audiences what the space program might be like in 2030 or 2040.

Jessica Chastain represented another Ridley Scott strong woman. In her position as ship commander, she is smart, capable, vulnerable but strong, a natural leader. Scott rarely misses an opportunity to include a strong woman character in his films.

Damon enjoyed playing his solitary scenes. It was basically just him and Ridley Scott; they appreciated each other's company. Damon commented that even if they weren't making a movie, he would still like to hang out with Scott. A key challenge in the solo scenes was that Damon had long monologues. The first one he got perfect in one take. Two moving cameras were used for others. Damon performed a lot of voice-over. To thoroughly capture every expression and action of Damon's performance, Ridley Scott had up to fifty GoPro cameras all over the areas where Mark Watney was stranded. GoPro cameras are manufactured by an American technology company founded by Nick Woodman in 2002; they are small, light cameras, easy to position and reposition, that come with different lenses and the capability to shoot in various formats.

Ridley Scott still drew his own storyboards, and a voluminous book of Ridleygrams was an integral part of the preparation. Illustrators also made renderings of the Red Planet and some of the events in the film. One day Ridley Scott took a draft of *The Martian* screenplay and made a pencil sketch of the Mark Watney character in his space suit standing in the sands of Mars; there are two vehicles in the background. In a cartoon balloon above the character are the trademark words spoken by Matt Damon—"I'm going to have to science the *shit* out of this." NASA saw the sketch and asked Scott if it could put the script in a rocket destined for a space journey of fifty-six thousand miles, a four-hour test flight that was to precede an eventual manned mission to Mars. The little comic strip character made the trip on December 5, 2014.

Scott was able to move quickly on the film because he knew what he wanted and his team had done the research to make the film highly realistic and true to the science. This extended even to minor details. Roger Holden, the greensman who had worked with Ridley Scott on many pictures, grew potatoes using indoor lights for three months before production began, employing the same techniques as cultivating marijuana inside. The potatoes were grown in plastic bags rolled down and covered with soil. No artificial potatoes were used during the filming.

When the filmmakers shot on location for the terrain representing Mars, there was no infrastructure—everything they needed had to be brought with them. They took lots of wide shots that re-created what was done back in the studio. They used aerial shots over everything in the area on location.

To create the massive storm that strands Mark, large fans blew dirt and a special mix all over. Five minutes before shooting, particles from the mix— but not dust, which would clump up—would be chucked at the fans. Not much acting was required in these sequences because Scott had placed his actors in a real environment in which it was hard to see out of their helmets. In the specials included in the DVD set of *The Martian,* Scott explained his approach, "To make it even more high wind, I had people in black suits and black covers on their heads with a line on each person, so each actor had to pull against added weight walking about 150 feet behind them, well you couldn't see them in the storm, just holding them back."

Scott's drawing ability is applied to every aspect in the making of his films, and especially so when the movie has many special effects. On *The Martian* he and his editor did temporary visual effects shots in the Avid digital editing platform known as temp VFX shots. Scott was committed to finding the best structure for the film, so many ideas and concepts were tried; scenes and sequences were edited and reedited. Editor Pietro Scalia recounts that because he has worked with Ridley Scott for so long, a lot of discussion during the editing process usually isn't necessary: "I just do it and present it to Ridley. I am very close to the film; I know what needs to be done and he trusts me. We like the same performances or camera angles. Sometimes we disagree on things but that's part of the process. Ultimately Ridley gives me a lot of creative freedom and just lets me do it. The goal is to make the right choices and not be boring. . . . Ultimately it's the emotional pulse of the story that keeps the audience interested."[1]

The advertising tagline rivaled *Alien*'s—"In space no one can hear you scream"—with "Help is only 140 million miles away." The film premiered at the Toronto International Film Festival on September 12, 2015, and there was a sneak preview at the New York Film Festival on September 27, 2015. *The Martian* was a rousing success with audiences. As always for a Ridley Scott film, the picture received many good reviews, but there were some detractors he couldn't please.

Chris Matthews of the MSNBC cable network show *Hardball* was moved by the film's humanity: "You'll be inspired by it . . . feel proud to be a human being. Proud that people like you can do good things, and overall beat the spread. . . . It's about the prevalence of the human spirit through the forge of individual courage and human loyalty. . . . This movie says that people aspire to be something better. We want to see people rising up to their great moral potential as human beings. And this is what the film's director, Ridley Scott, bet on. And it's what I predict people here and around the world are ready to prove him right on."

Manohla Dargis of the venerable *New York Times* wrote that *The Martian* "involves a dual journey into outer and inner space, a trip that takes you into that immensity called the universe and deep into the equally vast landscape of a single consciousness. For this accidental castaway, space is the place where he's physically marooned, but also where his mind is set free." Dargis characterized Ridley Scott as a film director whose "great, persistent theme is what it means to be human."

On the negative side, Stephanie Zacharek of the *Village Voice* found that the actors "are treated as accessories" and that Ridley Scott was "workmanlike in his approach to science, which always trumps magic in *The Martian*— that's the point. But if we can't feel a sense of wonder at the magnitude and mystery of space, why even bother?"

The Martian was nominated for Academy Awards in several categories including Best Picture, Matt Damon for Best Actor, sound editing and sound mixing, Arthur Max for Best Production Design, visual effects, and adapted screenplay.

On January 15, 2015, the pilot for the epic series *The Man in the High Castle,* based on the award-winning novel by author Philip K. Dick, who wrote the story that became *Blade Runner,* ran on Amazon Prime. The reaction was positive and strong, and Amazon promptly ordered a season of the series. The concept is an alternate universe in which the United States has lost World War II to Germany and Japan, which take over the US and divide it between them. The first season began in November 2015.

Originally *The Man in the High Castle* was to be a single series, but strong positive interest prompted a season 2 beginning in December 2016 and con-tinuing the dystopian story with the emergence of the American Resistance and the death of Adolf Hitler. Season 3 is expected in the fall of 2018, and a fourth season is anticipated.

Ridley Scott is a lifelong fan of rugby and football. He read the troubling reports of crippling or deadly concussions sometimes suffered by players of contact sports. This was affecting not just NFL players but semi-professionals, amateur players, and youngsters who played the game. Many players suffered memory loss. Scott and Facio let it be known that they were looking for an A-list screenwriter to create a story about this. The structure they were interested in was that used for *The Insider* (1999), directed by Michael Mann, a story in which one man takes on the powerful tobacco industry and exposes the link between serious health problems, including lung cancer, and cigarettes. Scott wanted to focus on the physical and psychological effects of concussions caused by crushing contact between players during a football game. When Scott decided to direct *The Martian* he abandoned the idea of directing *Concussion* and instead became one of the producers along with Giannina Facio and others.

Early in 2015 Ridley Scott made a major philanthropic contribution of memorabilia to the University of Southern California's School of Cinematic Arts. The gift includes scripts, awards, photography, storyboards and production design boards, editing notes, and various other materials and film elements. The school's dean, Elizabeth M. Daley, stated that the gift covers Scott's feature film career from *The Duellists* in 1977 through 2012, more than twenty films. She stated, "This is a most incredible gift, and we are tremendously grateful. Ridley's storied career is really unparalleled. He has traversed genres and historical periods, mixed fantasy with biographical dramas, epics with small personal stories. There is no one like him, and his legacy of memorabilia will be kept close to our hearts for generations to come."[2] In presenting this gift Ridley Scott said, "I continue to be impressed by the USC School of Cinematic Arts. Perhaps if I had gone there, my film career would have started much sooner."[3]

On July 3, 2015, at the Royal Albert Hall, Sir Ridley Scott received an honorary doctorate degree from his alma mater, the Royal College of Art. He was granted this distinction in recognition of his lifelong artistic contributions to the art and craft of film.

On November 29, 2016, the president of the Directors Guild of America, Paris Barclay, announced that the guild's top honor, the Lifetime Achievement Award for Distinguished Achievement in Motion Picture Direction, would be presented to Ridley Scott. In the guild's eighty-year history, only thirty-four directors have been given this honor, including Scott's idol, Stanley Kubrick, Orson Welles, David Lean, John Huston, Alfred Hitchcock, Ingmar Bergman, and Akira Kurosawa.

25

SON OF *PROMETHEUS*

Alien: Covenant

The compact which exists between the North and the South is a
covenant with death and an agreement with hell.

William Lloyd Garrison

In November 2015, Ridley Scott stated that *Alien: Covenant* would be the first
of three additional films in the *Alien* prequel series before the story was
linked up to the original *Alien*. Scott proclaimed that the *Prometheus* sequels
would reveal who created the xenomorph Aliens.

Ridley Scott has said on several occasions he doesn't believe in sequels.
When asked how *Alien: Covenant* would differ from the earlier *Alien* films,
Scott indicated it would be "gorier and scarier. . . . We raise some interesting
questions about the position and possibility of AI against human condition,
and it crosses into the zone of apartheid—kind of how Roy Batty was treated
as a second–class citizen [in *Blade Runner*]."[1] The timeline for the early part
of this franchise is: *Prometheus,* set in 2093; *Alien: Covenant,* which follows
Prometheus and takes place in 2104; and the original 1979 *Alien,* set in 2122.

Ridley Scott told *New York Times* reporter Mekado Murphy the reason
he was returning to the *Alien* franchise after the many versions that had followed his original film: "I was frustrated by the fact that the ones that followed never once asked the question 'Who would make this, and for what
reason?' So I went back to Fox saying, 'Listen I have a solution to resurrect the
old dog pretty well.'"[2]

Sigourney Weaver, who appears as Ripley in all the films in the *Alien*
franchise except for *Prometheus* and *Alien Covenant,* progresses from a
young brave and wily woman to a full-fledged hero, the kind usually played
by men in action movies. This character type inspired Jodie Foster's Dr. Eleanor "Ellie" Ann Arroway in the 1997 *Contact* and Sandra Bullock as Dr. Ryan
Stone in *Gravity,* released in 2013. In *Prometheus* Noomi Rapace, as archeolo-

gist Elizabeth Shaw, becomes a warrior when a threat arises, and in *Alien: Covenant* Katherine Waterson as Daniels takes on the Alien in its newest form.

In *Alien: Covenant* the *Covenant* heads for a remote planet with two thousand colonists and one thousand embryos. The mission is to create a new society, better than the one the crew left on earth. The ship becomes damaged, the captain is killed, and the crew is awakened from its suspended sleep state. During repairs the ship receives radio transmissions that seem to be from humans, and the crew decides to investigate the supposedly lifeless planet. The crew discovers that the signal comes from an Engineer ship piloted by Elizabeth Shaw, veteran of the disastrous mission undertaken by *Prometheus*. A few crew members are infected with alien spores and locked into the landing vehicle to quarantine them from the others. The crew discovers that the sole inhabitant of the planet is the synthetic android David from the *Prometheus* mission. David becomes an enemy of the *Covenant*. Throughout *Alien: Covenant* there is an onslaught of creature attacks of all sizes and shapes, making the film violent and bloody.

The cast includes Michael Fassbender as Walter, an android who assists the *Covenant*. Katherine Waterson, daughter of accomplished actor Sam Waterson, plays Daniels, a terraforming expert on the *Covenant* and the wife of the captain Jacob Branson, in the Ripley-like role. Much of the humor in *Alien: Covenant* comes from the character of Tennessee, played by Danny McBride, who has appeared in many movies and TV series, often in comedic roles. Billy Crudup portrays Captain Oran.

The film's first cut was two hours and twenty-three minutes, ultimately edited down to the released version of two hours and three minutes. The film, with a budget of $97 million, was a popular success, with a worldwide box office total of $240 million. Many critics and audiences thought *Alien: Covenant* was a return to the form and spirit of the original film and that Ridley Scott had created a worthy contribution to the *Alien* franchise.

Alien: Covenant is less stimulating than *Prometheus*, and although it has some philosophical aspects, in the main it is more a straightforward science fiction/horror thriller. The cast is strong but not as memorable as the 1979 lineup. Katherine Waterson eventually becomes captain as her colleagues fall, and she is the one who finally kills the big Alien, but unlike in the original she is not alone but has a comrade backing her up. The picture belongs to Michael Fassbender in the double android role of Walter and a reprise of David from *Prometheus*.

Scott still talks with pride about the power of *Alien* to scare the audience and how it has become an icon in movie history. In the majority of the interviews conducted around the release of *Alien: Covenant,* Scott describes the monster as beautiful in its sleek design and its murderous efficiency. To Scott beauty is in the essence of design and the conceptual perfection of a being from another place and time.

Peter Bradshaw, writing for the *Guardian,* said that *Alien: Covenant* was "a greatest hits compilation of the other *Alien* films' freaky moments. The paradox is that you are intended to recognize these touches, you won't really be impressed unless you happen to be seeing them for the first time. For all of this, the film is very capably made, with forceful, potent performances from Waterson and Fassbender."

Geoffrey McNab, writing in the *Independent,* criticized the writing and the adequacy of the production, saying the film "certainly delivers what you expect from an *Aliens* film—spectacle, body horror, strong Ripley-like female protagonists and some astonishing special effects—but there is also a dispiriting sense that the film isn't at all sure of its own identity. The very portentous screenplay co-written by John Logan . . . throws in references to Shelley and Byron, Wagner and Michelangelo, and lots of philosophizing about human origins and identity. In the meantime the crew members pitted against the monstrous creatures are trying their darndest to blast them to kingdom come, just as they would in any run of the mill sci-fi B movie."

A. O. Scott of the *New York Times* remarked,

When the larval alien at last explodes out of a human torso, you may experience, along with the expected jolt of fright, a curious sensation of relief, even affection. So much has changed in the world, and in movies, since the first *Alien* freaked out audiences in 1979, that the appearance of a chittering, scurrying, fast-spawning extraterrestrial predator feels like a visit from an old friend. Humanity may have lapsed into terminal tedium or hubristic stupidity, but that creature, with long, slender limbs and a cranium like a speed skater's helmet, remains interesting. The same can be said about *Alien: Covenant,* which follows *Prometheus* in Ridley Scott's 21st-century refurbishing of the franchise he initiated (with the crucial contributions of Sigourney Weaver and the graphic artist H. R. Giger) almost 40 years ago. It's an interesting movie. I wish I could be more effusive, but *Covenant,* for all its interplanetary ranging, commits itself above all to the canny management of expectations.

On April 3, 2017, the film reporter of *Variety,* Dave McNary, stated, "Ridley Scott is in early development at Fox to direct and produce a 'Battle of Britain' World War II movie. The Battle of Britain commenced on July 10, 1940 when the Luftwaffe, Hitler's air force relentlessly bombed the British Isles through October of that year. They began bombarding the airfields of the Royal Air Force (RAF) and launching nightly attacks on London. The Nazis were not able to overcome the British which was the first major defeat for Germany. As a young survivor of the Blitz, Ridley Scott has long been interested in directing a film of what Winston Churchill referred to as 'their finest hour.'"

Ridley Scott has one genre that he would like to explore—the western. He had an opportunity to direct an adaptation of Cormac McCarthy's novel *Blood Meridian* but passed because of the explicit violence of the story. Then in May 2016 it was announced that Scott would direct *Wraiths of the Broken Land,* an adaptation of S. Craig Zahler's western novel. Ironically, this novel also has elements of extreme horror, noir, and ultra-violence; it concerns two kidnapped sisters forced into prostitution. It is a difficult read that lacks a sense of humanity. There is no further information on the status of this project.

26

TRUE CRIME AGAIN
All the Money in the World

Money is a mechanism for control.

David Korten

On March 31, 2017, Deadline.com reported that after considering numerous projects, Ridley Scott would follow *Alien: Covenant* with *All the Money in the World*, a real-life drama about the kidnapping of John Paul Getty's grandson. At the time, in 1973, Getty was the richest man in the world. Shifting to this project, Scott put an adaptation of Don Winslow's 2015 novel *The Cartel* on hold.

Scott liked the David Scarpa script, based on the book *Painfully Rich: The Outrageous Fortunes and Misfortunes of the Heirs of J. Paul Getty* by John Pearson. (The book was retitled *All the Money in the World* after the film's release.) Scott knew of the kidnapping and found the story provocative; the portrayal of J. P. Getty, who was adamant about not paying the ransom, was an intriguing study. He also saw the Gail Harris character, mother of the kidnapped boy, as a woman of exceptional depth.

Production began in Italy in June 2017. Scott's choices for the cast were Kevin Spacey as John Paul Getty Jr., Michelle Williams as Gail Harris, the divorced wife and mother of J. Paul Getty III, to be portrayed by Charlie Plummer. Charlie Plummer (no relation to actor Christopher Plummer) was just seventeen. Mark Wahlberg was cast as Fletcher Chase, an ex-CIA agent sent to Rome to assist on the case. Timothy Hutton is J. P. Getty's lawyer.

Scott said after reading the script, "In my mind, I saw Kevin Spacey. Kevin's a brilliant actor, but I never worked with him and I always knew I would have to have him portray Getty in the film, he was so obsessed with what he was doing. . . . He wasn't giving people a second thought."[1]

In October 2017 powerful, Oscar-winning film mogul Harvey Weinstein had a colossal "open secret" broken wide open into an international scandal.

Ridley Scott directs Mark Wahlberg and Christopher Plummer on the set of *All the Money in the World.*

The *New York Times* and the *New Yorker* detailed the stories of more than a dozen women who said they had been sexually abused by Weinstein.

Reports of sexual misconduct involving other powerful individuals quickly followed. On October 29, 2017, stage and film actor Anthony Rapp (*Rent*), a member of the television show *Star Trek Discovery,* came forth and said that when he was fourteen years old and Kevin Spacey twenty-six, the actor invited the teenager to a party at his home and attempted to have unwanted sex with him. Spacey, a fine and respected actor onstage, in films, and on television, claimed that he didn't remember the incident, but he apologized to Rapp and the public.

Spacey tweeted his response to the Rapp allegations the same day they were made:

> I have a lot of respect and admiration for Anthony Rapp as an
> actor. I'm beyond horrified to hear his story. I honestly do not
> remember the encounter, it would have been over 30 years ago. But
> if I did behave then as he describes, I owe him the sincerest apology
> for what would have been deeply inappropriate drunken behavior
> and I am sorry for the feelings he describes having carried with
> him all these years.

This story has encouraged me to address other things about my life. I know that there are stories out there about me and that some have been fueled by the fact that I have been so protective of my privacy. As those closest to me know, in my life I have had relationships with both men and women. I have loved and had romantic encounters with men throughout my life, and I choose now to live as a gay man. I want to deal with this honestly and openly and that starts with examining my own behavior.

Dan Savage, syndicated author of the sex advice column *Savage Love,* and editor in chief of the feminist magazine *Wear Your Voice* transwoman Ashlee Marie Preston were quick to point out that Spacey joined being a closeted gay with the molestation of a child and criticized him for confusing the topics.

Further allegations of Kevin Spacey's aggressive sexual misconduct toward teenage boys followed. A lawyer representing Kevin Spacey denied the allegations. Spacey's publicist stated the actor was getting treatment but did not specify its nature, and then parted ways with the actor.

Weinstein and Spacey became part of a wave of important men who were outed by the individuals they abused. The list grew day by day and came to include Louis C. K., Matt Lauer, Charlie Rose, Roy Moore, and Brett Ratner.

All the Money in the World was prepared for a December 22, 2017, release date, but now the director/producer was about to face a challenge of historical proportions. The film had already been completed when the Spacey scandal broke. As awards season approached, Ridley Scott faced some hard decisions about a film he had big hopes for. After discussing this sensitive situation with producers from Imperative Entertainment and with the complete support of Sony Pictures, a moral and financial position was established. Kevin Spacey, who had a supporting but critically important role playing the legendary John Paul Getty in a masterful and complex makeup application, would be cut out of the film totally. This was decided despite the fact that the actor had been generating Oscar buzz for his strong performance, and a marketing plan to support this was in the works.

Every shot containing Spacey would be deleted from the completed film and reshot with a new actor. The cost was estimated at $10 million, a quarter of the original $40 million budget. Spacey had had to play older in the role, but to recast it Scott went back to his original choice, eighty-seven-year-old Christopher Plummer. The studio originally rejected Scott's choice of Plummer as Getty, asking instead for a current, younger big box office name, but eventually agreed.

Scott announced he was sticking to the original release date for the film. Many believed the task was impossible: the film had to be reshot, remixed, and color graded; the poster and trailers that had already been circulated with Spacey's physical image had to be redone and redesigned. And everything had to be done in six weeks to maintain the original release date. The announcement to reshoot came on November 8, 2017, with the reshoots planned for Thanksgiving week, November 20–29.

Despite the difficulty of the mission, the mood on the set was high—the dedicated cast and crew were all committed to Ridley Scott. Michelle Williams told Sara Vilkomerson of *Entertainment Weekly*, "I'm so very proud to be a part of this—we're all here for Ridley. When this idea was hatched I immediately started to feel better. This doesn't do anything to ease the suffering of people who were all too personally affected by Kevin Spacey, but it is our little act of trying to right a wrong and it sends a message to predators—you can't get away with this anymore. Something *will* be done."[2]

When the scandal broke, Ridley Scott was in England at the Abbey Road recording studio finalizing the music. He told Sara Vilkomerson, "I sat and thought about it and realized we *cannot*. You cannot tolerate any kind of behavior like that. And it will affect the film. We cannot let one person's action affect the good work of all these other people. It's that simple." Scott had no idea of Spacey's conduct before it was revealed. He had been pleased with the actor's performance and found him to be a very talented actor. They got along well.

Scott was not obliged to contact Spacey about the decision to edit him out of the film, so he didn't call him, nor did he receive a call from the actor. "I waited for Mr. Spacey to call me up," Ridley Scott told Michele Manelis of News.com.au, "and say what he wanted to say but I got nothing, not even from his representatives, which left me free to 'just move forward dude.'"[3] Scott says that if he had gotten a call from an apologetic Spacey he would have appreciated it—but still would have reshot the film.

When Plummer was approached to play John Paul Getty in the reshoots, he said to Ridley Scott, "God, I don't even have to read the script. I'd love to come and do something with you," according to Michele Manelis. "I'd always wanted to work with Ridley." Four days later he was on set delivering lines from the dialogue-heavy role. "It seemed so impossible to do it in such a short period of time," Plummer told Manelis, "so there was no point in being nervous." Spacey had needed a lot of makeup to look Getty's age at the time, but Plummer did not.

Scott reports that when he called the actors they all agreed wholeheartedly to come back for reshoots because of their commitment to the project and their director. Michelle Williams didn't draw any additional salary but received a small per diem for the time she worked on the reshoots. Due to complications with his contract and input from agents and advisers, Mark Wahlberg was to receive $1.5 million for his work on the reshoots. Wahlberg donated the money in Michelle Williams's name to the Time's Up legal fund, which supports women's safety from sexual abuse in the workplace.

"When Ridley came to me, I said to him, 'In all honesty it's a brilliant idea but it can't be done,' Tom Rothman, chairman of Sony Pictures, told Michelle Manelis. "But Ridley said, 'I can do it.' Maybe three or four filmmakers in the world could do it, but I think only one of them would have the balls to try it, and he did."

Instead of shooting many takes of a shot, Scott did one for himself and one to allow the actors to refine their performance or to give a different reading. As always, everything was storyboarded so the reshoot was, as Scott called it, "pre-filmed . . . in his head." He takes pride in listening to and trusting his intuition.

On November 8 it was announced that two weeks of reshoots, budgeted at $10 million, had been scheduled. The cast and crew would be away from their families on Thanksgiving Day, so the production arranged for roasted turkey with all the trimmings during a break at Hatfield House, a seventeenth-century Jacobean mansion. Scott, just days from his eightieth birthday, was full of his usual energy. As usual Scott scrutinized every aspect of a shot, moving background vases and photo frames where he wanted them. He was not at all stressed—Scott is always most alive and happy when he is working on a movie, regardless of the circumstances.

History was made. Scott had accomplished the seemingly impossible.

On Monday, November 11, it was announced that the film's release date had been moved from December 22 to Christmas Day. The reasons had nothing to do with Scott's ability to finish the film: Christmas is the biggest moviegoing day of the year, and it also allowed a little extra time to publicize the picture.

The reviews were strong and positive. Scott's decision to reshoot parts of the movie to remove Spacey was applauded. Christopher Plummer was especially singled out for a multifaceted performance. The structure of the film, that allows for moving back and forth in time, was also considered a plus as it enhances the narrative excitement.

Manohla Dargis of the *New York Times* wrote, "Mr. Scott conjures up entire worlds and sensibilities with visual precision. . . . Each new scene adds another layer of meaning, thickening the slow-building sense of dread. . . . As the story shifts from farmhouse to manor, from the kidnappers to Getty Sr. (each side armed, impatient, brutal), a parallelism develops and it becomes clear that he took his family hostage long before the kidnapping."

Kenneth Turan of the *Los Angeles Times* said, "With as visual a director as Scott at the helm, the film is especially good at re-creating the frenzy and chaos the Italian press whipped up around the kidnapping, and it never loses sight of the pain Getty's inflexibility about his fortune causes his family."

David Eagan of *Film Journal International* wrote, "That very reasonable question the movie tries to answer by showing exactly what it meant to be J. Paul Getty is: As F. Scott Fitzgerald wrote, and as Paul echoes in the narration, the rich are different from you and me. Not just in what they have, but in how they see themselves. Getty is self-absorbed to a monstrous degree, and his behavior, as depicted here, is jaw-dropping."

On December 11, 2017, the Golden Globe 2018 nominations were announced. *All the Money in the World* received three nominations: Christopher Plummer for Best Supporting Actor, Michelle Williams for Best Actress, and Ridley Scott for Best Director. The American Academy of Arts and Sciences recognized Christopher Plummer's valiant effort and professionalism by nominating him for Best Supporting Actor.

As with other dramatic representations based on true events, this film takes some liberties with the facts. Scott's tendency to change true stories is prevalent here. In reality Gail didn't accompany Fletcher to collect the boy. In the movie the grandfather dies the night the boy was released by the kidnappers; in fact, he died three years later. The real Paul Getty did not stage an escape as shown in the film. The film depicts a doctor cutting the kidnapped boy's ear off with the use of chloroform. The truth is there was no doctor; the kidnappers themselves executed the savage act, and no chloroform was applied.

There are black-and-white moments in the film, and at times the color is drained a bit—a perfect depiction of time period. All the visual details are carefully rendered; even the lighting evokes the early 1970s.

Although this is an American movie, many sequences take place in Italy and were produced there. Scott has a good feel for the parts of the country where the film was shot. The casting is impeccable, as is the depiction of the customs and lifestyle of the kidnappers and other Italian characters in the story.

Christopher Plummer gives a riveting performance, but he doesn't play the character as totally evil. Clearly, he is an evil man in that he refuses to pay the ransom for his grandson's freedom although he is the richest man in the world. Yet he is a multilayered character: crafty, stingy, greedy, and cheap, with a distorted view of wealth and the world around him; he is also charming. Mark Wahlberg shows command and worldliness as the man hired by Getty to resolve the situation. Michelle Williams appears to underplay Gail Harris. At times she seems to lack the emotion the situation warrants and is as low key as possible under the circumstances. Charlie Plummer is vulnerable, bewildered, and quirky as the grandson, managing to find nuances well beyond being frustrated.

All the Money in the World is a stylish and grueling thriller, with a steady pace that doesn't let up. The narrative goes back and forth in time, with deft intercutting by editor Claire Simpson. The location and time of most scenes are identified by on-screen text.

All the Money in the World made $2.6 million on the first day of release, Christmas. Opening box office was $5,584,000, and gross $14,342,632.

A few minutes into the film the viewer is caught up in the world it portrays; forgotten are the costs and troubles of replacing a significant part of the movie at the end of production. For this achievement, this film holds a special place in the Ridley Scott oeuvre.

EPILOGUE

I never dwell. I have a shelf of productions and I occasionally look at
them but not often, I'm already looking down the road.

Ridley Scott

At any given time Ridley Scott has dozens and dozens of titles listed in Imdb
.pro under "Projects in Development." Most are producing projects. Some are
just options, others have screenplays, and some have names attached. They
are feature films, TV movies, television series, miniseries, and short films.
Early in his career Scott decided he needed a well of projects on hand so he
could choose what he would do next whenever he was ready. Once he chooses
his next feature, everything required to make a motion picture is completed:
preproduction and planning on a project are well developed, and cast and
crew are selected. A project that has a screenwriter assigned moves up the
ladder; one with a completed first or more advanced screenplay draft is even
higher on the food chain. Those in-development projects have included
Aldous Huxley's *Brave New World,* which takes place in a high-tech, dystopian Britain of the future; *Gucci,* about the man who built an empire out of
leather handbags and shoes; *The Passage,* part of a trilogy set in the near
future when an apocalyptic and postapocalyptic world is confronted by vam-
pire-like creatures infected with a deadly virus; *Reykjavik,* about a meeting
between President Ronald Reagan and Soviet leader Mikhail Gorbachev that
led to the end of the Cold War; *The Terror,* based on the novel by Dan Sim-
mons, a fictionalized account of an expedition to find a lost ship; *Fog,* about
a family's battle with a supernatural higher power during a trip to London;
and *The Color of Lightning,* a story of a son avenging his father, a freed slave
killed by Native American warriors.

On July 11, 2015, the drug lord Joaquín Guzmán, known as El Chapo,
escaped for a second time from a Mexican federal prison. His story gained a
lot of attention. Before this event, Don Winslow, an accomplished crime
writer, had written *The Cartel,* a novel about the violence and death

Executive producer Ridley Scott and Harrison Ford on the set of *Blade Runner 2049*.

connected with drug dealing on an enormous scale, and as of February 2018 an adaptation is slated to be Ridley Scott's next movie.

Scott is pragmatic, a businessman and an artist with sharp instincts. There could be multiple projects developing for Scott Free, but Scott makes sure there are at least six to eight on deck.

On March 3, 2011, Alcon Entertainment announced it was in final discussions to secure the film, television, and ancillary franchises to produce prequels and sequels to the legendary science fiction film *Blade Runner*. At this time Christopher Nolan was sought as director. In November 2014 Ridley Scott announced that he would not direct the film but would be the executive producer. On February 26, 2015, Denis Villeneuve (*Prisoners,* 2013, *Sicario,* 2015, *Arrival,* 2016) was slated to direct. It was confirmed that Harrison Ford would return as Deckard. One of the two original writers, Hampton Fancher, was returning as well.

In November 2015 Ryan Gosling was cast in the lead role as the replicant blade runner "K." He was drawn to the project because of Villeneuve and director of photography Roger Deakins. Villeneuve wanted to cast David Bowie as Niander Wallace, but the iconic performer died before production began. The part was given to Jared Leto. Edward James Olmos reprised his role as Gaff in the *Blade Runner* sequel.

Blade Runner 2049 is a worthy sequel to *Blade Runner*. It is artful in execution and more conceptual in design, space, and text than the original. Time has passed, and while Los Angeles is disintegrating further, replicant technology has advanced. The story is logical in a science fiction sense, and it also remains true to Philip K. Dick. The use of color is strong and otherworldly.

Visual effects technology has grown enormously since the release of the original *Blade Runner*, which was stunning and inventive for its time given what was available. The sequel manages to expand the imagery while paying respect to Ridley Scott and his team. John Nelson, the visual effects supervisor of *Blade Runner 2049*, and director Denis Villeneuve achieved what many thought was impossible: continuing the story of a landmark film, one of science fiction's best.

At the historic Ninetieth Academy Awards, held on March 4, 2018, *Blade Runner 2049* won two awards. Legendary director of photography Roger Deakins was given the statue for Best Cinematography. He had previously been nominated thirteen times in this category. John Nelson, Paul Lambert, Richard R. Hoover, and Gerd Nefzer received Oscars for their work in visual effects on the film.

Ridley Scott is the essence of a filmmaker. He is admired around the world. Oscar-winning director James Cameron told Scott Foundas of *Variety*, "Ridley has continued to be someone I admire more than almost any other director out there. Even his minor films I'll see as promptly as I can, and his major films—his spectacles, or whatever he deigns to do, something in science fiction—I'll be the first in line. Here's a guy who's been vigorous over five decades, and is still going strong. Ridley is who I still aspire to be."[1]

Scott inspires great loyalty. Film editor Dody Dorn, who worked with Ridley Scott on three films, professes, "I would throw down and do anything if Ridley wanted me to work with him again, because it's such a wonderful gratifying experience."[2]

David Puttnam believes Ridley Scott is a remarkable director, but that he has spent his career portraying the outside of life rather than delving into what is inside. As other critics, scholars, and audience members have said, so far Scott has left behind ravishingly beautiful images, but is there true meaning in his work?

Scott himself has talked about being a creator of mainstream cinema. He has discussed the art, craft, and process of motion pictures and seems torn between making films for sheer entertainment value and exploring serious subjects. The truth appears to be that he has accomplished both. He has approached such subjects as history, war, the future, mythology, class structures, cultural issues, feminism, true-life stories, crime, what it means to be alive, neurosis, international conflicts, and the evil in the hearts of men and women.

Who is Ridley Scott? How does one define his career? What has driven him through all these decades of directing and producing commercials, television, and especially feature films? He is a tireless worker with a flawless eye for images and the skill to get them on the screen. After twenty-five major feature films and in apparent good health at just over eighty years old, he proceeds as if he were ageless. He runs a major company, frequently develops television projects, shoots commercials, and directs feature films. How does he do it? One answer is his stamina, which he talked about with Mr. Showbiz in 1996. "I think the first requirement of a director, now that I've done a few films and maybe over 2,000 commercials is stamina. Because without stamina, it's a bit like being a long-distance runner—you don't complete the course, you're wobbling as opposed to coming in with a good finish. I think that's a good metaphor."[3]

When Mr. Showbiz asked Scott what the director needs to contribute to a film in order to call it a true "Ridley Scott Film," he responded, "I don't really think about that. I'm sometimes accused of being over-visual. In a recent film, somebody referred to me as a visual-holic, which is odd because I really tried to pull my horns in on that one. If anything I try to allow the obvious aspects of what I bring to a film, which I guess is an eye, to overpower the story and the narrative. I now realize that's what I do, that's what I bring, that's one of my fortes and so it's something I don't really concern myself about. I guess that's part and parcel of my stamp."

Ridley Scott is a slightly stocky five foot eight. He has blue eyes, red, wavy hair mixed with a generous amount of white and gray, and sports a trim mustache and beard. He used to be a cigarette smoker, but nowadays can most often be seen smoking a fine Cuban cigar like a Cohiba. He speaks in a moderately toned British accent most of the time, but earlier in his career he was known as a terror—a screamer. His work uniform is generally a high-quality T-shirt or sweater and dungarees or casual khakis. His sense of humor is usually dry. Above all, he is very intense, especially when directing or looking through the eyepiece of a motion picture camera. He has an estimated net worth of approximately $180 million.

The *Guardian* writer Stephen Moss calls Scott's communication style more visual than verbal: "Scott is strangely inarticulate—or rather, the articulacy comes and goes. He proceeds not through rounded sentences, but via shafts of verbal light."[4]

Some have insisted that Scott is an entertainer, not an auteur, not a writer/director but more like an oldtime Hollywood studio director. It is perhaps appropriate to look beyond his enormous technical skills as a filmmaker to perceive the artist. Scott says, "Everyone . . . ought to be in the business of entertainment. I'm uneasy about the word 'auteur' but I do wonder why filmmaking isn't as legitimate as painting. I used to say, 'It's just a movie.' But actually it's not really. A lot of artistic decisions have gone into it."[5]

Ridley Scott has been a cineaste since first seeing films as a boy. He continues to watch films and says he can't sleep without seeing a movie. "I start at 11 and if I'm still watching at 1 that means it's a good film."[6]

Ridley Scott considers his experience in directing commercials as his "film school" where he learned the importance of working fast, which served him well then and later in making his feature films. "Fast and on the clock. There's a clock going tick, tick, tick, and that's costing you. And then at the end you have the agency tut-tutting on the side, so they're the studio. The agency is the pressure of the studio; they're always trying to intervene and say, 'Why do you want to . . .'. I learned to deal with that by saying 'Good idea.' If you say, good idea, you've just diffused the bomb. So I learned all my politics from advertising and walking the tightrope. Because film is walking the tightrope," Scott told Kenneth Turan, referring to the line between art and commerce in the making of a major feature film. "Anyone giving me that much money to spend on my intuition and whim deserves respect, they deserve to be listened to. If I were an investor I'd want to have a say as well. I think at the end of the day, filmmaking is a team, but eventually there's got to be a captain. Therefore that will finally boil down to saying, 'Let's do this, we're going to go this way. No more talk, we're going to do that.'"[7] Ridley Scott has been known to make as many as fifty to a hundred setups a day.

"People have no idea how physically tough doing a film is," he told Stephen Moss. "I do pretty big movies and you have to drive the bus—that's the job. My crews average anywhere between 400 and 500 people, but I never even think about it. It's like walking into an army camp every morning. You have to go, 'Right' (he claps his hands), and everybody moves. You've got to embrace the manpower and embrace your department heads. If I'm excited it tends to leak out. I think that's what I'm good at. I'm good at pushing the pace and suddenly everyone is running."

He is a master of lighting comparable to the paintings of Rembrandt and other Old Masters. He knows when to employ light and dark and when to create texture. He often lights areas of fog to illustrate atmosphere and mood. There have been directors who have done their own storyboards, but not with the amount of detail and visual complexity characteristic of a Ridleygram. He utilizes these drawings on the set to make a movie shot for shot. He told Moviesonline, "If I get lost, I just sit there and . . . doodle. . . . I spent a long time in art school so I can really draw. So I'll doodle and suddenly I'll find the beginning of the movie in one picture. Right by the telephone I've got a book of doodles. When I'm on the phone I'll be doing a drawing eventually this big [demonstrates a full-sized drawing with his hands] if the phone session's long." Russell Crowe has revealed that if Scott wants to draw something for someone else, he can place the paper in front of that person and draw the image backward. Every director must deal with the background of a shot, and Scott puts as much visual attention there as he devotes to the foreground. "The location is always like the other character. It's up to me to create a proscenium that's so real that when the actor walks into that proscenium he's actually affected by it. . . . I always remember the first time walking on a battlefield in Germania [on *Gladiator*]. We walked over the hill and into the front and that proscenium was pretty impressive. . . . It becomes part of the world. The locations are the work."[8]

During the shooting of a film, Scott retires to his trailer during the lunch period and puts up a "Do Not Disturb" sign. He eats in eight minutes or so, then takes around a forty-minute nap to recharge himself. Lately, he has put his productions on what is known as French hours. There is no lunch, and so two hours are saved. He found under the previous system that some crew members ate too much at lunch and thus were sleepy and less effective until around 3:30. Under the French system, Scott eats a good breakfast, has something like lunch on the run during the day, and then wraps at 6:00. The downside of this system is that while he is driving home he is observing great light—which he is unable to get on film.

Space and size are critical aspects for Ridley Scott and his director's vision. As he told *Empire* magazine:

It [the stage] . . . never is big enough. . . . You stand at one end and put a viewfinder on and get someone to go down and stand at the

Epilogue

other end. You go, "Uh, it's not that big." I'm a great recycler. I
wanted to recycle spaces so the more big spaces I've got, the bigger
my film will appear to be. I'll recycle every goddamn space. I'll
reshoot a corridor 13 different ways, and you'll never recognize
them. It's like in *Gladiator*. . . . The senate where they stood talking
and Joaquin spun his sword on the marble that is later his office, his
bedroom, his living room, and her [the character Lucilla] quarters.
That was simply by moving around dressing, changing the angles,
and changing the drapes. If you look carefully, you'll realize the
columns are the same on all those sets.[9]

Ridley Scott likes to think he comes from the "school of everything," a
total approach to filmmaking that has drawn him to the work of David Lean,
Stanley Kubrick, and Orson Welles. "Everything was important, not just the
script and the story and the actors, but everything on the screen was suited to
the subject," he told Scott Foundas of *Variety*.

The most distinctive characteristic that identifies a Ridley Scott film is
his uncanny ability to realize and create what *Empire* magazine calls "world-
building," a feat applied to every place from ancient Rome in *Gladiator* to
future environments in *Alien* and *Prometheus*.

There is darkness in some of Ridley Scott's movies. Tony Scott explained
to Ariel Leve, "All around us was darkness when we were younger—rain and
the industrial moors. That's where Ridley got *Blade Runner* from."[10]

Ridley Scott still runs Ridley Scott Associates. He is still involved in TV series,
TV movies, and miniseries. He also produces motion picture and television
projects for others. Ridley Scott has two films in the National Film Registry:
Blade Runner, which made the list in 1993, and *Alien* in 2002. Ridley Scott is
considered to be the finest director of television commercials ever. He is also
the most successful director of commercials to transition to feature films
ever. He has dedicated his life to moving images and moving-image
storytelling.

Ridley Scott has a home in an exclusive area in Los Angeles, an estate and
vineyard in Provence, and a stately home with a manicured garden in Hampstead in the UK. Scott does not take vacations and doesn't like not working.
He loves his family and works with his relatives in the family businesses. He
has nurtured and supported them throughout their careers. His long-term
relationship and collaboration with Giannina Facio endures.

Scott talks about his legacy to Tim Walker of the *Independent*. "It's a family business. They didn't want to be part of RSA originally, but now they are. I told them, 'Fundamentally, it's your company.' If I were an actor, then I wouldn't encourage my child to be an actor, because it's really hard. Being a director is not quite so bad although, honestly, it's nearly as bad. But they decided to follow me."[11]

"I'm constantly telling dad to slow down and, of course, I worry when he goes off to the desert for five months to film. But he loves working and is much happier on the set than not. Take that away from him and oooh," Jordan Scott stated to the *London Evening Standard,* shaking her head in dismay.[12]

Ridley Scott considers himself lucky, as he told John Patterson of the *Guardian.* "I'm sorry for people who never knew what they wanted to be. There aren't many lucky enough to know—but I'm one of them."[13]

In the late 1970s and early 1980s, an era that saw the American New Wave and the Australian New Wave, there was a movement, never really named or codified, that consisted of British film directors Adrian Lyne, Hugh Hudson, Alan Parker, and others, who all began their careers in advertising and television commercials. Their films made a sizable international impression. Since 2015, only one of these men continues to direct film after film and receive worldwide attention—Ridley Scott. He is the last man standing.

On the commentary track for the *Exodus: Gods and Kinds* DVD, Ridley Scott explained how difficult it is for a director to get started in his or her career:

> There is a lot lost frequently because a lot of people aren't in my
> position, experience, longevity, success, so it's hard for a first-time,
> second-time director today, [who can] get pushed and [strung
> along] by less informed executives. It's a tricky thing because half
> the time you've got to let the man run . . . providing he's not going
> over budget or going out of control. Let the man run—that's why
> you brought him in—you bought the horse, let him run, There's
> more films ruined by being looked at too early, saying, "I don't
> think he's going to get there," rather than say, "Let him run, let him
> run." You know what the difference is if someone is scared to death
> and they don't know what they are doing. Then you have to do
> something, but talented people have been knocked and hurt today.
> You've got to be strong—you have to fight your cause.

On the other hand, too many films are given to . . . people who aren't ready—they give somebody a $10 million, a $20 million movie, but [you] don't go from a commercial to a $180 million movie. . . . Are you crazy? Because the stakes are so high they think they are going to get a bargain. . . . It ain't cool if you can't play tennis and you are getting trashed by the old geezer at the other end of the court.

I am always amazed that I couldn't do a film until I was forty. I was ready to do a film when I was twenty-seven. . . . I had done . . . three or four hundred commercials. . . . I started *The Duellists* in my thirty-ninth year because I paid for the completion bond, and I got no fee. People say it's really hard today. I say . . . you know what it was like to get a movie going then? Jesus, it was impossible.

Many ask how long Ridley Scott can go on. Why does he plan so far into the future at this stage in his life? How many more films can he make? The answer is as many as he can.

He has lost two brothers before their time. One can only rationalize that Ridley Scott must keep going because he believes, in the words of the Nobel Prize–winning author Samuel Beckett in *The Unnamable*, "I can't go on. I'll go on."[14]

ACKNOWLEDGMENTS

First and foremost, I want to thank my wife Harriet Morrison for her unflagging support of this project and for her generous contributions to the creation of this book.

My son Alexander Morrison has long been an avid fan of the films of Ridley Scott. His inspiration and our spirited discussions have been enlightening and motivating.

Thanks to my daughter Rebecca Roes; I remember the day I referred to my first book as "just a little book" and she took issue, replying, "No, it's not just a *little* book." Her steadfast appreciation of my professional efforts is of great personal value.

At the School of Visual Arts I thank all my students—past, present, and future—for their support and contributions. Thanks to Rob Barton for talking to me for hours on end about movies and life. My gratitude to Robert Lobe, the school's chief librarian, for his untiring enthusiasm. Although Ridley Scott is not officially a maverick filmmaker, I thank the students in the 2015 American Film Mavericks class for being so insightful about movies and for proving to me once again that the art of discussion is not dead.

To Dr. Jain I extend my appreciation and admiration for her help during the writing of this biography.

To Pat McGilligan my gratitude for being a constant friend, for looking out for me, for being a pro and a helluva film biographer—maybe the best there is. Also, I thank Pat for his patience and care when I really needed it.

To Anne Dean Dotson, senior acquisitions editor, my gratitude for her steady support, expertise, and care.

To my copyeditor Robin DuBlanc, my thanks for her great skill and the totality of her approach to the completion of this book.

I thank Bailey Johnson, the original acquisitions assistant, for always answering my questions with precision and goodwill and Patrick O'Dowd for continuing assistance.

Acknowledgments

To Peter Tonguette, writer of film books and other media in print and on the net, my thanks for his unflagging friendship and support of my work.

To Harry Northup, many thanks for engaging conversations on cinema and for thoughtful insights about Ridley Scott's first film *Boy and Bicycle*.

My sincere appreciation to Maestro Hans Zimmer for talking to me about Ridley Scott for *CinemaEditor* magazine. I thank Lawrence G. Paull for his generous interview concerning *Blade Runner* that appears in my book *By Design: Interviews with Film Production Designers*.

I thank the masterful film editor Dody Dorn for talking to me about the films she edited for Ridley Scott.

Filmmaking is a collaborative process; so is writing a book. I thank everyone for their contributions and encouragement.

FILMOGRAPHY

Abbreviations

P	Producer
EP	Executive producer
D	Director
SC	Screenplay
M	Music
PD	Production designer
DP	Director of photography
SUE	Supervising editor
E	Editor
C	Costumes
SSE	Supervising sound editor
SE	Sound editor
S	Sound
VES	Visual effects supervisor

The Duellists (1977)

Enigma Productions, Paramount Pictures, 100 minutes, rated PG

P: David Puttnam; D: Ridley Scott; SC: Gerald Vaughan-Hughes, based on the story "The Duel" by Joseph Conrad; M: Howard Blake; PD: Peter J. Hampton; DP: Frank Tidy; E: Pamela Power; C: Tom Rand; SSE: Michael Bradsell; S: Derrick Leather

Cast: D'Hubert (Keith Carradine), Féraud (Harvey Keitel), Fouché (Albert Finney), Colonel (Edward Fox), Adele (Christina Raines), General Treillard (Robert Stephens), Doctor Jacquin (Tom Conti), Laura (Diana

Quick), maid (Gay Hamilton), Chevalier (Alan Webb), Mme. de Lionie (Jenny Runacre), narrator (Stacy Keach)

Alien (1979)

Brandywine Productions, 20th Century Fox, 117 minutes, rated R
P: Gordon Carroll, David Glier, Walter Hill; D: Ridley Scott; SC: Story by Dan O'Bannon, Ronald Shusett; M: Jerry Goldsmith; PD: Michael Seymour; DP: Derek Vanlint, E: David Crowther, Terry Rawlings, Peter Weatherley; C: John Mollo; SE: Jim Shields; S: Derek Leather; VES: Nick Allder
Cast: Dallas (Tom Skerritt), Ripley (Sigourney Weaver), Lambert (Veronica Cartwright), Brett (Harry Dean Stanton), Kane (John Hurt), Ash (Ian Holm), Parker (Yaphet Kotto), Alien (Bolaji Badejo), voice of Mother (Helen Morton)

Blade Runner (1982)

Ladd Company, Warner Bros., 117 minutes, rated R
P: Michael Deeley, Charles de Lauzirka; D: Ridley Scott; SC: Hampton Fancher, David Webb Peoples, based on the novel *Do Androids Dream of Electric Sheep?"* by Philip K. Dick; M: Vangelis; PD: Lawrence G. Paull; DP: Jordan Cronenweth; SUE: Terry Rawlings; E: Marsha Nakashima; C: Michael Kaplan, Charles Knode; SE: Peter Pennell; S: Gordon K. McCallum; VES: Ian Hunter
Cast: Rick Deckard (Harrison Ford), Roy Batty (Rutger Hauer), Rachael (Sean Young), Gaff (Edward James Olmos), Bryant (M. Emmet Walsh), Pris (Daryl Hannah), J. F. Sebastian (William Sanderson), Leon Kowalski (Brion James), Dr. Eldon Tyrell (Joe Turkel), Hannibal Chew (James Hong), Holden (Morgan Paull)

Legend (1985)

Legend Production Company, MCA/Universal Home Video, 94 minutes, rated PG
P: Arnon Milchan; D: Ridley Scott; SC: William Hjortsberg; M: Jerry Goldsmith, Tangerine Dream; PD: Assheton Gorton; DP: Alex Thomson; E: Terry Rawlings; C: Charles Knode; S: Roy Charman; VES: Nick Allder

Cast: Jack (Tom Cruise), Lili (Mia Sara), Darkness (Tim Curry), Gump (David Bennent), Blix (Alice Playten), Screwball (Billy Barty), Brown Tom (Cork Hubbert), Pox (Peter O'Farrell), Blunder (Kiran Shah), Oona (Annabella Lanyon), Meg Mucklebones (Robert Picardo)

Someone to Watch over Me (1987)

Columbia Pictures Corporation, 106 minutes, rated R

P: Thierry de Ganay, Harold Schneider; EP & D: Ridley Scott; SC: Howard Franklin; M: Michael Kamen; PD: James D. Bissell; DP: Steven Poster; E: Claire Simpson; C: Colleen Atwood; SE: Jim Shields; S: Gene Cantamessa

Cast: Detective Mike Keegan (Tom Berenger), Claire Gregory (Mimi Rogers), Ellie Keegan (Lorraine Bracco), Lieutenant Garber (Jerry Orbach), Neil Steinhart (John Rubenstein), Joey Venza (Andreas Katsulas), T. J. (Tony Di Benedetto), Win Hockings (Mark Moses), Tommy Keegan (Harley Cross)

Black Rain (1989)

Paramount Pictures, Jaffe-Lansing, Pegasus Film Partners, 125 minutes, rated R

P: Stanley R. Jaffe, Sherry Lansing; D: Ridley Scott; SC: Craig Bolotin, Warren Lewis; M: Hans Zimmer; PD: Norris Spencer; DP: Jan de Bont; E: Tom Rolf; C: Ellen Mirojnick; SSE: Milton C. Burrow; S: Keith A. Wester

Cast: Nick Conklin (Michael Douglas), Charlie Vincent (Andy Garcia), Masahiro (Ken Takakura), Joyce (Kate Capshaw), Sato (Yûsaku Matsuda), Ohashi (Shigeru Kôyama), Katayama (Guts Ishimatsu), Nashida (Yûya Uchida), Sugai (Tomisaburô Wakayama), Miyuki (Miyuki Ono), Frankie (Luis Guzmán)

Thelma & Louise (1991)

Pathé Entertainment, Metro-Goldwyn-Mayer, 130 minutes, rated R

P: Mimi Polk, Ridley Scott; D: Ridley Scott; SC: Callie Khouri; M: Hans Zimmer; PD: Norris Spencer; DP: Adrian Biddle; E: Thom Noble; C: Elizabeth McBride; SSE: Jim Shields; S: Keith A. Wester

Cast: Louise Sawyer (Susan Sarandon), Thelma Dickinson (Geena Davis), Hal (Harvey Keitel), Jimmy (Michael Madsen), Darryl (Christopher McDonald), Max (Stephen Tobolowsky), J.D. (Brad Pitt), Harlan (Timothy Carhart), Lena the waitress (Lucinda Jenney)

1492: Conquest of Paradise (1992)

Gaumont, Paramount Pictures, 154 minutes, rated PG-13

P: Alain Goldman, Ridley Scott; D: Ridley Scott; SC: Roselyne Bosch; M: Vangelis; PD: Norris Spencer; DP: Adrian Biddle; E: William M. Anderson, Francoise Bonnot, Leslie Healey, Armen Minasian, Deborah Zeitman; C: Charles Knode, Barbra Rutter; SSE: Jim Shields; S: John Hayward; VES: Yves De Bono

Cast: Columbus (Gérard Depardieu), Sanchez (Armand Assante), Queen Isabella (Sigourney Weaver), older Fernando (Loren Dean), Beatrix (Ángela Molina), Marchena (Fernando Rey), Moxica (Michael Wincott), Santangel (Frank Langella), Bobadilla (Mark Margolis), young Fernando (Billy L. Sullivan)

White Squall (1996)

Hollywood Pictures, Buena Vista Pictures, Largo Entertainment, Scott Free Productions, 129 minutes, rated PG-13

P: Mimi Polk Gitlin, Rocky Lang; EP & D: Ridley Scott; SC: Todd Robinson, based on the book *The Last Voyage of the Albatross* by Charles Gieg Jr. and Felix Sutton; M: Jeff Rona; PD: Peter J. Hampton, Leslie Tomkins; DP: Hugh Johnson; E: Gerry Hambling; C: Judianna Makovsky; SSE: Campbell Askew; S: Ken Weston

Cast: Captain Christopher "Skipper" Sheldon (Jeff Bridges), Dr. Alice Sheldon (Caroline Goodall), McCrea (John Savage), Charles "Chuck" Gieg/narrator (Scott Wolf), Frank Beaumont (Jeremy Sisto), Gil Martin (Ryan Phillipe), Francis Beaumont (David Selby), Girard Pascal, (Julio Mechoso), Coast Guard captain Sanders (Zeljko Ivanek), Tod Johnstone (Balthazar Getty), Middy Gieg (Libeth Mackay) Peggy Beaumont (Jill Larson), Danish schoolgirl (Jordan Scott)

G.I. Jane (1997)

Caravan Pictures, Buena Vista Pictures, Scott Free Productions, 125 minutes, rated R

P: Roger Birmbaum, Demi Moore, Ridley Scott, Suzanne Todd; D: Ridley Scott; SC: Danielle Alexander, David Twohy, M: Trevor Jones; PD: Arthur Max; DP: Hugh Johnson; E: Pietro Scalia: C: Marilyn Vance; SSE: Campbell Askew; S: Keith A. Wester; VES: Steve Galich

Cast: Jordan O'Neill (Demi Moore), Master Chief John James Urgayle (Viggo Mortensen), Lillian DeHaven (Anne Bancroft), Royce (Jason Beghe), Chief of Staff (John Michael Higgins), instructor Pyro (Kevin Gage), instructor Johns (David Warshofsky), Cortez (David Vadim), McCool (Morris Chestnut), Flea (Josh Hopkins), Slovnik (Jim Caviezel), C. O. Salem (Scott Wilson), Admiral O'Connor (Stephen Mendillo), barber (Arthur Max)

Gladiator (2000)

Universal Pictures, DreamWorks SKG, Scott Free Productions, 155 minutes, rated R

P: David Franzoni, Branko Lustig, Douglas Wick; EP: Laurie MacDonald, Walter F. Parkes, Ridley Scott; D: Ridley Scott; SC: David Franzoni, John Logan, William Nicholson; M: Lisa Gerrad, Hans Zimmer; PD: Arthur Max; DP: John Mathieson; E: Pietro Scalia; C: Janty Yates; SSE: Per Hallberg: S: Ken Weston, Bob Beemer, and Scott Millan; VES: Terry Glass, David Hunter, Trevor Wood

Cast: Maximus (Russell Crowe), Commodus (Joaquin Phoenix), Lucilla (Connie Nielsen), Proximo (Oliver Reed), Marcus Aurelius (Richard Harris), Gracchus (Derek Jacobi), Juba (Djimon Hounsou), Lucius (Spencer Treat Clark), Cassius (David Hemmings), Hagen (Ralf Moeller), narrator (Billy Dowd), Maximus's wife (Giannina Facio)

Hannibal (2001)

Metro Goldwyn Mayer, Dino De Laurentiis Company, Scott Free Productions, 131 minutes, rated R

P: Dino De Laurentiis, Martha De Laurentiis, Ridley Scott; D: Ridley Scott; SC: David Mamet, Steven Zaillian, based on the book *Hannibal* by

Thomas Harris; M: Hans Zimmer; PD: Norris Spencer; DP: John Mathieson; E: Pietro Scalia; C: Janty Yates; SSE: Karen M. Baker, Per Hallberg; S: Danny Michael; VES: Renato Agostini (Florence), Kevin Harris

Cast: Hannibal Lecter (Anthony Hopkins), Clarice Starling (Julianne Moore), Mason Verger (Gary Oldman), Paul Krendler (Ray Liotta), Nurse Barney (Frankie R. Faison), Inspector Rinaldo Pazzi (Giancarlo Giannini), Allegra Pazzi (Francesca Neri), Dr. Cordell Doemling (Zeljko Ivanek), Verger's fingerprint technician (Giannina Facio)

Black Hawk Down (2001)

Revolution Studios, Jerry Bruckheimer Films, Scott Free Productions, 144 minutes, rated R

P: Jerry Bruckheimer, Ridley Scott; D: Ridley Scott; SC: Ken Nolan, based on the book *Black Hawk Down: A Story of Modern War* by Mark Bowen; M: Hans Zimmer, PD: Arthur Max; DP: Slawomir Idziak; E: Pietro Scalia, C: David Murphy, Sammy Sheldon; SSE: Karen M. Baker, Per Hallberg; S: Chris Munro; VES: Tim Burke

Cast: Eversmann (Josh Hartnett), Grimes (Ewan McGregor), McKnight (Tom Sizemore), Hoot (Eric Bana), Garrison (Sam Shepard), Wex (Kim Coates), Schmid (Hugh Dancy), Durant (Ron Eldard), Harrell (Zeljko Ivanek), Wolcott (Jeremy Piven), Blackburn (Orlando Bloom), Wilkinson (Ty Burrell)

Matchstick Men (2003)

Warner Bros., Scott Free Productions, 116 minutes, rated PG-13

P: Sean Bailey, Ted Griffin, Jack Rapke, Ridley Scott, Steve Starkey; D: Ridley Scott; SC: Nick Griffin, Ted Griffin, based on the book *Matchstick Men: A Novel about Grifters with Issues* by Eric Garcia; M: Hans Zimmer; PD: Tom Foden; DP: John Mathieson; E: Dody Dorn; C: Michael Kaplan; SSE: Per Hallberg, Karen Baker Landers; S: Lee Orloff; VES: Sheena Duggal

Cast: Roy Waller (Nicolas Cage), Frank Mercer (Sam Rockwell), Angela (Alison Lohman), Dr. Klein (Bruce Altman), Chuck Frechette (Bruce McGill), laundry lady (Beth Grant), Kathy (Sheila Kelley), slacker boyfriend (Fran Kranz), bank teller (Giannina Facio)

Kingdom of Heaven (2005)

20th Century Fox, Scott Free Productions, 144 minutes, rated R
P & D: Ridley Scott; SC: William Monahan; M: Harry Gregson-Williams; PD: Arthur Max; DP: John Mathieson; E: Dody Dorn; C: Janty Yates; SSE: Per Hallberg; S: David Stephenson: VES: Raúl Romanillos (Spain), Wesley Sewell
Cast: gravedigger (Martin Hancock), priest (Michael Sheen), Balian's wife (Nathalie Cox), Hospitaler (David Thewlis), Godfrey de Ibelin (Liam Neeson), Balian de Ibelin (Orlando Bloom), Sibylla (Eva Green), Reynald de Chatillon (Brendan Gleeson), Muslim Grandee (Nasser Memarzia), Tiberias (Jeremy Irons), Guy de Lusignan (Marton Csokas), Jerusalem (Jon Finch), King Baldwin (Edward Norton), Saladin (Ghassan Massoud), Saladin's sister (Giannina Facio)

A Good Year (2006)

Fox 2000 Pictures, Scott Free Productions, 117 minutes, rated PG-13
P & D: Ridley Scott; SC: Marc Klein, based on the novel *The Good Year* by Peter Mayle; M: Marc Streitenfeld; PD: Sonja Klaus; DP: Phillipe Le Sourd; E: Dody Dorn, Robb Sullivan; C: Catherine Leterrier; SSE: Per Hallberg, Karen Baker Landers; S: Jean-Paul Morrill; VES: Wesley Sewell, Steven Warner
Cast: young Max (Freddie Highmore), Uncle Henry (Albert Finney), Max Skinner (Russell Crowe), Gemma (Archie Panjabi), maitre d' (Giannina Facio), Charlie Willis (Tom Hollander), Gemma's friend (Maria Papas), Francis Duflot (Didier Bourdon), Fanny Chenal (Marion Cotillard), Christie Roberts (Abbie Cornish), Fanny's mother (Catherine Vinatier), young Fanny (Marine Casto)

American Gangster (2007)

Universal Pictures, Imagine Entertainment, Relativity Media, Scott Free Productions, 157 minutes, rated R
P: Brian Grazer, Ridley Scott; D: Ridley Scott; SC: Mark Jacobson, Steve Zaillian, based on Jacobson's article "The Return of Superfly"; M: Marc Streitenfeld; PD: Arthur Max; DP: Harris Savides; E: Pietro Scalia; C: Janty

Yates; SSE: Per Hallberg, Karen Baker Landers; S: William Sarokin; VES: Samson Panichsuk

Cast: Frank Lucas (Denzel Washington), Richie Roberts (Russell Crowe), Huey Lucas (Chiwetel Ejiofor), Detective Trupo (Josh Brolin), Eva (Lymari Nadal), Lou Toback (Ted Levine), Nate (Roger Guenveur Smith), Moses Jones (RZA), Mama Lucas (Ruby Dee), Doc (Ruben Santiago-Hudson), Laurie Roberts (Carla Gugino), Michael Roberts (Skyler Fortgang), Dominic Cattano (Armand Assante), Mrs. Dominic Cattano (Kathleen Garrett), Charlie Williams (Joe Morton), Joe Louis (Bari K. Willerford), Tango (Idris Elba), Jimmy Zee (Malcolm Goodwin), Nicky Barnes (Cuba Gooding Jr.), Turner Lucas (Common), Melvin Lucas (Warren Miller), Terrance Lucas (Albert Jones), Dexter Lucas (L. Kyle Manzay), Stevie Lucas (Tip Harris), Redtop (Melissa Hill), Rossi (Jon Polito), Joe Louis (Bari K. Willeford), funk band singer (Anthony Hamilton), Bumpy Johnson (Clarence Williams III)

Body of Lies (2008)

Warner Bros., Scott Free Productions, 128 minutes, rated R

P: Donald De Line, Ridley Scott; D: Ridley Scott; SC: David Ignatius, William Monahan, based on Ignatius's novel *Penetration*; M: Marc Streitenfeld; PD: Arthur Max; DP: Alexander Witt; E: Pietro Scalia; C: Janty Yates; SSE: Per Hallberg, Karen Baker Landers, Richard Van Dyke; VES: Paul Corbould

Cast: Roger Ferris (Leonardo DiCaprio), Ed Hoffman (Russell Crowe), Hani (Mark Strong), Aisha (Golshifteh Farahani); Bassam (Oscar Isaac), Omar Sadiki (Ali Suliman), Al-Saleem (Alon Aboutboul), Nizar (Mehdi Nebboum), Holiday (Michael Gaston), Mustafa Karami (Kais Nashif), Aisha's sister Cala (Lubna Azabal), Hoffman's wife (Giannina Facio)

Robin Hood (2010)

Universal Pictures, Imagine Entertainment, Relativity Media, Scott Free Productions, 140 minutes, rated PG-13

P: Russell Crowe, Brian Grazer, Ridley Scott; D: Ridley Scott; SC: Brian Helgeland, Ethan Reiff, Cyrus Voris; M: Mark Streitenfeld; PD: Arthur Max; DP: John Mathieson; E: Pietro Scalia; C: Yanty Yates, SSE: Mark P. Stoeckinger; S: Tony Dawe; VES: Dick Edwards, Michael Kennedy, Steve Street, Edson Williams, Trevor Wood

Cast: Robin Longstride (Russell Crowe), Marion Loxley (Cate Blanchett), Sir Walter Loxley (Max Von Sydow), William Marshall (William Hurt), Godfrey (Mark Strong), Prince John (Oscar Isaac), King Richard the Lionhearted (Danny Huston), Eleanor of Aquitaine (Eileen Atkins), Friar Tuck (Mark Addy), sheriff of Nottingham (Matthew Macfayden), Little John (Kevin Durand)

Prometheus (2012)

20th Century Fox, Dune Entertainment, Scott Free Productions, Brandywine Productions, 124 minutes, rated R

P: David Glier, Walter Hill, Ridley Scott; D: Ridley Scott; SC: Dan O'Bannon, David Lindelof, Ronald Shusett, Jon Spaihts; M: Marc Streitenfeld; PD: Arthur Max; DP: Dariusz Wolski; E: Pietro Scalia, C: Janty Yates; SSE: Victor Ray Ennis, Mark P. Stoeckinger; S: Simon Hays; VES: Jamie Dixon, Charles Henley, Martin Hill, Matt Homes, Vivek Joshi, Lara Lom, Jignesh Meh, Stefano Pepin, Craig Saunders, Richard Stammers, James Turner, Nisha Vijayan

Cast: Elizabeth Shaw (Noomi Rapace), David (Michael Fassbender), Meredith Vickers (Charlize Theron), Janek (Idris Elba), Peter Weyland (Guy Pearce), Charles Holloway (Logan-Marshall Green), young Shaw (Lucy Hutchinson), Shaw's mother (Giannina Facio)

The Counselor (2013)

Nick Wechsler Productions, Scott Free Productions, 117 minutes, rated R

P: Paula Mae Schwartz, Steve Schwartz, Ridley Scott, Nick Wechsler; D: Ridley Scott; SC: Cormac McCarthy; M: Daniel Pemberton; PD: Arthur Max; DP: Darius Wolski; E: Pietro Scalia; C: Janty Yates; SSE: Oliver Tarney; S: Simon Hayes; VES: Charles Henley, Stefano Pepin, Richard Stammers

Cast: counselor (Michael Fassbender), Laura (Penélope Cruz), Malkina (Cameron Diaz), Reiner (Javier Bardem), diamond dealer (Bruno Ganz), Westray (Brad Pitt), Ruth (Rosie Perez), woman with mobile phone (Giannina Facio), Jefe (Rubén Blades), banker (Goran Visnjic), cartel man (Arthur Max), coverall man Randy (John Leguizamo), buyer (Dean Norris)

Exodus: Gods and Kings (2014)

Chernin Entertainment, 20th Century Fox, Scott Free Productions, 150 minutes, PG-13

P: Peter Chernin, Mohamed El Raie, Mark Huffam, Michael Schaefer, Ridley Scott, Jenno Topping; D: Ridley Scott, SC: Jeffrey Caine, Bill Collage, Adam Cooper, Steve Zaillian, M: Alberto Iglesias, PD: Arthur Max, DP: Darius Wolski; E: Billy Rich; C: Janty Yates; SSE: Oliver Tarney, S: Jorge Adrados; VES: Caimin Bourne, Simon Cockren, Pau Costa, Neil Coubould

Cast: Moses (Christian Bale), Ramses (Joel Edgerton), Seti (John Tuturro), Joshua (Aaron Paul), Viceroy Hegep (Ben Mendelsohn), Zipporah (Maria Valverde), Tuya (Sigourney Weaver), Nun (Ben Kingsley), Nefertari (Golshifteh Farahani), Ramses' grand vizier (Ghassan Massoud), Jethro's sister (Gianinna Facio), Malak (Isaac Andrews)

The Martian (2015)

20th Century Fox, Genre Films, Scott Free Productions, 130 minutes, PG-13

P: Mark Huffman, Simon Kinberg, Michael Schaefer, Ridley Scott, Aditya Sood; D: Ridley Scott; SC: Drew Goddard, based on the novel *The Martian* by Andy Weir; M: Harry Gregson-Williams; PD: Arthur Max; DP: Darius Wolski; E: Pietro Scalia; C: Janty Yates; SSE: Oliver Tarney; S: Mac Ruth; VES: Tom Barber, Aaron Baudin, Sara Bennett, Miguel Castrillo, Justin Cornish, Peter Hartless, Alberto Herrera, Brooke Lyndon-Stanford, Toby White

Cast: Beth Johanssen (Kate Mara), Mark Watney (Matt Damon), Melissa Lewis (Jessica Chastain), Annie Montrose (Kristen Wiig), Chris Beck (Sebastian Stan), Mitch Henderson (Sean Bean), Venkat Kapoor (Chiwetel Ejiofor), Mindy Park (Mackenzie Davis), Teddy Sanders (Jeff Daniels), Rich Purnell (Donald Glover), Rick Martinez (Michael Peña)

Alien: Covenant (2017)

Brandywine Productions, 20th Century Fox, 122 minutes, rated R

P: David Giler, Walter Hill, Mark Huffman, Michael Schaefer, Ridley Scott; D: Ridley Scott; SC: Michael Green, John Logan, Jack Paglen; M: Harry Gregson-Williams; PD: Chris Seagers; DP: Dariusz Wolski; E: Pietro Scalia; C: Yanty Yates; VES: Charlie Henley

Cast: David/Walter (Michael Fassbender), Elizabeth Shaw (Noomi Rapace), Tennessee (Danny McBride), Oran (Billy Crudup), Daniels (Katherine Waterson)

All the Money in the World (2018)

Imperative Entertainment, Scott Free Productions, TriStar Pictures, 132 minutes, rated R

P & D: Ridley Scott; SC: David Scarpa, based on the book *Painfully Rich: The Outrageous Fortunes and Misfortunes of the Heirs of J. Paul Getty* by John Pearson; M: Daniel Pemberton; PD: Arthur Max; DP: Dariusz Wolski; E: Claire Simpson; C: Janty Yates; SSE: Oliver Tarney; S: Gary Dodkin; VES: Gary Brozenich

Cast: Gail Harris (Michelle Williams), J. Paul Getty (Christopher Plummer), Fletcher Chase (Mark Wahlberg), Cinquanta (Romain Duris), Oswald Hinge (Timothy Hutton), John Paul Getty III (Charlie Plummer), John Paul Getty II (Andrew Buchan)

NOTES

Introduction

1. Tim Walker, "Is Ridley Scott the Most Macho Man in Movies?" *Independent*, May 26, 2012.

2. Lynn Barber, "Ridley Scott: 'Talking to Actors Was Tricky—I Had No Idea Where They Were Coming From,'" *Guardian*, January 6, 2002.

1. Mother's Milk

1. Steve Szkotak, "Scott Brothers Capture Civil War in *Gettysburg*," Associated Press, May 28, 2011.

2. John Patterson, "Ridley Scott: Creator of Worlds," *Guardian*, May 10, 2010.

3. Paul M. Sammon, *Ridley Scott, Close Up: The Making of His Movies* (New York: Thunder's Mouth, 1999), 9.

4. Patterson, "Ridley Scott: Creator of Worlds."

5. Lindesay Irvine, "'$225 Million Isn't Bad, I Guess,'" *Guardian*, October 6, 2005.

6. Stephen Galloway, "Return of the 'Alien' Mind," *Hollywood Reporter*, May 15, 2012.

7. Kenneth Turan, "Man of Vision," *Directors Guild of America Quarterly* (Fall 2010).

8. Lynn Barber, "Ridley Scott: 'Talking to Actors Was Tricky—I Had No Idea Where They Were Coming From,'" *Guardian*, January 6, 2002.

9. Galloway, "Return of the 'Alien' Mind."

10. *Eye of the Storm: Ridley Scott, Omnibus*, season 30, episode 6, directed by Nadia Haggar (British Broadcasting Company, October 13, 1992).

11. "Sir Ridley Scott: Interview," Royal College of Art, https://www.rca.ac.uk/studying -at-the-rca/the-rca-experience/student-voices/rca-luminaries/sir-ridley-scott/.

2. Brother and Brother

1. Kenneth Turan, "Man of Vision," *Directors Guild of America Quarterly* (Fall 2010).

2. "Sir Ridley Scott: Interview," Royal College of Art, https://www.rca.ac.uk/studying -at-the-rca/the-rca-experience/student-voices/rca-luminaries/sir-ridley-scott/.

3. Scott Foundas, "*Exodus: Gods and Kings*' Director Ridley Scott on Creating His Vision of Moses," *Variety,* November 25, 2014.

3. The Professional

1. *Eye of the Storm: Ridley Scott, Omnibus,* season 30, episode 6, directed by Nadia Haggar (British Broadcasting Company, October 13, 1992).

2. Chris Lee, "The Beautiful Bromance between Filmmakers Tony Scott and Ridley Scott," *Daily Beast,* August 21, 2012.

3. Lynn Barber, "Ridley Scott: 'Talking to Actors Was Tricky—I Had No Idea Where They Were Coming From,'" *Guardian,* January 6, 2002.

4. Kenneth Turan, "Man of Vision," *Directors Guild of America Quarterly* (Fall 2010).

5. John Patterson, "Ridley Scott: Creator of Worlds," *Guardian,* May 10, 2010.

6. Joel McIver, "Tony Scott Obituary," *Guardian,* August 20, 2012.

7. David Geffner, "Ridley Scott–Robin Hood," *International Cinematographers Guild Magazine,* May 26, 2010.

8. Scott Foundas, "*Exodus: Gods and Kings*' Director Ridley Scott on Creating His Vision of Moses," *Variety,* November 25, 2014.

9. Danny Peary, ed., *Omni's Screen Flights/Screen Fantasies: The Future According to Science Fiction* (New York: Doubleday, 1984).

10. Sean Woods, "Ridley Scott on His New Movie *Prometheus, Mad Men,* and a *Blade Runner* Sequel," *Rolling Stone,* May 23, 2012.

11. *Eye of the Storm;* Richard Natale, "Commercial Break," in *Ridley Scott Interviews,* edited by Lawrence F. Knapp and Andrea F. Kulas (Jackson: University of Mississippi Press, 2005).

12. Tim Walker, "Is Ridley Scott the Most Macho Man in Movies?" *Independent,* May 26, 2012.

4. Fencers

1. Trevor Hogg, "Hard to Replicate: A Ridley Scott Profile (Part 1)," *Flickering Myth* (blog), April 21, 2010, https://www.flickeringmyth.com/2010/04/hard-to-replicate-ridley-scott-profile-2/.

2. Paul M. Sammon, *Ridley Scott, Close Up: The Making of His Movies* (New York: Thunder's Mouth, 1999), 41.

3. Lawrence Raw, *The Ridley Scott Encyclopedia* (Lanham, MD: Scarecrow, 2009), 169.

4. Sara C. Nelson, "Ridley Scott's Hovis Bicycle Boy Returns to the Scene 40 Years Later," *Huffington Post,* April 12, 2013, https://www.huffingtonpost.co.uk/2013/12/04/ridley-scotts-hovis-bicycle-boy-pictures-_n_4383223.html.

5. Michael Sragow, "Ridley Scott's Brilliant First Film," *New Yorker,* May 29, 2012.

6. Rick Sincere, "Keith Carradine Discusses *The Duellists* at Virginia Film Festival," *YouTube,* November 3, 2012, https://www.youtube.com/watch?v=12_pLyS8j0I.

7. Marlow Stern, "Ridley Scott Opens Up about *Prometheus*, Kick-Ass Women, and *Blade Runner 2*," *Daily Beast*, May 17, 2012.

8. Kenneth Turan, "Man of Vision," *Directors Guild of America Quarterly* (Fall, 2010).

9. Donald Chase, "Ridley Scott Directs *The Duellists*," *Millimeter*, May 1978, 142–47.

10. *Eye of the Storm: Ridley Scott, Omnibus*, season 30, episode 6, directed by Nadia Haggar (British Broadcasting Company, October 13, 1992).

11. Tom Milne, "*The Duellists*," *Monthly Film Bulletin*, December 1977, 258.

12. Dave Kehr, "*The Duellists*," *Chicago Reader*, May 17, 1985.

13. Mark Chalon Smith, "Film: *The Duellists* Misfires Because of Miscasting," *Los Angeles Times*, February 13, 1992.

14. Vincent Canby, "New Movie, *The Duellists* Is Set during Napoleonic Wars," *New York Times*, January 14, 1978.

15. John Patterson, "Ridley Scott: Creator of Worlds," *Guardian*, May 10, 2010.

5. Alienation

1. Paul M. Sammon, *Ridley Scott, Close Up: The Making of His Movies* (New York: Thunder's Mouth, 1999), 52.

2. *Eye of the Storm: Ridley Scott, Omnibus*, season 30, episode 6, directed by Nadia Haggar (British Broadcasting Company, October 13, 1992).

3. John Monaghan, "Detroit Native Tom Skerritt Come Home Tuesday to Reflect on His Life," *Detroit Free Press*, April 20, 2014.

4. Ryan Gilbey, "HR Giger Obituary," *Guardian*, May 13, 2004.

5. *Cinefantastique* (Autumn 1979).

6. Vincent Canby, "Screen: *Alien* Brings Chills from the Far Galaxy: A Gothic Set in Space," *New York Times*, May 25, 1979.

7. Lynn Barber, "Ridley Scott: 'Talking to Actors Was Tricky—I Had No Idea Where They Were Coming From,'" *Guardian*, January 6, 2002.

8. "A Reel Life: Jordan Scott," *London Evening Standard*, November 19, 2009.

6. Electric Ladyland

1. Vincent LoBrutto, *Becoming Film Literate: The Art and Craft of Motion Pictures* (Westport, CT: Praeger, 2005), 41.

2. Vincent LoBrutto, *By Design: Interviews with Film Production Designers* (Westport, CT: Praeger, 2005).

3. Ibid.

4. Ibid.

5. Paul Gallagher, "Nothing Matches *Blade Runner*: Philip K. Dick Gets Excited about Ridley Scott's Film," dangerousminds.net, posted April 8, 2012.

6. Harlan Kennedy, "*Blade Runner*: 21st Century Nervous Breakdown; Interview with Ridley Scott," *Film Comment* (July/August 1982).

7. Trevor Hogg, "Hard to Replicate: A Ridley Scott Profile (Part 2)," *flickeringmyth .com*, April 2010.

8. Forster Hirsch, *Detours and Lost Highways: A Map of Neo-Noir* (New York: Limelight, 1999), 315.

9. Gallagher, "Nothing Matches *Blade Runner*."

7. Mythology

1. *Eye of the Storm: Ridley Scott, Omnibus,* season 30, episode 6, directed by Nadia Haggar (British Broadcasting Company, October 13, 1992).

2. Harlan Ellison, *Harlan Ellison's Watching* (Los Angeles: Underwood-Miller, 1989), 320.

3. Roger Ebert, "*Legend,*" rogerebert.com, April 18, 1986, https://www.rogerebert .com/reviews/legend-1986.

8. Noir One/Noir Two

1. Paul M. Sammon, *Ridley Scott, Close Up: The Making of His Movies* (New York: Thunder's Mouth, 1999), 89.

2. *Eye of the Storm: Ridley Scott, Omnibus,* season 30, episode 6, directed by Nadia Haggar (British Broadcasting Company, October 13, 1992).

3. Sean Woods, "Ridley Scott on His New Movie *Prometheus, Mad Men* and a *Blade Runner* Sequel," *Rolling Stone,* May 23, 2003.

4. Eric Walkuski, "Reel Action: Ridley Scott's *Black Rain,* Starring Michael Douglas," *Joblow.com,* August 19, 2011.

9. Male Feminist

1. Syd Field, "Callie Khouri on Creating Character: *Thelma & Louise,*" in *Syd Field: The Art of Visual Storytelling,* June 1, 2000, https://sydfield.com/articles/callie-khouri -on-creating-character-thelma-louise/.

2. Sheila Weller, "The Ride of a Lifetime," *Vanity Fair,* March 2011.

3. *Eye of the Storm: Ridley Scott, Omnibus,* season 30, episode 6, directed by Nadia Haggar (British Broadcasting Company, October 13, 1992).

4. Raina Lipsitz, "*Thelma & Louise:* The Last Great Film about Women," *Atlantic,* August 31, 2011.

5. Weller, "The Ride of a Lifetime."

10. Columbus Days

1. Alex von Tunzelmann, "*Conquest of Paradise*: New World—Old Tosh," *Guardian,* October 9, 1992.

13. Ridley Scott's *Spartacus*

1. Vincent LoBrutto, "Interview with Hans Zimmer," *CinemaEditor* 54, no. 3 (2004): 30.

2. Edgar Burcksen, "Interview with Pietro Scalia," *CinemaEditor* 51, no. 2 (2001).

3. LoBrutto, "Interview with Hans Zimmer."

4. Kenneth Turan, "Man of Vision," *Directors Guild of America Quarterly* (Fall 2010).

15. The Burden of Men

1. Jeremy Kagan, ed., *Director's Close-Up: Interviews with Directors Nominated for Best Film by the Directors Guild of America* (Lanham, MD: Scarecrow, 2006), 19.

2. James Chapman, *War and Film* (London: Reaktion Books, 2008).

16. Con Job

1. Rebecca Murray, "Nicholas Cage Plays a Con Man in *Matchstick Men*," *About .com*, September 2003, http://movies.about.com/cs/matchstickmen/match/nicholas.htm.

2. "Queen Knights Gladiator Director," *BBC News*, July 8, 2003.

17. Crusades and Romantic Comedy

1. Jonathan Riley-Smith, "Crusade against Scott's *Kingdom*—Historians Cry Distortion," *Daily Telegraph*, January 19, 2014.

2. Thomas F. Madden, medievalists.net, December 27, 2009.

19. I Spy

1. Nancy O'Dell, "Russell Crowe Talks Bulking Up for *Body of Lies*: 'Bring on the Burgers, Baby!'" *Access Hollywood*, September 29, 2008.

2. Sheila Roberts, "Interview with Russell Crowe, Ridley Scott & Leonardo DiCaprio," moviesonline, November 2008.

3. Patricia Thompson, "Middle East Intrigue," *American Cinematographer*, October 2008.

20. Revisonist Robin

1. Terrence Rafferty, *The Thing Happens: Ten Years of Writing about the Movies* (New York: Grove, 1993), 298.

2. Steve Rose, "Sorry Russell Crowe, but Only the Greats Can Improvise," *Guardian*, April 28, 2010.

3. David Carr, "English Legends: That Robin Guy and Sir Ridley Scott," *New York Times*, May 7, 2010.

4. John Hiscock, "Ridley Scott and Russell Crowe, Collaborators in Anger," *Telegraph*, April 29, 2010.

5. *Live with Regis and Kelly*, season 22, May 7, 2010.

6. A. O. Scott, "Rob the Rich? Give to the Poor? Oh, Puh–*leeze!*" *New York Times*, May 14, 2010.

7. Peter Travers, "*Robin Hood*," *Rolling Stone,* May 13, 2010.

8. Gabriel Snyder, "Going for Gold," *W Magazine,* November 1, 2007.

9. Steve "Frosty" Weintraub, "Russell Crowe and Director Ridley Scott Interview: *Robin Hood,*" *Collider,* May 11, 2010.

21. Prequel?

1. Phil de Semlyen, "Exclusive: Ridley Scott on *Prometheus,*" *Empire,* March 28, 2012.

2. Eric Spitznagel, "Q+A: Ridley Scott's *Star Wars,*" *Esquire,* June 4, 2012.

3. Stephen Galloway, "Return of the *Alien* Mind," *Hollywood Reporter,* May 25, 2012.

4. Sean O'Connell, "*Prometheus* Star Noomi Rapace on Ridley Scott, *Alien,* and Possible Sequels," cinemablend.com, n.d.

22. At Law

1. Helen O'Hara, "Exclusive: Scott Talks *Blood Meridian:* Sir Ridley on His Dark Western," *Empire,* November 2008.

2. Film4, "*The Counselor* Interview Special," *YouTube,* November 11, 2013, https://www.youtube.com/watch?v=mxz6xvHiaPs.

3. Scott Foundas, "*Exodus: Gods and Kings*' Director Ridley Scott on Creating His Vision of Moses," *Variety,* November 25, 2014.

4. Jeff Dawson, *Quentin Tarantino: The Cinema of Cool* (New York: Applause Theatre & Cinema, 2000), 58, 101.

5. Pamela McClintock, "'No Better Person in the Trenches': Hollywood Remembers Tony Scott," *Hollywood Reporter,* August 22, 2012.

6. Ariel Leve, "Tony Scott," *Sunday Times,* 2016.

7. Chris Lee, "The Beautiful Bromance between Filmmakers Tony Scott and Ridley Scott," *Daily Beast,* August 21, 2012.

8. Foundas, "*Exodus: Gods and Kings*' Director Ridley Scott on Creating His Vision of Moses."

9. ScreenSlam, "*The Counselor:* Penelope Cruz Official Movie Interview," *YouTube,* October 7, 2013, https://www.youtube.com/watch?v=j7jWn6XDok8.

10. Lynn Barber, "Ridley Scott: 'Talking to Actors Was Tricky—I Had No Idea Where They Were Coming From,'" *Guardian,* January 6, 2002.

11. Film4, "*The Counselor* Interview Special."

12. Scott Foundas, "Why *The Counselor* Is One of Ridley Scott's Best Films," *Variety,* October 28, 2013.

13. ScreenSlam, "*The Counselor:* Director Ridley Scott Official Movie Interview," *YouTube,* October 7, 2013, https://www.youtube.com/watch?v=f6fdVhaUYuk.

23. Not Otto Preminger's *Exodus*

1. Willam Diem, "In the Hands of Director Ridley Scott, Tale of *Exodus* Is Given Life," *San Francisco Examiner,* December 8, 2014.

2. Kim Masters, "*Exodus:* How Ridley Scott Chose His 11-Year-Old Voice of God," *Hollywood Reporter,* November 21, 2014.

3. Scott Foundas, "*Exodus: Gods and Kings'* Director Ridley Scott on Creating His Vision of Moses," *Variety,* November 25, 2014.

4. Don Steinberg, "Special Effects Enliven *Exodus* Epic," *Wall Street Journal,* March 16, 2015.

5. Justin Chang, "Film Reviews," *Variety,* December 2, 2014.

6. Richard Corliss, "Don't Let Your People Go See *Exodus: Gods and Kings,*" *Time,* December 13, 2014.

24. Red

1. Pietro Scalia, "*The Martian,*" *CinemaEditor* 65 (2015).

2. Katherine Vu, "Filmmaker Ridley Scott's Collection Coming to USC School of Cinematic Arts," *USC News,* February 11, 2015.

3. Greg Kilday, "Ridley Scott Donates Collection to USC School of Cinematic Arts," *Hollywood Reporter,* January 29, 2015.

25. Son of *Prometheus*

1. Mitchell Corner, "*Alien: Covenant* Sequel Gets Title: Returning Character Confirmed," *Geek,* March 21, 2017.

2. Mekado Murphy, "How *Alien* Spawned So Many Others," *New York Times,* May 4, 2017.

26. True Crime Again

1. Kayleigh Donaldson, "*All the Money in the World:* The Last–Minute, Spacey-Removing Reshoots Explained," *Screen Rant,* December 30, 2017.

2. Sara Vilkomerson, "Ridley Scott's *All the Money in the World* Moves to Christmas," *Entertainment Weekly,* December 6, 2017.

3. Michele Manelis, "Ridley Scott Was Furious at Kevin Spacey after Allegations of Sexual Harassment," news.com.au, December 13, 2017, http://www.news.com.au /entertainment/movies/upcoming-movies/ridley-scott-was-furious-at-kevin-spacey -after-allegations-of-sexual-harassment/news-story/b0e87e88f8312a4fc89a967f601 e2990.

Epilogue

1. Scott Foundas, "*Exodus: Gods and Kings'* Director Ridley Scott on Creating His Vision of Moses," *Variety,* November 25, 2014.

2. Author's interview with film editor Dody Dorn, February 23, 2018.

3. Mr. Showbiz, posted on the *Blade Runner: The Replicant* site, www.brmovie.com /Articles/MrShowbiz_RS_1996.htm. 1996.

4. Stephen Moss, "The Late Developer," *Guardian,* November 11, 2007.

5. Ibid.

6. Ibid.

7. Kenneth Turan, "Man of Vision," *Directors Guild of America Quarterly* (Fall 2010).

8. Sheila Roberts, "Interview with Russell Crowe, Ridley Scott & Leonardo DiCaprio," *moviesonline*, November 2008.

9. Phil de Semlyen, "Why Are We Here?" *Empire,* March 28, 2012.

10. Ariel Leve, *Sunday Times Magazine,* 2012.

11. Tim Walker, "Is Ridley Scott the Most Macho Man in Movies?" *Independent,* May 26, 2012.

12. "A Reel Life: Jordan Scott," *London Evening Standard,* November 11, 2009.

13. John Patterson, "Ridley Scott: Creator of Worlds," *Guardian,* May 10, 2010.

14. Samuel Beckett, *The Unnamable* (New York: Grove, 1958).

SELECTED BIBLIOGRAPHY

Armes, Roy. *A Critical History of British Cinema*. New York: Oxford University Press, 1978.

Ballinger, Alexander. *New Cinematographers*. New York: Collins Design, 2004.

Barkman, Adam, Ashley Barkman, and Nancy Kang, eds. *The Culture and Philosophy of Ridley Scott*. Lanham, MD: Lexington Books, 2013.

Barnwell, Jane. *Production Design: Architects of the Screen*. London: Wallflower, 2004.

Begleiter, Marcie. *From Word to Image: Storyboarding and the Filmmaking Process*. Studio City, CA: Michael Wiese Productions, 2001.

Boorstin, Jon. *The Hollywood Eye: What Makes Movies Work*. New York: Cornelia & Michael B. Bessie Books, 1990.

Bowden, Mark. *Black Hawk Down: A Story of Modern War*. New York: Penguin Books, 2000.

Brosan, John. *Movie Magic: The Story of Special Effects in the Cinema*. New York: St Martin's, 1974.

Brown, Royal S. *Overtones and Undertones: Reading Film Music*. Berkeley: University of California Press, 1994.

Callan, Michael Feeney. *Anthony Hopkins: The Unauthorized Biography*. New York: Charles Scribner's Sons, 1993.

Chapman, James. *War and Film*. London: Reaktion Books, 2008.

Christopher, Nicholas. *Somewhere in the Night: Film Noir and the American City*. New York: Henry Holt, 1997.

Chutkow, Paul. *Depardieu: A Biography*. New York: Knopf, 1994.

Clarens, Carlos. *Crime Movies: An Illustrated History*. New York: Norton, 1980.

———. *An Illustrated History of the Horror Film*. New York: Perigee Trade, 1968.

Clarke, James. *Ridley Scott*. London: Virgin Film, 2002.

Conrad, Mark T., ed. *The Philosophy of Film Noir*. Lexington: University Press of Kentucky, 2007.

Cristiano, Giuseppe. *Storyboard Design Course: Principles, Practices and Techniques: The Ultimate Guide for Artists, Directors, Producers, and Scriptwriters*. London: Barron's, 2007.

Dawson, Jeff. *Quentin Tarantino: The Cinema of Cool*. New York: Applause Theatre & Cinema, 2000.

Deeley, Michael. *Blade Runners, Deer Hunters, and Blowing the Bloody Doors Off: My Life in Cult Movies*. New York: Pegasus Books, 2009.

Dick, Philip K. *Do Androids Dream of Electric Sheep?* New York: Doubleday, 1968.

Dickos, Andrew. *Street with No Name: A History of the Classic American Film Noir.* Lexington: University Press of Kentucky, 2013.

Ebert, Roger. *The Great Movies II.* New York: Broadway Books, 2005.

Ellison, Harlan. *Harlan Ellison's Watching.* Los Angeles: Underwood-Miller, 1989.

Gerstner, David A. *Manly Arts: Masculinity and Nation in Early American Cinema.* Durham: Duke University Press, 2006.

Goldberger, Paul. *Building Up and Tearing Down: Reflections on the Age of Architecture.* New York: Monacelli, 2009.

Granzotto, Gianni. *Christopher Columbus: The Dream and the Obsession—A Biography.* New York: Doubleday, 1985.

Hamilton, Edith. *Mythology.* Boston: Little, Brown, 1942.

Harris, Thomas. *Hannibal.* New York: Delacorte, 1999.

Hart, John. *The Art of the Storyboard: Storyboarding for Film, TV, and Animation.* Boston: Focal, 1999.

Hirsch, Foster. *Detours and Lost Highways: A Map of Neo-Noir.* New York: Limelight, 1999.

Hutchison, David. *Film Magic: The Art and Science of Special Effects.* New York: Prentice Hall, 1987.

Jackson, Pamela, and Jonathan Lethem, eds. *The Exegesis of Philip K. Dick.* Boston: Houghton Mifflin Harcourt, 2011.

Johnson, William, ed. *Focus on the Science Fiction Film.* Englewood Cliffs, NJ: Prentice Hall, 1972.

Kagan, Jeremy, ed. *Directors Close-Up: Interviews with Directors Nominated for Best Film by the Directors Guild of America.* Lanham, MD: Scarecrow, 2006.

Katz, Steven D. *Film Directing Shot by Shot: Visualizing from Concept to Screen.* Studio City, CA: Michael Wiese Productions, 1991.

Kauffmann, Stanley. *Field of View: Film Criticism and Comment.* New York: PAJ, 1986.

Khouri, Callie. *Thelma & Louise and Something to Talk About: Screenplays.* New York: Grove, 1991.

Klein, Norman M. *The Vatican to Vegas: A History of Special Effects.* New York: New Press, 2004.

Knapp, Lawrence F., and Andrea F. Kulas, eds. *Ridley Scott Interviews.* Jackson: University of Mississippi Press, 2005.

Lamster, Mark, ed. *Architecture and Film.* New York: Princeton Architectural Press, 2000.

LoBrutto, Vincent. *Becoming Film Literate: The Art and Craft of Motion Pictures.* Westport, CT: Praeger, 2005.

———. *By Design: Interviews with Film Production Designers.* Westport, CT: Praeger, 1992.

———. *Selected Takes: Film Editors on Editing.* New York: Praeger, 1991.

McGilligan, Patrick. *Backstory 5: Interviews with Screenwriters of the 1990s.* Berkeley: University of California Press, 2010.

McGrath, Declan. *Screencraft: Editing and Post-production.* Boston: Focal, 2001.

Selected Bibliography

Morton, Andrew. *Tom Cruise: An Unauthorized Biography.* New York: St. Martin's, 2008.

Naha, Ed. *The Making of* Dune. New York: Berkley Books, 1984.

Neumann, Dietrich, ed. *Film Architecture: Set Designs from Metropolis to Blade Runner.* Munich: Prestel, 1999.

Parrill, William B. *Ridley Scott: A Critical Filmography.* Jefferson, NC: McFarland, 2011.

Perkins, Roy, and Martin Strollery. *British Film Editors: The Heart of the Movie.* London: BFI, 2004.

Pinteau, Pascal. *Special Effects: An Oral History.* New York: Harry N. Abrams, 2004.

Piper, David, ed. *The Genius of British Painting.* New York: William Morrow, 1975.

Pyle, Howard. *The Merry Adventures of Robin Hood.* Ann Arbor, MI: Borders Classics, 2008.

Rafferty, Terrence. *The Thing Happens: Ten Years of Writing about the Movies.* New York: Grove, 1993.

Raw, Lawrence. *The Ridley Scott Encyclopedia.* Lanham, MD: Scarecrow, 2009.

Rickitt, Richard. *Special Effects: The History and Technique.* New York: Billboard Books, 2000.

Rogers, Pauline B. *Art of Visual Effects: Interviews on the Tools of the Trade.* Boston: Focal, 1999.

Rosenblum, Naomi. *A World History of Photography.* New York: Abbeville, 1984.

Sammon, Paul M. *Future Noir: The Making of Blade Runner.* New York: Harper Paperbacks, 1996.

———. *Ridley Scott, Close Up: The Making of His Movies.* New York: Thunder's Mouth, 1999.

Sanders, Steven M., ed. *The Philosophy of Science Fiction Films.* Lexington: University Press of Kentucky, 2008.

Sawicki, Mark. *Filming the Fantastic: A Guide to Visual Effects Cinematography.* Amsterdam: Focal, 2007.

Schwartz, Richard A. *The Films of Ridley Scott.* New York: Praeger, 2001.

Shapiro, Marc. *Susan Sarandon.* Amherst: Prometheus Books, 2001.

Silver, Alain, and Elizabeth Ward, eds. *Film Noir: An Encyclopedic Reference to the American Style.* 3rd ed. Woodstock, NY: Overlook, 1979.

Simon, John. *On Film: Criticism, 1982–2001.* New York: Applause Theatre & Cinema, 2005.

Simon, Mark. *Storyboards: Motion in Art.* Boston: Focal, 2000.

Thomson, David. *"Have You Seen . . .?"* New York: Knopf, 2008.

Vineyard, Jeremy. *Setting Up Your Shots: Great Camera Moves Every Filmmaker Should Know.* Studio City, CA: Michael Wiese Productions, 2000.

Walker, Alexander. *National Heroes: British Cinema in the Seventies and Eighties.* London: Harrap, 1965.

Washington, Denzel. *A Hand to Guide Me.* Des Moines: Meredith Books, 2006.

Wells, Paul. *The Horror Genre: From Beelzebub to Blair Witch.* London: Wallflower, 2000.

Yule, Andrew. *Fast Fade: David Puttnam, Columbia Pictures, and the Battle for Hollywood.* New York: Delacorte, 1989.

INDEX

Index

Index

Index

Index

Index

Index

Index

Tarkovsky, Andrei, 3, 144
technical advisors, 111
Technicinol, 30
television, 29, 69, 158, 214, 217; Danielle
  Alexandra, 114; Australian TV series,
  121; cable, 76; commercials, 25, 218;
  Drew Goddard, 194; *The Good Wife*,
  149, 165–66; Roland Kibbe, 74; *1984*,
  78; production designer, 66; *The
  Vatican*, 187
television movies, 54, 119
Temple, Amanda, 93
Temple, Julian, 93
temp shots, 197
Ten Commandments, The, 189, 191, 192
Terror, The, 211
Texas, 117
Texas Chainsaw Massacre, The, 50
Thailand, northern, 155
Thelma & Louise, 79, 93–104, 129, 139, 164
Thewlis, David, 144
*Thing Happens, The: Ten Years of Writing
  about the Movies*, 164
Things to Come, 61
Third Man, The, 18, 145
Thompson, Jack, 121
Those About to Die, 120
3D, 191
3D hologram, 177
Three Musketeers, The (1973 film), 40, 44
thriller genre, 161
Throne of Blood, 16
Thunderbird, Ford, 98, 100, 101
Tidy, Frank, 24, 35
Tiffen, 35
tigers, 125
Tillis, Pam, 93
Time's Up Legal Fund, 208
TNT, 119
Toccafondo, Gianluigi, 145
Tokyo International Film Festival, 170
Tomita, 55
Tonight (TV show), 19–20
Top Gun, 182
Toronto International Film Festival, 197
Total Recall, 61
tracking shot, 100
Train, The, 77

Training Day, 152
Tripoli, 139
Tristan and Isolde (2006 film), 48
Tristan and Isolde (medieval poem), 45
Tristan and Isolde (movie project), 45, 46,
  47, 48, 80
Triumph of the Will, 122
True Romance, 181
Truffaut, François, 81
Truman, Harry, 89
Trumbull, Douglas, 68–69, 72
Turner, J. M., 176
20th Century Fox, 47, 49, 50, 66, 114, 144,
  147, 174, 177, 189, 194
Twohy, David, 114
2001: A Space Odyssey, 47, 61, 68
Tyneside (region in England), 8

Ufland, Harry, 36
Uhis, Jim, 77
UNICEF, 144
United Arab Emirates, 161, 192
Universal Studios, 82, 122, 130, 153,
  157–58
University of Southern California's School
  of Cinematic Arts, 199
Unnamable, The, 219
Unstoppable, 182
Ulysses, 15
US Defense Department, 135

Vangelis, 74, 108
Van Lint, Derek, 25, 52
Van Sant, Gus, 195
Variety, 183, 188, 189, 190, 203
Vatican, The, 187
Vaughan-Hughes, Gerald, 29, 30, 45, 45
Venice Film Festival, 158
Verhoeven, Paul, 61
Vermeer, Johannes, 34, 67
Vernet, Carle, 34
video assist, 136
video monitors, 52, 70
Vietnam, 155, 156
Villeneuve, Denis, 212
Vincent Thomas Bridge, 180
Vine-Miller, Bosie, 21
Virginia Film Festival, 36

SCREEN CLASSICS

Screen Classics is a series of critical biographies, film histories, and analytical studies focusing on neglected filmmakers and important screen artists and subjects, from the era of silent cinema to the golden age of Hollywood to the international generation of today. Books in the Screen Classics series are intended for scholars and general readers alike. The contributing authors are established figures in their respective fields. This series also serves the purpose of advancing scholarship on film personalities and themes with ties to Kentucky.

Series Editor

Patrick McGilligan

Books in the Series

Olivia de Havilland
Victoria Amador

Mae Murray: The Girl with the Bee-Stung Lips
Michael G. Ankerich

Hedy Lamarr: The Most Beautiful Woman in Film
Ruth Barton

Rex Ingram: Visionary Director of the Silent Screen
Ruth Barton

Conversations with Classic Film Stars: Interviews from Hollywood's Golden Era
James Bawden and Ron Miller

You Ain't Heard Nothin' Yet: Interviews with Stars from Hollywood's Golden Era
James Bawden and Ron Miller

Von Sternberg
John Baxter

Hitchcock's Partner in Suspense: The Life of Screenwriter Charles Bennett
Charles Bennett, edited by John Charles Bennett

Hitchcock and the Censors
John Billheimer

My Life in Focus: A Photographer's Journey with Elizabeth Taylor and the Hollywood Jet Set
Gianni Bozzacchi with Joey Tayler

Hollywood Divided: The 1950 Screen Directors Guild Meeting and the Impact of the Blacklist
Kevin Brianton

He's Got Rhythm: The Life and Career of Gene Kelly
Cynthia Brideson and Sara Brideson

Ziegfeld and His Follies: A Biography of Broadway's Greatest Producer
Cynthia Brideson and Sara Brideson

The Marxist and the Movies: A Biography of Paul Jarrico
Larry Ceplair

Dalton Trumbo: Blacklisted Hollywood Radical
Larry Ceplair and Christopher Trumbo

Warren Oates: A Wild Life
Susan Compo

Improvising Out Loud: My Life Teaching Hollywood How to Act
Jeff Corey and Emily Corey

Crane: Sex, Celebrity, and My Father's Unsolved Murder
Robert Crane and Christopher Fryer

Jack Nicholson: The Early Years
Robert Crane and Christopher Fryer

My Life as a Mankiewicz: An Insider's Journey through Hollywood
Tom Mankiewicz and Robert Crane

Hawks on Hawks
Joseph McBride

Showman of the Screen: Joseph E. Levine and His Revolutions in Film Promotion
A. T. McKenna

William Wyler: The Life and Films of Hollywood's Most Celebrated Director
Gabriel Miller

Raoul Walsh: The True Adventures of Hollywood's Legendary Director
Marilyn Ann Moss

Veit Harlan: The Life and Work of a Nazi Filmmaker
Frank Noack

Harry Langdon: King of Silent Comedy
Gabriella Oldham and Mabel Langdon

Charles Walters: The Director Who Made Hollywood Dance
Brent Phillips

Some Like It Wilder: The Life and Controversial Films of Billy Wilder
Gene D. Phillips

Ann Dvorak: Hollywood's Forgotten Rebel
Christina Rice

Michael Curtiz: A Life in Film
Alan K. Rode

Arthur Penn: American Director
Nat Segaloff

Claude Rains: An Actor's Voice
David J. Skal with Jessica Rains

Barbara La Marr: The Girl Who Was Too Beautiful for Hollywood
Sherri Snyder

Buzz: The Life and Art of Busby Berkeley
Jeffrey Spivak

Victor Fleming: An American Movie Master
Michael Sragow

Hollywood Presents Jules Verne: The Father of Science Fiction on Screen
Brian Taves

Thomas Ince: Hollywood's Independent Pioneer
Brian Taves

Carl Theodor Dreyer and Ordet: *My Summer with the Danish Filmmaker*
Jan Wahl

Clarence Brown: Hollywood's Forgotten Master
Gwenda Young